THE STONES
OF VENICE

JOHN RUSKIN
THE STONES OF VENICE

EDITED & INTRODUCED BY
JAN MORRIS

Little, Brown and Company
Boston   Toronto

ISBN: 0-316-76190-7

Library of Congress Catalogue card no. 81-80862

First American edition 1981

Designed and produced for Little, Brown and Company by
Bellew & Higton Publishers Ltd
19–21 Conway Street, London W1P 6JD

Published simultaneously in Canada
by Little, Brown & Company (Canada) Limited

Printed in Great Britain

CONTENTS

INTRODUCTION

O N November 10, 1849, John Ruskin the art critic arrived in
Venice with his wife Effie, her friend Charlotte Ker and their
servant John Hobbs, to start work on a monumental book,
The Stones of Venice. He was in his thirty-first year, and was already
known for his uncompleted *Modern Painters*, of which two volumes
had so far appeared, and for a hortatory treatise called *The Seven Lamps of
Architecture*. With these works he had established a precocious reputation as a
writer of remarkable didactic powers, a heady stylist and something of an
oracle, whose opinions were often dogmatic but whose vision was startlingly
fresh and provocative. *The Stones of Venice* was to be more ambitious still. With
it Ruskin proposed to change the attitudes of a nation—and that the most
powerful and complacent of the age, Great Britain—towards the very meaning
of architecture, through the artistic, moral, social and historical example of a
single city—and that a city in the depths of failure, Venice.

This terrific purpose Ruskin was to work out in an extraordinary elabora-
tion of thought and feeling, illustrating his book with his own drawings,
dignifying it with passages of loftiest prose, and infusing it with a growing
awareness of the relationship between style, history, the morale of States and
the progress of peoples. It was a new kind of book. Smith, Elder and Company
of London published it in three volumes, the last appearing in the autumn of
1853, and it has been honoured ever since (though sometimes ridiculed too) as
a seminal work of artistic analysis and social philosophy, as an incomparable
evocation of Venice, and as a monument to its author, one of the strangest and
grandest geniuses of the Victorian age.

The Venice in which Ruskin and his young wife unpacked their bags that
day (they had rooms at Danieli's Hotel) was in a condition of tragedy from
which it has never entirely extricated itself. Rather more than half a century
had passed since the island Republic of Venice, for a thousand years a
Sovereign Power within its inviolate lagoon, had abjectly surrendered its
independence to the forces of Napoleon. By then, though it had become in its
last decades a very image of stylish gaiety, it had long lost all pretensions to

political greatness: its eastern empire had been lost to the Turks, its once pre-eminent navy was in decay, its proud oligarchal system, for so long the envy of Europe, was emasculated by age, changing times and lost convictions. Napoleon, despising this sad wreck of ancient glories, declared himself 'an Attica to the State of Venice', and in 1797 he seized the city, looted it, made a few alterations to its structures and put paid to the Venetian Republic. With his own fall in 1815 Venice passed to the Austrians, who made it their principal arsenal and naval base on the Adriatic. They maintained a garrison there, and all Austrian naval officers were trained at the Venetian Naval Academy. Venice became absolutely subject to the imperial authority of Vienna, and in 1846 the Austrians, by building a railway causeway across the lagoon from Mestre, even ended its insular status too.

The Venetians had been too demoralized to resist these events, and had settled into a fairly surly quiescence. All the brilliance of the Republic was lost, and the reckless excesses of carnival, which had so fascinated the world even in its last decrepitude, were replaced by very different social *mores*. The officers of the Austrian fleet and army provided a more sober elite now, together with a few collaborationist Venetian families, and that stream of visiting swells which, whatever the fortunes of Venice, always filters through her salons. The gulf between Austrian and Venetian grew deeper as the years passed, and here as in so many parts of Europe in the 1840s, a nationalist movement came secretly into being.

In the year before Ruskin arrived to start his work, the city burst into revolution: 1848 had been a year of revolutions, in which the forces of liberal disaffection rose to arms against the Empires then lying like great upholstered muffles across the body of Europe. North Italy rebelled in a particular fury of patriotic feeling, and in Venice the people responded in a last splendid demonstration of the old spirit. Their leader was a lawyer of partly Jewish descent, Daniele Manin, and at first they were startlingly successful. They drove the garrison out, cut the railway line, and proclaimed the restoration of the Republic. They printed their own currency, they flew the Lion of St. Mark, the thrilling emblem of old Venice, from the great bronze flagstaffs in the Piazza. The Austrians, massing guns on the mainland only three miles away and blockading the city from the sea, settled down to besiege them.

Manin appealed for help to the liberals of Europe, but nothing happened. Systematically the Austrians wore down the defences of the city, bombarding it, floating bomb-balloons over it, rigidly controlling its sea-approaches: and as one by one the other risings of 1848 spluttered out in despair and reprisal, so Venice sank for a second time slowly into defeat. The city was scarred by shell-fire, depressed by lack of food and fuel, ravaged by cholera, but it resisted longer than any of the other rebellious Italian centres. Only after a full year of siege, on August 22, 1849, did Venice surrender. Manin left the city for permanent exile, Marshal Joseph Radetzky the 83-year-old Austrian Governor was rowed up the Grand Canal through shuttered windows and silent quays, to a Piazza San Marco absolutely empty but for his own soldiers. The

George Richmond PORTRAIT OF JOHN RUSKIN

J. M. W. Turner THE BRIDGE OF SIGHS AND THE DUCAL PALACE
During his first visit to Venice, Ruskin wrote in his diary that
'this place is quite beyond everybody but Turner'.

eagle of the Hapsburgs once more replaced the winged lion on the ceremonial flag-staffs.

Three months later, the Ruskins arrived. John Ruskin had known the city since boyhood, but it had greatly changed since his first visit with his parents fourteen years before. Not only had the railway been built since then, but the temper of the place, so recently emerged from its terrible and heroic ordeal, was very different now. Bitterness was everywhere, and poverty too. There was the rubble of bombardment here and there–half the palaces of the Grand Canal were chipped by shrapnel. The evening crowds in the Piazza held themselves angrily aloof from the Austrians, and when imperial bigwigs arrived in the city from Vienna, the Venetians ostentatiously ignored them. Manin, far away in Paris, was mourned still as a lost prince of Venice.

Nevertheless, as civic life returned begrudgingly to normal, café and salon society was reviving too. The officers of the garrison proceeded heedlessly enough with their own pleasures. The bands played again in the Piazza cafés–to Venetians on one side, to Austrians on the other. The European aristocracy resumed its visits to the city. Venice once more cast her magnetic spell across Europe, and Ruskin, so soon after the conflagration, deemed it safe and proper to start his work.

It was a humiliated city, but then to the Victorians, and especially perhaps to the British, the habitual sadness of Venice was part of its allure. Its history powerfully fascinated a generation addicted to success, progress and Example, and the British saw in its condition an ultimate figure of the picturesque *tristesse* that so attracted them. Wordworth mourned, that

. . . even the Shade
Of that which once was great is pass'd away.

Shelley, looking out from the Eugeanean Hills, saw the towers of Venice as

Sepulchres, where human forms,
Like pollution-nourished worms
To the corpse of greatness cling,
Murdered, and now mouldering . . .

Byron toyed with the tragic fantasy of Venice's last physical extinction, sinking slowly beneath the waters that gave her birth–

A cry of nations o'er thy sunken halls,
A loud lament along the sweeping sea!

To the British, too, Venice provided all too obvious parallels. The Venetian Republic had been, so to speak, the Britain of its day, mistress of a maritime empire built upon trade and technology. Like Britain, Venice had been a Power unique to itself, an aristocratic society of famous stability, dependent upon mutual trust between its classes, and intensely patriotic. Like Britain, she had proclaimed herself in quirk and pageantry: and she too was set in a silver sea, moat-like, which set her apart from her less happy neighbours of the mainland shore.

But look at her now! Venice seemed to have ruined herself by her own hedonism. All the goings-on of eighteenth-century Venice, the display and the debauch, seemed to the British like the scenes of a morality play, or the successive plates in those improving narrative pictures which demonstrated the wastrel's inevitable decline from prosperous paternity to gin-sodden abandon. The story of Venice was a rake's progress with a vengeance, and offered the British enjoyable *frissons* of warning and comparison. *Thy lot* (Byron apostrophized the unhappy city)

> *is shameful to the nations—most of all,*
> *Albion! to thee . . .*
> *in the fall*
> *of Venice think of thine.*

Anglo-Saxon visitors then, in the first decades of Queen Victoria's reign, went to Venice pre-conditioned. They saw it, as Ruskin said of his own earlier visits, through Byron's eyes. They went expecting no more than the shade of that which once was great. 'Melancholy' was the most familiar epithet of their reportage—the melancholy line of the marshes, the melancholy wastes of the lagoon, the melancholy decay of palaces, the melancholy in the eye of the Venetian citizen, or in the light that settled in winter evenings upon the neglected structures of the city.

Ruskin hurried there, so soon after the collapse of Manin's revolution, because he feared many buildings had been severely damaged in the fighting, and he wanted to record as much as he could before they were restored out of recognition. In fact the damage was not cataclysmic, and physically the city was much the same as the city we know today. The works begun by Napoleon's regime had been finished—the completion of the Piazza San

The Fondaco de' Turchi from a nineteenth-century photograph:
'The unsightly heap is festering to its fall.'

Marco as we know it now, the creation of the Public Gardens at the eastern tip of the city. The Arsenal was an active naval base under the Austrians, and deep-sea shipping sailed up the Grand Canal as far as the Rialto bridge, but the docks were already concentrated at the western end of the Zattere, as they are today. There were gas lights in the city squares, steamboats were plying the lagoon, and the trains were running again over the patched-up causeway from Mestre.

Many of the institutions which are familiar to modern visitors to Venice were already active then – cafés like Florian's and Quadri's, on their respective sides of the Piazza, the Marciana Library around the corner in the Piazzetta, the Accademia art gallery, the Danieli and Luna hotels. Some of the buildings

Ruskin's worksheet on the Fondaco de' Turchi.

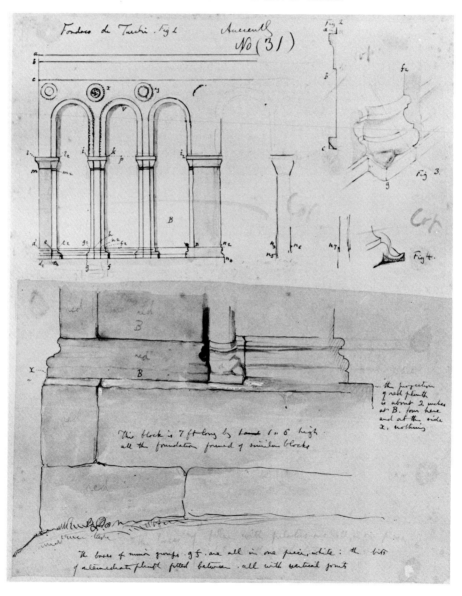

that Ruskin inspected have since been restored or greatly altered, but very few have been demolished, and the vast majority are more or less as they were in his time: even the campanile of San Marco, which fell down in 1902, was put up again ten years later *com' era, dov' era* – as it was, where it was – and is still available for purposes of comparison, as Ruskin used it in 1849, with the tower of 'the lately built college at Edinburgh' (one of the twin towers, actually, of William Playfair's New College, completed in 1846).

Such then was the Venice, shabby, bruised, reproachful, occupied by a conquering army, veiled in its own reputation, that awaited Ruskin's attentions. He set to work at once upon his detailed analysis in the raw grey days of the Adriatic winter. The task was harder than he had expected. Written records were scanty, local antiquarians differed wildly over the simplest questions of origin or chronology. Ruskin soon discovered, like many a Venetian inquirer after him, that almost nothing in the blurred and evasive city was absolutely certain.

But all that winter he slaved away, measuring, sketching, taking daguerreotypes, clambering up ladders and scaffolds, peering at dim-lit paintings and mouldy tombs, spending long hours in meticulous study of the mosaics in the Basilica, or the columns of the Doge's Palace. Soon he was well-known in the city. 'John excites the liveliest atonishment', wrote Effie, 'to all and sundry in Venice, and I do not think they have made up their minds yet whether he is very mad or very wise. Nothing interrupts him and whether the Square is crowded or empty he is either seen with a black cloth over his head taking Daguerreotypes or climbing about the capitals covered with dust, or else with cobwebs exactly as if he had just arrived from taking a voyage with the old woman on her broomstick . . .'

Ruskin's notes on the Casa Loredan from 'Housebook 2'.

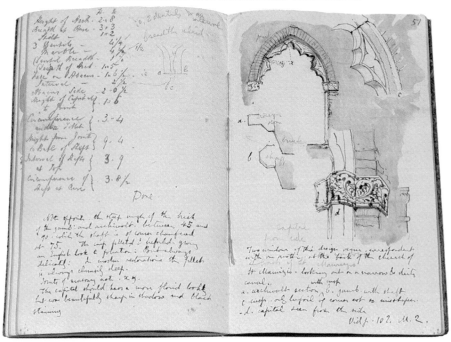

Whether he was very mad or very wise would puzzle people always and everywhere, for Ruskin was a character of fluctuating extremes and contradictions, now displaying all the symptoms of the genuine sage, now behaving and talking like a perfect ass. A writer of magnificent powers, a fine draughtsman, a thinker with a truly noble range of interest and reference, he was prone to silly exaggerations and generalizations, dogmatic assertions and flights of foolish rhetoric. He was also a man of debilitating inner torments, and when in 1849 he embarked upon *The Stones of Venice*, his complex personality was only just reaching its frustrated and brilliant maturity.

Ruskin at thirty was a tall slim man of rather fragile bearing, just beginning to stoop. His hair was yellow, his eyes were blue beneath heavy beetling eyebrows, his nose and cheek-bones were prominent. His mouth, though slightly deformed at one corner from a dog-bite in childhood, seemed habitu-

Notes on the Fondaco de' Turchi from Ruskin's 'Gothic Book'.

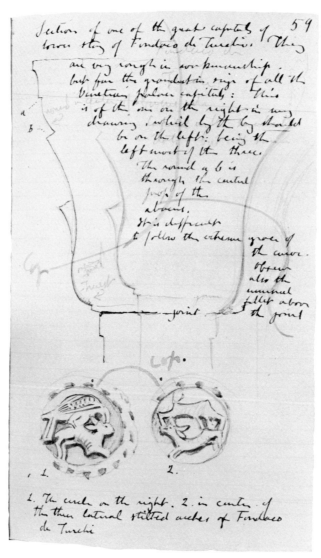

ally to settle into the wistful suggestion of a smile, and his general expression, so everybody said, was gentle and kindly. He had been brought up with excessive care, and this had left him, except in matters of the mind, always dependent upon others, and gave him a motherable and valetable appeal: no sooner was he down from those cobwebby pillars, Effie reported, than he was 'standing very meekly to be brushed down by [his manservant] Domenico'.

Ruskin was exactly a Victorian, in that he was born in the same year as the Queen, 1819, and he was in many ways a true child of his age. His father John James Ruskin, a prosperous wine merchant, personified several of the Victorian virtues: he had worked his way up to a partnership from a humble clerkship, and after an eight-year engagement had married his own first cousin, Margaret Cox, the exceedingly pious and genteel daughter of the landlord of the Old King's Head at Croydon. John Ruskin Jr, who had no other Christian name, was their only child, and for half a century their every thought was to revolve around him. They knew him almost from the start as a boy of remarkable gifts, and expected him to be at once famous, fashionable and respectable: his father hoped he would be a great poet, his mother wanted him to be a man of God – preferably, no doubt, a bishop of fundamentalist persuasion. They loved him with an obsessive pride. They closely supervised his schooling; they took him on long trips abroad; when in 1836 he went to Oxford, where he was admitted as a gentleman-commoner among the foul-mouthed and cocksure young noblemen of Christ Church, his mother took rooms in the High Street to keep an eye on him.

Brought up in this bourgeois, evangelical, ambitious, well-heeled and possessive family, it was natural that the young Ruskin should be of an earnest frame of mind. He thought deeply about Life, God and Art, and shared his mother's evangelical zeal, but even at Oxford his less conventional genius was stirring. He had already developed an extraordinary eye for landscape, for the structure of mountains in particular, and he had learnt to draw uncommonly well. 'A very wonderful gentleman-commoner', is how one of his Oxford tutors, Henry Liddell, described him, 'living in quite his own way among the odd set of hunting and sporting men that gentlemen-commoners usually are. Ruskin tells them that they like their own way of living and he likes his; and so they go on, and I am glad to say that they do not bully him, as I should have been afraid they would.'

His Oxford career was interrupted by an unrequited and novelettish love affair, which so affected him that his parents took him off for a long trip to Italy, curing his doubtless psychosomatic sore throats and giving him some intoxicating new experiences of art and terrain. When he returned he abandoned any attempt to get an Honours Degree and was given instead a Double Fourth Pass Degree in Classics and Mathematics – one of the oddest of all Oxford's odd denouements. At once his mother was urging him to Higher Things: 'Believe me John you will never know permanent happiness in this world ever if you do not seek it in ... loving and obeying your God.'

But though Ruskin toyed for years with the idea of ordination, in fact immediately after Oxford he embarked upon his life's career: that of the inspired dilettante. He was the supreme amateur, for he was a teacher too, and he came in time to see as his true vocation the instruction of his compatriots in those marginal areas of thought that embraced aesthetics, morality and social economy.

He was always an *enthusiast* – 'better the errors of affection', he was to say in answer to criticism of his frequent mistakes, 'than the accuracy of apathy' – and in the years after Oxford he founded his reputation upon a defiant enthusiasm for the painter William Turner, whose landscape pictures, he believed, penetrated like no others to the very meaning of Nature itself. From landscape art he moved on to architecture, and he became increasingly concerned with the historical and moral allusions of buildings. His views were pronounced, his interpretations often startling, and more and more he saw in the development of architecture the development of human society itself.

In particular he came to think that the Gothic architecture of pre-Renaissance Europe represented the apex of human achievement. It was a precipitate conclusion, for he had never been to Greece, to Germany or to Spain, let alone any of the countries of the East. He expressed it though with a persuasive energy. He was not an admirer of the sort of artificial Gothic already popular in England, which he thought synthetic and contrived. Charles Barry's Houses of Parliament, completed in 1843, he once described as 'the most effeminate and effectless heap of stones ever raised by man', and Gothic Revival buildings as a whole suggested to him meat that somebody else had chewed. It was the real thing he loved, with all its fantasies of the grotesque and the ornamental, its unrepentant asymmetries, its grand imperfections, the sense it gave of a lofty common purpose, master and man, architect and common labourer pouring their devotion, their skill and their imagination into the mighty churches of mediaeval Christendom. It was a pity of course that they were Catholic structures: but recognizing their splendour and their virtue did not mean that, like Ruskin's arch-rival Gothicist, the architect Augustus Pugin, one must embrace Papistry as well.

In *The Seven Lamps of Architecture*, which he wrote in his late twenties, he detailed the seven particular qualities he saw in the Gothic style: its sense of sacrifice or dedication, its truthfulness or lack of sham, its power, its beauty (which was essentially the beauty of nature itself) its faithfulness to the past, its obedience to honourable rules, and finally its life, its revelation of the fallible but inspired human spirit that lay behind it, never to be rivalled by mere copies or machine work. By 1849 he had come to see all these characteristics most magnificently exemplified in the buildings of Venice, which was not only the most beautiful of European cities, but seemed to Ruskin the very centre of all history – the place where east and west met, where the cold of the north met the warmth of the south, and where Gothicism in all its meanings could best be analysed in rise, climax and decay.

Intellectually, then, he had arrived in Venice with his mind cleared and ordered for the job. Emotionally he was not so composed, for in the previous year he had embarked upon a marriage which was a failure from the start. Twenty-eight years old then, intensely introverted, in matters of sex Ruskin was altogether innocent, masturbation it seems being his only experience. No young man was ever more assiduously protected by his parents, and it is unlikely that Ruskin had ever set eyes on a naked woman – unlikely perhaps that he had ever lusted after one in any carnal sense. His unhappy adolescent affair had been of a strictly poetical kind, and on his family journeys through Europe he had been more interested in the shapes of mountains than of girls. He was the virgin of virgins. He married, he said himself, 'in order to have a companion – not for passion's sake'.

Euphemia Gray, on the other hand, bubbled with sexuality. The daughter of a Scottish lawyer, she had first entered the Ruskin home in 1841, when she was thirteen, and over the years she and John had gradually slipped into an engagement, alternately encouraged and disapproved by Ruskin's parents (for though Effie was not much of a catch for a gentleman-commoner of Christ Church, she seemed likely to make an affectionate and presentable wife). Effie was bright, pretty, a vivacious dancer, a bit of a snob and something of a flirt. Ruskin thought that in time she might, too, develop scholastically, and be happy contemplating at his side the subtleties of cusps or the derivations of architraves: but Effie was not really the contemplative kind, being cheerfully gregarious, happily conscious of male attentions, and not overwhelmingly concerned with Gothic ornamentation. She knew hardly more than Ruskin did about sexual intercourse, never having been told, she once said, 'the duties of married persons to each other', but she was certainly hoping for more than intellectual companionship.

It is perhaps not surprising that when, in April 1848, they took to their honeymoon bed at Blair Atholl in the Scottish Highlands, Ruskin failed in his husbandly duty. Perhaps when it came to the point the very nature of the sexual act repelled him – it is suggested that he was taken aback to find that women had pubic hair. Perhaps all the years of maternal shelter were taking their toll, and denying him, at his moment of male fulfilment, command of the male prerogatives. Whatever the cause, the marriage was not consummated, and never would be.

At first they made the best of it. Effie suggested kindly that the next time they might both be less frightened. Ruskin proposed that they postpone consummation by mutual agreement – until Effie was twenty-five, say, in four years' time. It was not immediate disaster. They did not want children yet in any case, since Ruskin wished to continue his life of scholarly travel, and Effie doubtless hoped to enjoy a full social life among those she liked to call 'the nobs'. 'It will be much nicer next time', Ruskin assured his wife a year later. 'He really is the kindest creature in the world,' Effie wrote of him, 'and he is so pleased with me . . .'

So they were happy enough during that first winter in Venice, if only because they did not interfere too much with one another. Effie, chaperoned by Charlotte Ker, threw herself with gusto into the social life of the city, found herself admirers and wrote lively letters home. Ruskin worked away all day long, returning to the hotel to work up his sketches and arrange his notes. He was, reported Effie to her parents, kinder and fonder every day; however, 'we ladies like to see and know everything', and she was perfectly happy, she said, following her own pursuits, 'never troubling John, nor he me'.

In the following March, 1851, they went home to England, and Ruskin presented to his publishers the first volume of his book, sub-titled 'The Foundations'. Almost at once, on May 1, while Effie went off with four gentlemen friends to the opening of the Great Exhibition at the Crystal Palace, he started work on the second volume–'may God help me to finish it', he wrote in his diary, 'to His glory and man's good'. His researches were unfinished, though, and in September he and Effie returned to Venice for another winter's work. This time they took an apartment on the Grand Canal, in the house which is now the Gritti Palace Hotel, and they had their own gondoliers, Carlo and Beppo, whom they dressed in red and blue, and Effie became very much part of *le beau monde*, and consorted constantly with nobs.

By now Venice was socially flourishing again, and the Viennese aristocracy turned up in full fig to keep her happy. She was flattered by princes, complimented by archdukes, taken notice of by Radetsky himself and authentically fought over by duellists. Ruskin went along to her balls and parties sometimes, but generally, as before, husband and wife looked after themselves, and now a trace of sourness entered their marriage. Ruskin hated the trumpery ceremonial that Effie loved so much–when the Emperor Franz Joseph was received by Radetzky in the city, he described the pair as looking like 'a great white baboon and a small brown monkey'. Effie accused him of sulking on such occasions, and told her parents that he was writing long accounts of the social state of the Venetians, 'and thinks himself an excellent judge though he knows no-one and never stirs out'.

Still, the work got done. During their last weeks in Venice the Ruskins moved into an apartment actually in the Piazza San Marco, on its north side–very convenient for Effie's café amusements and for Ruskin's never-ending examinations of the Basilica and the Doge's Palace. Their stay in the city was prolonged for an extra week or two by a tiresome and ludicrous affair involving the theft of Effie's jewels and the challenging of Ruskin to a duel: but by the middle of July, 1852, they were home in London. They moved into a house in Herne Hill, the London suburb which had been Ruskin's boyhood home (Effie hated it), and there, working diligently all through that autumn and winter, Ruskin completed *The Stones of Venice*. The second and third volumes, *The Sea-Stories* and *The Fall*, were both published in the following year. 'A strange, unexpected, and I believe, most true and excellent *Sermon* in Stones', Carlyle called the 450,000 words of the completed work.

'Don't frown over it', Carlyle advised a reader about another Ruskinian book. 'Read it again till you understand it.' There is no denying that *The Stones of Venice* is a demanding work. It requires in its readers not just interest and diligence, but a particular frame of mind–a willingness to listen, an earnest sharing of the inquiry, which was perhaps easier to summon in the 1850s than it is today. Ruskin is often infuriating, sometimes ridiculous, but that is not the point. He asks you only to listen, and observe, and think, and so to learn: the reader of *The Stones of Venice* must be prepared to enter the experience (for it really is more than just the reading of a book) *in statu pupillaris*.

This edition is not the first to be abridged. Ruskin supervised his own 'Travellers' Edition' in 1877, and in doing so he himself recognized the uncompromising structure of the work. Not only was it divided into three more or less self-contained volumes, but each long chapter was split inexorably into numbered paragraphs, which gave it at first sight rather the air of a

John Ruskin THE SOUTH SIDE OF ST. MARK'S FROM THE LOGGIA OF THE DUCAL PALACE

Bible, a text-book or perhaps a builder's catalogue. Added to this were sundry appendices – 'Divisions of Humanity', 'Answer to Mr Garbett', 'Theology of Spenser', 'Proper Use of the Word Idolatory' – and a lengthy Venetian gazetteer which included 'every building of importance in the city of Venice itself, or near it'. The reader dipping into this massive work for the first time might well be puzzled to know into what genre of literature it was intended to fall. Was it a guide-book? Was it a technical manual? Was it art criticism? Was it philosophy?

It was really all four, and far more besides, and it doubtless developed as its author wrote it. In later years Ruskin himself defined its principal purposes. First he said, and most importantly, the book showed 'how the rise and fall of the Venetian builders' art depended on the moral or immoral temper of the State'. Secondly, it examined 'the relation of the life of the workman to his work in mediæval times, and its necessary relation to it at all times'. Thirdly, it traced 'the formation of Venetian Gothic from the earliest Romanesque types until it perished in the revival ... of classical principles in the 16th century'. Fourthly, it contained 'an analysis of the best structures of stone and brick building, on a simple and natural scale'.

These serious purposes were embedded in a portrait of the city itself, its history, its setting and its style, which remains perhaps the greatest ever written. Not all of it is strictly accurate in the fact, but it is wonderfully true in the sensation. Ruskin's Venice is an infinitely suggestive sort of dream, and after more than a century his descriptions still capture better than any others, I think, the essential strangeness of Venice, the veiled emanation of privacy that even now accompanies one's first sight of the city.

Ruskin clearly loved his purple passages. When he is about to burst into full lyric voice one feels the joyous spasm approaching in advance, as the tread of the prose shifts, the Degradation of the Crocket finds its proper period, and with a modest break of paragraph the glorious tide of prose is released. Into such passages, perhaps, his deeper passions were channelled; to this day a powerful sensuality emerges from them; we are thrilled as by some seductive temptation to the vision of Torcello in its 'waste of wild sea moor'; there is something orgasmic to the moment when, as our boat is poled through the rank grasses of the Mestre foreshore, we see far in the distance those four or five pale domes beyond the causeway, that sullen cloud of black smoke brooding, and realize it to be Venice.

Ruskin described the buildings of Venice so thoroughly and so fascinatingly that generations of travellers used the work as a sort of handbook, and the Englishman or American following Ruskin column by column along the arcade of the Doge's Palace became a familiar figure of Venetian tourism. 'You may be doomed', John James Ruskin had told his son when he was ten years old, 'to enlighten a People by your Wisdom', and he was certainly conscientious even in his sightseeing advice: a traveller's interest, he once said, was 'too precious a thing to be heedlessly wasted', and he was not much in sympathy with John Murray's *Handbook to Northern Italy*, which contained suggestions on 'how to see all the remarkable objects in Venice in a single day'.

But almost imperceptibly the Victorian tourist, if he stayed the course, was being led on from mere entertainment to deeper things – matters to be mulled over long after the holiday, pondered in maidenly journals or argued about in clubs. Having established so to speak the *mis-en-scène*, 'a city which should surely be interesting to the men of London, as affording the richest existing examples of architecture raised by a mercantile community'–having introduced his readers to Venice as an archetype, Ruskin goes on to interpret the city as a parable.

He saw it as a figure of civilization betrayed. Not for him the exquisite pleasures of the forlorn. He looked back at Venice in her greatness, he looked around him at Venice in her debasement, and he deduced particular moral reasons for the fall. Venice had been great so long as she honoured honest and heroic values, dedicating herself to the glory of God and the common weal: when once she forsook these old loyalties, abandoned the grand ideals of brotherhood between rulers and ruled, rich and poor, so she declined as a State too, until after the sorry tomfooleries of the eighteenth century she subsided at last into the state of subjugation in which mid-Victorians found her.

Ruskin professed to identify the exact moment when the decline started–with the death of Carlo Zeno, one of the most splendid of the Venetian hero-admirals, on May 8, 1418. After that, he maintained, all was slow rot. The nobility of true faith deserted the city, impoverishing its rulers, its artists, its soldiers and its citizens alike. In Venetian architecture, the fine old Gothic gave way to effete neo-classicism: in Venetian art, 'mythologies, ill-understood at first, then perverted into feeble sensuality, [took] the place of the representations of Christian subjects'. In short, the Renaissance had come to Venice, and Ruskin saw it as degrading her style and fatally weakening her values. Art was the badge of morality: it was through the study of Venice, above all other cities, that 'effectual blows could be struck at this pestilential art of the Renaissance', and in the very stones of Venice, he claimed, its moral corruptions could be traced.

The theme is pursued through eleven of the twelve chapters of the present edition. In the first six chapters we observe the rise of Venice to grandeur, evolved in the Byzantine style which Ruskin admired as the worthy precursor of Gothic: in the last five we watch its decline, from the heroic climax of the fourteenth century to the last degradation, expressed in Renaissance buildings that were 'among the worst and basest ever built by the hands of men ... hardly otherwise defined than as the perpetuation in stone of the ribaldries of drunkenness'.

But in the centre of it all, Chapter 7 in this edition, Ruskin embedded an essay which was different in kind from all the others. 'The Nature of Gothic' was to be the most generally admired part of the whole book. It was Ruskin's *cri-de-coeur* about the meaning of the style, and with it the lost society, that he so revered. It forms the crux of the work, for it leads the inquiry into sociopolitical ideas of radical originality. William Morris, who later published it separately in a magnificent Kelmscott Press edition, called it 'one of the very

Overleaf: The Casa d'Oro from a nineteenth-century photograph taken after the
first restorations (compare with Ruskin's watercolour on p. 145):
'*Of what remains, the most beautiful portions are ... the capitals of the windows in the
upper story, most glorious sculpture of the fourteenth century.*'

few necessary and inevitable utterances of the century'. Proust was profoundly moved by it. Kenneth Clark, a century later, thought it 'one of the noblest things written in the 19th century'.

Ruskin now went far beyond his definitions of Gothic in *Seven Lamps*, for he had come to feel that the greatest distinctive character of the style lay in the minds and hearts of the workmen who built it. He had decided, chiefly on the example of the French cathedrals, that ordinary workmen, given freedom of spirit and opportunity, could produce work worthily reflecting the glory of God and the spirit of man. The myriad fantasies and surprises of Gothic architecture, what he called its 'playfulness', its sweet imperfections indeed, he now saw as a mirror of humanity's true nature. Gothic was the very antithesis of all those machine-made products, perfectly finished, absolutely regular, repeatable to order, which were the emblems of the industrial age ('a gross of kings sent down from Kensington', as Ruskin satirized Victorian church statuary).

Gothic was the style *organic*. It could tolerate mistakes, roughnesses, asymmetries, because it was derived strictly from Nature, which detested a straight line as it abhorred a vacuum. It had none of the servile perfection of the neo-classical. It was ornamented not with urns, but with fauna and flora. It was an architecture rude and wild, tinged with humour, joyful, spontaneous, strong, and never afraid of superfluity. It deserved 'our profoundest reverence'.

And what was true for the Middle Ages was true for the nineteenth century. In the course of this brilliant essay, full of life, enriched by Ruskin's love of analogy and synthesis, the deepest message of *The Stones of Venice* reveals itself. It concerns the sanctity of labour, a concept far ahead of its times. Ruskin reasons that the best of architecture, like civilization itself, depends upon the creative participation of ordinary people in its construction. In an era when the average English workman was hardly more than a mechanism himself, Ruskin was reading into the nature of Gothic the text of a time when every man used his heart, his head and his brain to the divine glory.

It was a romantic reading of course – not every labourer was a craftsman in mediaeval Europe, and not every mason was free to chisel how he would: but the very conception of it, the subtle grandeur of Ruskin's arguments, makes 'The Nature of Gothic' the crowning chapter of this book. It comes halfway through, and only after reading the whole work does one realize that *The Stones of Venice* is itself a paradigm of its vision – a mighty Gothic structure itself, obeying Ruskin's own rules with scrupulous splendour.

For it too is, as he would say, rude and wild of character – a soaring, profuse, tangled book, whose shape must be worried out from the spectacular richness of it all. It too scorns symmetry or unnecessary perfection ('either the inscriptions are defaced', Ruskin says endearingly of one of the Doge's Palace columns, 'or I have omitted to note them'). It is often quirky and whimsical. It is full of deductions drawn from Nature itself. It contains a thousand examples of the author's plain manual labour – not only the literary remains of his laborious scramblings and crawlings over monuments, but the drawings too which he executed so diligently throughout his time in Venice. The book is big, like the great fanes he admired so much. It is dappled, like them. It has its gargoyles and its flying buttresses, its mischievous misericordes, its high arches.

Above all, it is a work executed in faith. Ruskin often changed his mind, and was later to renege on some of his judgments in *The Stones of Venice*, not least his sectarian Christian judgments: but he worked always, right or wrong, in the fire of conviction, just as the mediaeval master-masons of his imagination stood on the dizzy scaffold of their towers, or paced their echoing vaults, in the certainty that they were doing the work of God.

The Stones of Venice met with mixed reactions. General readers, though nearly always captivated by its style, were often confused by its reasonings. Architects were affronted, especially by what they took to be Ruskin's claim that ornamentation in architecture was more important than structure. Nevertheless after a slow start the book went on to be a great popular success, and a mighty influence in several ways.

At the simplest level it gave to many thousands of Britons a new interest in the city of Venice. Hitherto travellers there had mostly been rich aristocrats, young men on the Grand Tour, peregrinating dukes. In no small part because of Ruskin's book, in the second half of the nineteenth century the city became a prime destination for the English bourgeoisie, the families of Ruskin's own kind who had risen to wealth on the proceeds of the Industrial Revolution: it was an ironic by-product of Ruskin's sterile married life that Venice became one of the most popular of all choices for middle-class English honeymooners.

To this day there is hardly an anthology of English writing about Venice that does not include some passages of Ruskin, and as recently as 1976 a collection of extracts from *The Stones of Venice* was published specifically for use as a guide-book. The great set-pieces of description are as effective today as they were when they were written—despite the motor-boats, the tankers, the roaring motor highway that now parallels the railway, all of which so amply confirm Ruskin's own bleak prophecy that St. Petroleum would presently outrank St. Peter.

Then again Ruskin's championship of Gothic shaped the attitude of the nation towards that style. If his contentions puzzled people at first, by the end of the nineteenth century they were accepted as neo-gospel. When Ruskin went to Venice in 1849 the Battle of the Styles in England—the fight between the champions of Gothic and of neo-classicism—was already in full swing: it was, though, his passionate advocacy of Gothic that dictated its conclusion, and made late Victorian Britain essentially a place of pointed arches and flying buttresses, rather than porticos and pediments.

He it was, above all others, who persuaded the British public that the Gothic style was the proper one for their historical condition, fit to express their greatness as it had expressed the greatness of Venice. Ruskin's emphasis on its moral content struck just the right chord. His argument that, in Venice at least, it represented the combination of mercantile success, social justice and godly thanksgiving happily indulged their self-image. (And what if Gothic Venice *had* been Catholic—was not Ruskin at pains to emphasize, probably as much for his own comfort as for theirs, that it had been Catholicism of a peculiarly independent kind, constantly at odds with the Papacy?)

Besides, he had convincingly demonstrated that it was a proper style for imperial supremacy—one need not, after all, rule an Empire with Roman forms. Four years after the publication of *The Stones of Venice* the British Crown assumed responsibility for the government of India, and the British felt themselves truly an imperial people. Nearly a quarter of the world would presently be in their possession, a quarter of its people would be their subjects. More than ever did the object-lesson of imperial Venice apply to them: muscular Christianity, *mens sana in corpore sano*, became not merely concepts of personal conduct, but political precepts too.

So Gothic became overwhelmingly the style of imperial Britain. The very look of it became an earnest of probity and success, and all over the British dominions, Canada to New Zealand, buildings arose directly reflecting Ruskinian thought. In later years Ruskin was to suggest that it was a duty of young Britons to migrate across the empty spaces of the world, taking their values with them: they obeyed in their thousands, and they took with them too, to be transmuted wherever they went into trefoil and ornamented gable, the lessons of this book.

These startling results did not always please Ruskin, for if the general conclusions of his arguments became widely known, the premises behind them were all too often ignored, especially by architects. Gothic was being built for the wrong reasons, for the wrong purposes, and in the wrong way. 'The relation of the art of Venice to her moral temper', he complained, 'which is the chief subject of the book, and that of the life of the workman to his work, which is the most important practical principle developed in it, have both been ignored ... by modern architectural readers.'

In a preface to the third edition of *The Stones of Venice*, in 1874, he declared himself horrified by such solecisms as a porch of best Italian Gothic attached to an English pub—'its total motive the provocation of thirst, and the encouragement of idleness'! There was not, he wrote severely, 'the remotest possibility of any success being obtained in any of the arts by a nation which ... mimics the architecture of Christians to promote the trade of poisoners', and he was re-issuing the book 'merely for the little pleasure which I hope it may yet give to readers, few and uninfluential, who still read books through, and wish to understand them ...'

Worse still, wherever he went in England he found God's nature defiled by industrial works, which not only ruined landscapes, but demeaned humanity too. His vision of Gothic after all, and of the society which he saw as its glorious sponsor, was essentially harmonious, a blend of the human, the natural and the divine. Industrial society in Victorian England was exactly the opposite. It was dividing man from Nature, from God and from himself.

Almost immediately after the publication of *The Stones of Venice*, in 1853, he persuaded the University of Oxford to decorate its new Museum according to the principles he enunciated in it, using 'the genius of the unassisted workman'. A family of Irish masons, the O'Sheas, were invited to carve the column-heads free-hand as the spirit moved, drawing upon the examples of

An early photograph of S. Giorgio Maggiore from the Ducal Palace:
'It is impossible to conceive a design more contemptible under every point of rational regard.'

Nature exactly as Ruskin imagined the masons of the Middle Ages working on the columns of the Doge's Palace.

Technically this was not altogether a success. The O'Sheas' owls, monkeys, fruits and vegetables were predictably below the standards of Chartres or Rouen, while their caricatures of University worthies, done in the true spirit of Gothic playfulness, were considered so impertinent than they were decapitated. Still, the enterprise was an effective practical demonstration of Ruskin's belief that the welfare of the workman, his acceptance as a partner, was an integral part of good architectural art, as it ought to be of industrial society. The workmen at the Museum were given their own mess-hall and library, were encouraged to form their own co-operative, and were frequently joined on the site by Ruskin himself, who put up a pillar with his own hands.

The pillar had to be taken down and put up again by professionals; the O'Sheas walked off the job and were replaced by less volatile employees; but the Gospel of Labour was, in the long run, the most compelling idea to come out of *The Stones of Venice*. Ruskin was really looking backwards, to an imaginary Golden Age of mediaevalism. To many readers, though, his notions sounded almost revolutionary in their modernism. Ruskin's father was horrified in his old age to find that his genius son was enlightening the People with proposals half-way to Communism: bourgeois audiences were dismayed when their expected lectures on aesthetic appreciation turned out to be egalitarian polemics—give up all your luxuries, Ruskin told one startled assembly of burghers in Bradford Town Hall, and live as simply as your workers!

It was an ironic message to be drawn, however indirectly, from the example of Venice in her glittering and predatory prime, when the Venetian aristocracy lived in unexampled luxury, and the entire existence of the Republic and its empire revolved around the acquisition of wealth. It was not, however, illogical. Ruskin believed in the unity of virtue: just as he could not believe in the injustice of a society so artistically creative as fifteenth-century Venice, so he could not believe that a society so reconciled to ugliness as Victorian Britain could ever be fair and happy.

And if the mill-owners of Bradford hardly rushed to dispossess themselves, Ruskin did find many disciples elsewhere. His ideas were eagerly taken up by the Christian Socialists of the day. The movement for working-men's education got much of its impetus from them, and when a working-men's college was founded at Oxford in 1899, it was named after him. The Independent Labour Party, which came into being in 1893, was animated largely by the idealistic belief in the nobility of labour which Ruskin preached; when he died it was an article in the Socialist weekly *Clarion*, almost alone among the myriad obituaries, which recognized the unity of all his ideas, artistic, moral and social.

Today many of the themes which Ruskin developed in *The Stones of Venice* seem as contemporary as ever. What modern sociologists call 'the quality of life', that element of fulfilment and self-respect which goes beyond mere economic welfare, was precisely what Ruskin had in mind when he urged the liberation of the working man's spirit. His reverence for Nature foreshadowed the twentieth-century yearning for a return to the God-given order of things.

His impassioned pleas for balance and restraint expressed, in better English, the concerns of today's anxious and embattled ecologists.

All this, from a work ostensibly about the long-dead architecture of a single distant city! *The Stones of Venice* grew in stature as Ruskin wrote it, and it has been growing ever since–in the depths of its meaning, in the range of its analogies, and in the relevance of its thought.

Ruskin lived for almost half a century after the publication of the book, dying in 1900, at his home on Lake Coniston in the English Lake District, after a series of mental breakdowns. His marriage to Effie had survived only another year: in 1854 she procured an annulment on the grounds of his 'incurable impotency' and married his friend the painter John Millais, by whom she had eight children. Ruskin went on to a tempestuous love affair with a girl thirty years his junior, Rose La Touche, ended only by her death insane in 1875, and developed in old age a rather embarrassing fondness for pubescent girls: but so far as is known he remained a celibate, and his creative powers were directed as always into a tumultuous out-pouring of books and pamphlets–books of criticism and philosophy, books of social comment, four more volumes of *Modern Painters*, a private magazine, *Fors Clavigera*, in which he published month by month his irrepressible ideas on every subject under the sun.

He became a vastly popular if eccentric Slade Professor of Art at Oxford, and founded the St. George's Guild, a utopian but unsuccessful instrument of social reform. He lost his Christian faith, and became in his old age, as he sank sporadically into madness, tragically disillusioned. The warning of Venice, he believed, had been disregarded; moral gloom had overcome the nation; wherever he looked in his last years, when Europe was lurching towards war, he saw fateful images of storm cloud and plague wind–'its sound ... a hiss instead of a wail'.

He never again wrote anything as complete, as majestic or as influential as *The Stones of Venice*, and his name is linked indissolubly with the city which had proved so marvellous a quarry for his mind. He often went back there, and later wrote a handbook to the city, *St. Mark's Rest*, and a guide to the pictures in the Accademia gallery, besides playing a leading role in the conservation of Venetian buildings. He was, he declared, a foster-child of Venice, and the city acknowledges it still. At the Danieli and Gritti Palace Hotels they still show you the rooms he occupied with Effie: on the Zattere a plaque marks the site of the house he occupied during later visits. Sometimes, even now, you may see people wandering around with copies of Ruskin in their hands: and those of imaginative turn may even occasionally glimpse the tall stooped figure of the sage himself–measuring, drawing and expostulating still, precarious on ladders in shadowy recesses, being dusted down by Domenico beneath the palace arcades, or waved at in a pre-occupied way, perhaps, by Effie from her seat among the *aides-de-camp* at Quadri's.

As to the city itself, Byzantine, Gothic and Renaissance alike, it has survived all that history and changing taste has brought to bear upon it, and proceeds still down the generations, as Ruskin would have wished it, from allegory to allegory.

John Ruskin PALAZZO DARIO
'The palaces in which Renaissance is engrafted on Byzantine . . . are characterized by
an ornamentation very closely resembling Byzantine work; namely groups of coloured
marble circles inclosed in interlacing bands.'

THE QUARRY

SINCE first the dominion of men was asserted over the ocean, three thrones, of mark beyond all others, have been set upon its sands: the thrones of Tyre, Venice, and England. Of the First of these great powers only the memory remains; of the Second, the ruin; the Third, which inherits their greatness, if it forget their example, may be led through prouder eminence to less pitied destruction.

The exaltation, the sin, and the punishment of Tyre have been recorded for us, in perhaps the most touching words ever uttered by the Prophets of Israel against the cities of the stranger. But we read them as a lovely song; and close our ears to the sternness of their warning: for the very depth of the Fall of Tyre has blinded us to its reality, and we forget, as we watch the bleaching of the rocks between the sunshine and the sea, that they were once 'as in Eden, the garden of God.'

Her successor, like her in perfection of beauty, though less in endurance of dominion, is still left for our beholding in the final period of her decline: a ghost upon the sands of the sea, so weak – so quiet, – so bereft of all but her loveliness, that we might well doubt, as we watched her faint reflection in the mirage of the lagoon, which was the City, and which the Shadow.

I would endeavour to trace the lines of this image before it be for ever lost, and to record, as far as I may, the warning which seems to me to be uttered by every one of the fast-gaining waves, that beat like passing bells, against the STONES OF VENICE.

It would be difficult to overrate the value of the lessons which might be derived from a faithful study of the history of this strange and mighty city: a history which, in spite of the labour of countless chroniclers, remains in vague and disputable outline, – barred with brightness and shade, like the far away edge of her own ocean, where the surf and the sandbank are mingled with the sky. The inquiries in which we have to engage will hardly render this outline clearer, but their results will, in some degree, alter its aspect; and, so far as they bear upon it at all, they possess an interest of a far higher kind than that usually belonging to architectural investigations. I may, perhaps, in the outset, and in a few words, enable the general reader to form a clearer idea of the importance of every existing expression of Venetian character through Venetian art, and of the breadth of interest which the true history of Venice embraces, than he is likely to have gleaned from the current fables of her mystery or magnificence.

Venice is usually conceived as an oligarchy: She was so during a period less than the half of her existence, and that including the days of her decline; and it is one of the first questions needing severe examination, whether that decline was owing in any wise to the change in the form of her government, or altogether, as assuredly in great part, to changes in the character of the persons of whom it was composed.

The state of Venice existed Thirteen Hundred and Seventy-six years, from the first establishment of a consular government on the island of the Rialto, to the moment when the General-in-chief of the French army of Italy pronounced the Venetian republic a thing of the past. Of this period, Two Hundred and Seventy-six years were passed in a nominal subjection to the cities of old Venetia, especially to Padua, and in an agitated form of democracy, of which the executive appears to have been entrusted to tribunes, chosen, one by the inhabitants of each of the principal islands. For six hundred years, during which the power of Venice was continually on the increase, her government was an elective monarchy, her King or doge possessing, in early times at least, as much independent authority as any other European sovereign, but an authority gradually subjected to limitation, and shortened almost daily of its prerogatives, while it increased in a spectral and incapable magnificence. The final government of the nobles, under the image of a king, lasted for five hundred years, during which Venice reaped the fruits of her former energies, consumed them, – and expired.

Let the reader therefore conceive the existence of the Venetian state as broadly divided into two periods: the first of nine hundred, the second of five hundred years, the separation being marked by what was called the 'Serrar del Consiglio'; that is to say, the final and absolute distinction of the nobles from the commonalty, and the establishment of the government in their hands to the exclusion alike of the influence of the people on the one side, and the authority of the doge on the other.

Then the first period, of nine hundred years, presents us with the most interesting spectacle of a people struggling out of anarchy into order and power; and then governed, for the most part, by the worthiest and noblest man whom they could find among them, called their Doge or Leader, with an aristocracy gradually and resolutely forming itself around him, out of which, and at last by which, he was chosen; an aristocracy owing its origin to the accidental numbers, influence, and wealth of some among the families of the fugitives from the older Venetia, and gradually organising itself, by its unity and heroism, into a separate body.

This first period includes the Rise of Venice, her noblest achievements, and the circumstances which determined her character and position among European powers; and within its range, as might have been anticipated, we find the names of all her hero princes – of Pietro Urseolo, Ordalafo Falier, Domenico Michieli, Sebastiano Ziani, and Enrico Dandolo.

The second period opens with a hundred and twenty years, the most eventful in the career of Venice—the central struggle of her life—stained with her darkest crime, the murder of Carrara—disturbed by her most dangerous internal sedition, the conspiracy of Falier—oppressed by her most fatal war, the war of Chiozza—and distinguished by the glory of her two noblest citizens (for in this period the heroism of her citizens replaces that of her monarchs), Vittor Pisani and Carlo Zeno.

I date the commencement of the Fall of Venice from the death of Carlo Zeno, 8th May, 1418; the *visible* commencement from that of another of her noblest and wisest children, the Doge Tomaso Mocenigo, who expired five years later. The reign of Foscari followed, gloomy with pestilence and war; a war in which large acquisitions of territory were made by subtle or fortunate policy in Lombardy, and disgrace, significant as irreparable, sustained in the battles on the Po at Cremona, and in the marshes of Caravaggio. In 1454, Venice, the first of the states of Christendom, humiliated herself to the Turk: in the same year was established the Inquisition of State, and from this period her government takes the perfidious and mysterious form under which it is usually conceived. In 1477, the great Turkish invasion spread terror to the shores of the lagoons; and in 1508 the league of Cambrai marks the period usually assigned as the commencement of the decline of the Venetian power; the commercial prosperity of Venice in the close of the fifteenth century blinding her historians to the previous evidence of the diminution of her internal strength.

Now there is apparently a significative coincidence between the establishment of the aristocratic and oligarchical powers, and the diminution of the prosperity of the state. But this is the very question at issue; and it appears to me quite undetermined by any historian, or determined by each in accordance with his own prejudices. It is a triple question: first, whether the oligarchy established by the efforts of individual ambition was the cause, in its subsequent operation, of the Fall of Venice; or (secondly) whether the establishment of the oligarchy itself be not the sign and evidence, rather than the cause, of national enervation; or (lastly) whether, as I rather think, the history of Venice might not be written almost without reference to the construction of her senate or the prerogatives of her Doge. It is the history of a people eminently at unity in itself, descendants of Roman race, long disciplined by adversity, and compelled by its position either to live nobly or to perish:—for a thousand years they fought for life; for three hundred they invited death: their battle was rewarded, and their call was heard.

Throughout her career, the victories of Venice, and, at many periods of it, her safety, were purchased by individual heroism; and the man who exalted or saved her was sometimes (oftenest) her king, sometimes a noble, sometimes a citizen. To him no matter, nor to her: the real question is, not so much what names they bore, or with what powers they were entrusted, as how they were trained, how they were made masters of themselves, servants of their country, patient of distress, impatient of dishonour; and what was the true reason of the change from the time when she could find saviours among those whom she had cast into prison, to that when the voices of her own children commanded her to sign covenant with Death.

On this collateral question I wish the reader's mind to be fixed throughout all our subsequent inquiries. It will give double interest to every detail: nor will the interest be profitless; for the evidence which I shall be able to deduce from the arts of Venice will be both frequent and irrefragable, that the decline of her political prosperity was exactly coincident with that of domestic and individual religion.

I say domestic and individual; for – and this is the second point which I wish the reader to keep in mind – the most curious phenomenon in all Venetian history is the vitality of religion in private life, and its deadness in public policy. Amidst the enthusiasm, chivalry, or fanaticism of the other states of Europe, Venice stands, from first to last, like a masked statue; her coldness impenetrable, her exertion only aroused by the touch of a secret spring. That spring was her commercial interest – this the one motive of all her important political acts, or enduring national animosities. She could forgive insults to her honour, but never rivalship in her commerce; she calculated the glory of her conquests by their value, and estimated their justice by their facility. The fame of success remains, when the motives of attempt are forgotten; and the casual reader of her history may perhaps be surprised to be reminded – that the expedition which was commanded by the noblest of her princes, and whose results added most to her military glory, was one in which, while all Europe around her was wasted by the fire of its devotion, she first calculated the highest price she could exact from its piety for the armament she furnished, and then, for the advancement of her own private interests, at once broke her faith and betrayed her religion, by directing the arms of the Crusaders against a Christian prince.

And yet, in the midst of this national criminality, we shall be struck again and again by the evidences of the most noble individual feeling. The tears of Dandolo were not shed in hypocrisy, though they could not blind him to the importance of the conquest of Zara. The habit of assigning to religion a direct influence over all *his own* actions, and all the affairs of *his own* daily life, is remarkable in every great Venetian during the times of the prosperity of the state; nor are instances wanting in which the private feeling of the citizens reaches the sphere of their policy, and even becomes the guide of its course where the scales of expediency are doubtfully balanced. I sincerely trust that the inquirer would be disappointed who should endeavour to trace any more immediate reasons for their adoption of the cause of Alexander III against Barbarossa, than the piety which was excited by the character of their suppliant, and the noble pride which was provoked by the insolence of the emperor. But the heart of Venice is shown only in her hastiest councils; her worldly spirit recovers the ascendancy whenever she has time to calculate the probabilities of advantage, or when they are sufficiently distinct to need no calculation; and the entire subjection of private piety to national policy is not only remarkable throughout the almost endless series of treacheries and tyrannies by which her empire was enlarged and maintained, but symbolised by a very singular circumstance in the building of the city itself. I am aware of no other city of Europe in which its cathedral was not the principal feature. But the principal church in Venice was the chapel attached to the palace of her prince, and called the 'Chiesa Ducale'. The patriarchal church, inconsiderable in size and mean in decoration, stands on the outermost islet of the

Venetian group, and its name, as well as its site, are probably unknown to the greater number of travellers passing hastily through the city. Nor is it less worthy of remark, that the two most important temples of Venice, next to the ducal chapel, owe their size and magnificence, not to national efforts, but to the energy of the Franciscan and Dominican monks, supported by the vast organisation of those great societies on the mainland of Italy, and countenanced by the most pious, and perhaps also, in his generation, the most wise, of all the princes of Venice, Tomaso Mocenigo, who now rests beneath the roof of one of those very temples, and whose life is not satirized by the images of the Virtues which a Tuscan sculptor has placed around his tomb.

There are, therefore, two strange and solemn lights in which we have to regard almost every scene in the fitful history of the Rivo Alto. We find, on the one hand, a deep and constant tone of individual religion characterising the lives of the citizens of Venice in her greatness; we find this spirit influencing them in all the familiar and immediate concerns of life, giving a peculiar dignity to the conduct even of their commercial transactions, and confessed by them with a simplicity of faith that may well put to shame the hesitation with which a man of the world at present admits (even if it be so in reality) that religious feeling has any influence over the minor branches of his conduct. And we find as the natural consequence of all this, a healthy serenity of mind and energy of will expressed in all their actions, and a habit of heroism which never fails them, even when the immediate motive of action ceases to be praise-worthy. With the fulness of this spirit the prosperity of the state is exactly correspondent, and with its failure her decline, and that with a closeness and precision which it will be one of the collateral objects of the following essay to demonstrate from such accidental evidence as the field of its inquiry presents. And, thus far, all is natural and simple. But the stopping short of this religious faith when it appears likely to influence national action, correspondent as it is, and that most strikingly, with several characteristics of the temper of our present English legislature, is a subject, morally and politically, of the most curious interest and complicated difficulty; one, however, which the range of my present inquiry will not permit me to approach, and for the treatment of which I must be content to furnish materials in the light I may be able to throw upon the private tendencies of the Venetian character.

One more circumstance remains to be noted respecting the Venetian government, the singular unity of the families composing it,—unity far from sincere or perfect, but still admirable when contrasted with the fiery feuds, the almost daily revolutions, the restless successions of families and parties in power, which fill the annals of the other states of Italy. That rivalship should sometimes be ended by the dagger, or enmity conducted to its ends under the mask of law, could not but be anticipated where the fierce Italian spirit was subjected to so severe a restraint: it is much that jealousy appears usually unmingled with illegitimate ambition, and that, for every instance in which private passion sought its gratification through public danger, there are a thousand in which it was sacrificed to the public advantage. Venice may well call upon us to note with reverence, that of all the towers which are still seen rising like a branchless forest from her islands, there is but one whose office was other than that of summoning to prayer, and that one was a watch-tower only: from first to last, while the palaces of the other cities of Italy were lifted into sullen fortitudes of rampart, and fringed with forked battlements for the javelin and the bow, the sands of Venice never sank under the weight of a war tower, and her roof terraces were wreathed with Arabian imagery, of golden globes suspended on the leaves of lilies.

These, then, appear to me to be the points of chief general interest in the character and fate of the Venetian people. I would next endeavour to give the reader some idea of the manner in which the testimony of Art bears upon these questions, and of the aspect which the arts themselves assume when they are regarded in their true connection with the history of the state:

1st. Receive the witness of Painting.

It will be remembered that I put the commencement of the Fall of Venice as far back as 1418.

Now, John Bellini was born in 1423, and Titian in 1480. John Bellini, and his brother Gentile, two years older than he, close the line of the sacred painters of Venice. But the most solemn spirit of religious faith animates their works to the last. There is no religion in any work of Titian's: there is not even the smallest evidence of religious temper or sympathies either in himself, or in those for whom he painted. His larger sacred subjects are merely themes for the exhibition of pictorial rhetoric, – composition and colour. His minor works are generally made subordinate to purposes of portraiture. The Madonna in the church of the Frari is a mere lay figure, introduced to form a link of connection between the portraits of various members of the Pesaro family who surround her.

Now this is not merely because John Bellini was a religious man and Titian was not. Titian and Bellini are each true representatives of the school of painters contemporary with them; and the difference in their artistic feeling is a consequence not so much of difference in their own natural characters as in their early education: Bellini was brought up in faith; Titian in formalism. Between the years of their births the vital religion of Venice had expired.

The *vital* religion, observe, not the formal. Outward observance was as strict as ever; and doge and senator still were painted, in almost every important instance, kneeling before the Madonna or St. Mark; a confession of faith made universal by the pure gold of the Venetian sequin. But observe the great picture of Titian's, in the ducal palace, of the Doge Antonio Grimani kneeling before Faith: there is a curious lesson in it. The figure of Faith is a coarse portrait of one of Titian's least graceful female models: Faith had become carnal. The eye is first caught by the flash of the Doge's armour. The heart of Venice was in her wars, not in her worship.

The mind of Tintoret, incomparably more deep and serious than that of Titian, casts the solemnity of its own tone over the sacred subjects which it approaches, and sometimes forgets itself into devotion; but the principle of treatment is altogether the same as Titian's: absolute subordination of the religious subject to purposes of decoration or portraiture.

The evidence might be accumulated a thousandfold from the works of Veronese, and of every succeeding painter, – that the fifteenth century had taken away the religious heart of Venice.

Such is the evidence of Painting. To collect that of Architecture will be our

Giovanni Bellini MADONNA AND CHILD
'John Bellini and his brother Gentile close the line of sacred painters of Venice.
But the most solemn spirit of religious faith animates their works to the last.'

task through many a page to come; but I must here give a general idea of its heads.

Philippe de Commynes, writing of his entry into Venice in 1495, says, –

They placed me between these two Ambassadors, (for the midst in *Italy* is the honourablest place) and conveyed me along through the great street called the great channel, which is so large that the gallies pass to and fro through it, yea I have seen hard by the houses ships of four hundred tun and above. Sure in mine opinion it is the goodliest street in the world and the best built, and reacheth in length from the one end of the Towne to the other. Their buildings are high and stately, and all of fine stone. The ancient houses be all painted; but the rest that have been built within these hundred years, have their front all of marble, brought thither out of *Istria* a hundred miles thence, and are beautified with many great pieces of Porphire and Sarpentine.... It is the most triumphant City that ever I saw, and where Ambassadors and strangers are most honourably entertained, the Commonwealth best governed, and God most devoutly served; so far forth, that notwithstanding they have divers imperfections, yet think I verily that God prospereth them, because of the reverence they bear to the service of the Church.

This passage is of peculiar interest, for two reasons. Observe, first, the impression of Commynes respecting the religion of Venice: of which, as I have above said, the forms still remained with some glimmering of life in them, and were the evidence of what the real life had been in former times. But observe, secondly, the impression instantly made on Commynes' mind by the distinction between the elder palaces and those built 'within this last hundred years; which all have their fronts of white marble brought from Istria, a hundred miles away, and besides, many a large piece of porphyry and serpentine upon their fronts.'

The French ambassador was right in his notice of the distinction. There had indeed come a change over Venetian architecture in the fifteenth century; and a change of some importance to us moderns: we English owe to it our St. Paul's Cathedral, and Europe in general owes to it the utter degradation or destruction of her schools of architecture, never since revived. But that the reader may understand this, it is necessary that he should have some general idea of the connection of the architecture of Venice with that of the rest of Europe, from its origin forwards.

All European architecture, bad and good, old and new, is derived from Greece through Rome, and coloured and perfected from the East. The history of architecture is nothing but the tracing of the various modes and directions of this derivation. Understand this, once for all: if you hold fast this great connecting clue, you may string all the types of successive architectural

Wall-Veil Decoration from the Ca' Trevisian, *'in which a most curious and delicate piece of inlaid design is introduced into a band which is almost exactly copied from the church of Theotocos at Constantinople'*.

invention upon it like so many beads. The Doric and the Corinthian orders are the roots, the one of all Romanesque, massy-capitalled buildings–Norman, Lombard, Byzantine, and what else you can name of the kind; and the Corinthian of all Gothic, Early English, French, German, and Tuscan. Now observe: those old Greeks gave the shaft; Rome gave the arch; the Arabs pointed and foliated the arch. The shaft and arch, the framework and strength of architecture, are from the race of Japheth: the spirituality and sanctity of it from Ismael, Abraham, and Shem.

I have said that the two orders, Doric and Corinthian, are the roots of all European architecture. You have, perhaps, heard of five orders: but there are only two real orders; and there never can be any more until doomsday. On one of these orders the ornament is convex: those are Doric, Norman, and what else you recollect of the kind. On the other the ornament is concave: those are Corinthian, Early English, Decorated, and what else you recollect of that kind. The transitional form, in which the ornamental line is straight, is the centre or root of both. All other orders are varieties of these, or phantasms and grotesques, altogether indefinite in number and species.

This Greek architecture, then, with its two orders, was clumsily copied and varied by the Romans with no particular result, until they began to bring the arch into extensive practical service; except only that the Doric capital was spoiled in endeavours to mend it, and the Corinthian much varied and enriched with fanciful, and often very beautiful imagery. And in this state of things came Christianity: seized upon the arch as her own: decorated it, and delighted in it: invented a new Doric capital to replace the spoiled Roman one: and all over the Roman empire set to work, with such materials as were nearest at hand, to express and adorn herself as best she could. This Roman Christian architecture is the exact expression of the Christianity of the time, very fervid and beautiful–but very imperfect; in many respects ignorant, and yet radiant with a strong, childlike light of imagination, which flames up under Constantine, illumines all the shores of the Bosphorus and Ægean and the Adriatic Sea, and then gradually, as the people give themselves up to idolatry, becomes corpse-light. The architecture sinks into a settled form–a strange, gilded, and embalmed repose: it, with the religion it expressed; and so would have remained for ever,–so *does* remain, where its languor has been undisturbed. But rough wakening was ordained for it.

This Christian art of the declining empire is divided into two great branches, western and eastern; one centred at Rome, the other at Byzantium, of which the one is the early Christian Romanesque, properly so called, and the other, carried to higher imaginative perfection by Greek workmen, is distinguished from it as Byzantine. But I wish the reader, for the present, to class these two branches of art together in his mind, they being, in points of main importance, the same; that is to say, both of them a true continuance and sequence of the art of old Rome itself, flowing uninterruptedly down from the fountain-head, and entrusted always to the best workmen who could be found–Latins in Italy and Greeks in Greece; and thus both branches may be ranged under the general term of Christian Romanesque, an architecture which had lost the refinement of Pagan art in the degradation of the empire, but which was elevated by Christianity to higher aims, and by the fancy of the

Greek workmen endowed with brighter forms. And this art the reader may conceive as extending in its various branches over all the central provinces of the empire, taking aspects more or less refined, according to its proximity to the seats of government; dependent for all its power on the vigour and freshness of the religion which animated it; and as that vigour and purity departed, losing its own vitality, and sinking into nerveless rest, not deprived of its beauty, but benumbed, and incapable of advance or change.

Meantime there had been preparation for its renewal. While in Rome and Constantinople, and in the districts under their immediate influence, this Roman art of pure descent was practised in all its refinement, an impure form of it—a patois of Romanesque—was carried by inferior workmen into distant provinces; and still ruder imitations of this patois were executed by the barbarous nations on the skirts of the empire. But these barbarous nations were in the strength of their youth; and while, in the centre of Europe, a refined and purely descended art was sinking into graceful formalism, on its confines a barbarous and borrowed art was organising itself into strength and consistency. The reader must therefore consider the history of the work of the period as broadly divided into two great heads: the one embracing the elaborately languid succession of the Christian art of Rome; and the other, the imitations of it executed by nations in every conceivable phase of early organisation, on the edges of the empire, or included in its now merely nominal extent.

Some of the barbaric nations were, of course, not susceptible of this influence; and, when they burst over the Alps, appear, like the Huns, as scourges only, or mix, as the Ostrogoths, with the enervated Italians, and give physical strength to the mass with which they mingle, without materially affecting its intellectual character. But others, both south and north of the empire, had felt its influence, back to the beach of the Indian Ocean on the one hand, and to the ice creeks of the North Sea on the other. On the north and west the influence was of the Latins; on the south and east, of the Greeks. Two nations, pre-eminent above all the rest, represent to us the force of derived mind on either side. As the central power is eclipsed, the orbs of reflected light gather into their fulness; and when sensuality and idolatry had done their work, and the religion of the empire was laid asleep in a glittering sepulchre, the living light rose upon both horizons, and the fierce swords of the Lombard and Arab were shaken over its golden paralysis.

The work of the Lombard was to give hardihood and system to the enervated body and enfeebled mind of Christendom; that of the Arab was to punish idolatry, and to proclaim the spirituality of worship. The Lombard covered every church which he built with the sculptured representations of bodily exercises—hunting and war. The Arab banished all imagination of creature form from his temples, and proclaimed from their minarets, 'There is no god but God.' Opposite in their character and mission, alike in their magnificence of energy, they came from the North and from the South, the glacier torrent and the lava stream: they met and contended over the wreck of the Roman empire; and the very centre of the struggle, the point of pause of both, the dead water of the opposite eddies, charged with embayed fragments of the Roman wreck, is VENICE.

The Ducal palace of Venice contains the three elements in exactly equal

Titian THE MADONNA OF THE PESARO FAMILY
'*The Madonna in the Church of the Frari is a mere lay figure, introduced to form a
link of connection between the portraits of various members of the Pesaro family.*'

proportions—the Roman, Lombard, and Arab. It is the central building of the world.

The reader will now begin to understand something of the importance of the study of the edifices of a city which concludes, within the circuit of some seven or eight miles, the field of contest between the three pre-eminent architectures of the world:—each architecture expressing a condition of religion; each an erroneous condition, yet necessary to the correction of the others, and corrected by them.

The glacier stream of the Lombards, and the following one of the Normans, left their erratic blocks wherever they had flowed; but without influencing, I think, the Southern nations beyond the sphere of their own presence. But the lava stream of the Arab, even after it ceased to flow, warmed the whole of the Northern air; and the history of Gothic architecture is the history of the refinement and spiritualisation of Northern work under its influence. The noblest buildings of the world, the Pisan-Romanesque, Tuscan (Giottesque) Gothic, and Veronese Gothic, are those of the Lombard schools themselves, under its close and direct influence; the various Gothics of the North are the original forms of the architecture which the Lombards brought into Italy, changing under the less direct influence of the Arab.

Understanding thus much of the formation of the great European styles, we shall have no difficulty in tracing the succession of architectures in Venice herself. From what I said of the central character of Venetian art, the reader is not, of course, to conclude that the Roman, Northern, and Arabian elements met together and contended for the mastery at the same period. The earliest element was the pure Christian Roman; but few, if any, remains of this art exist at Venice; for the present city was in the earliest times only one of many settlements formed on the chain of marshy islands which extend from the mouths of the Isonzo to those of the Adige, and it was not until the beginning of the ninth century that it became the seat of government; while the cathedral of Torcello, though Christian Roman in general form, was rebuilt in the eleventh century, and shows evidence of Byzantine workmanship in many of its details. This cathedral, however, with the church of Santa Fosca at Torcello, San Giacomo di Rialto at Venice, and the crypt of St. Mark's, form a distinct group of building, in which the Byzantine influence is exceedingly slight; and which is sufficiently representative of the earliest architecture on the islands.

The Ducal residence was removed to Venice in 809, and the body of St. Mark was brought from Alexandria twenty years later. The first church of St. Mark was, doubtless, built in imitation of that destroyed at Alexandria, and from which the relics of the Saint had been obtained. During the ninth, tenth, and eleventh centuries, the architecture of Venice seems to have been formed on the same model, and is almost identical with that of Cairo under the caliphs, it being quite immaterial whether the reader chooses to call both Byzantine or both Arabic; the workmen being certainly Byzantine, but forced to the invention of new forms by their Arabian masters, and bringing these forms into use in whatever other parts of the world they were employed.

To this first manner of Venetian Architecture, together with such vestiges as remain of the Christian Roman, I shall devote the first division of the following inquiry. The examples remaining of it consist of three noble churches (those of Torcello, Murano, and the greater part of St. Mark's), and about ten or twelve fragments of palaces.

To this style succeeds a transitional one of a character much more distinctly Arabian; the shafts become more slender, and the arches consistently pointed, instead of round; certain other changes, not to be enumerated in a sentence, taking place in the capitals and mouldings. This style is almost exclusively secular. It was natural for the Venetians to imitate the beautiful details of the Arabian dwelling-house, while they would with reluctance adopt those of the mosque for Christian churches.

I have not succeeded in fixing limiting dates for this style. It appears in part contemporary with the Byzantine manner, but outlives it. Its position is, however, fixed by the central date, 1180, that of the elevation of the granite shafts of the Piazzetta, whose capitals are the two most important pieces of detail in this transitional style in Venice. Examples of its application to domestic buildings exist in almost every street of the city, and will form the subject of the second division of the following essay.

The Venetians were always ready to receive lessons in art from their enemies (else had there been no Arab work in Venice). But their especial dread and hatred of the Lombards appear to have long prevented them from receiving the influence of the art which that people had introduced on the mainland of Italy. Nevertheless, during the practice of the two styles above distinguished, a peculiar and very primitive condition of pointed Gothic had arisen in ecclesiastical architecture. It appears to be a feeble reflection of the Lombard-Arab forms, which were attaining perfection upon the continent, and would probably, if left to itself, have been soon merged in the Venetian-Arab school, with which it had from the first so close a fellowship, that it will be found difficult to distinguish the Arabian ogives from those which seem to have been built under this early Gothic influence. The churches of San Giacomo dell' Orio, San Giovanni in Bragora, the Carmine, and one or two more, furnish the only important examples of it. But, in the thirteenth century, the Franciscans and Dominicans introduced from the continent their morality and their architecture, already a distinct Gothic, curiously developed from Lombardic and Northern (German?) forms; and the influence of the principles exhibited in the vast churches of St. Paul and the Frari began rapidly to affect the Venetian-Arab school. Still the two systems never became united; the Venetian policy repressed the power of the church, and the Venetian artists resisted its example; and thenceforward the architecture of the city becomes divided into ecclesiastical and civil: the one an ungraceful yet powerful form of the Western Gothic, common to the whole peninsula, and only showing Venetian sympathies in the adoption of certain characteristic mouldings; the other a rich, luxuriant, and entirely original Gothic, formed from the Venetian-Arab by the influence of the Dominican and Franciscan architecture, and especially by the engrafting upon the Arab forms of the most novel feature of the Franciscan work, its traceries. These various forms of Gothic, the *distinctive* architecture of Venice, chiefly represented by the churches of St. John and Paul, the Frari, and San Stefano, on the ecclesiastical side, and by the Ducal palace, and the other principal Gothic palaces, on the secular side, will be the subject of the third division of the essay.

Now observe. The transitional (or especially Arabic) style of the Venetian work is centralised by the date 1180, and is transformed gradually into the Gothic, which extends in its purity from the middle of the thirteenth to the beginning of the fifteenth century; that is to say, over the precise period which I have described as the central epoch of the life of Venice. I dated her decline from the year 1418; Foscari became doge five years later, and in his reign the first marked signs appear in architecture of that mighty change which Philippe de Commynes notices as above, the change to which London owes St. Paul's, Rome St. Peter's, Venice and Vicenza the edifices commonly supposed to be their noblest, and Europe in general the degradation of every art she has since practised.

This change appears first in a loss of truth and vitality in existing architecture all over the world. All the Gothics in existence, southern or northern, were corrupted at once: the German and French lost themselves in every species of extravagance; the English Gothic was confined, in its insanity, by a strait-waistcoat of perpendicular lines; the Italian effloresced on the mainland into the meaningless ornamentation of the Certosa of Pavia and the Cathedral of Como (a style sometimes ignorantly called Italian Gothic), and at Venice into the insipid confusion of the Porta della Carta and wild crockets of St. Mark's. This corruption of all architecture, especially ecclesiastical, corresponded with, and marked the state of religion over all Europe–the peculiar degradation of the Romanist superstition, and of public morality in consequence, which brought about the Reformation.

Now Venice, as she was once the most religious, was in her fall the most corrupt, of European states; and as she was in her strength the centre of the pure currents of Christian architecture, so she is in her decline the source of the Renaissance. It was the originality and splendour of the palaces of Vicenza and Venice which gave this school its eminence in the eyes of Europe; and the dying city, magnificent in her dissipation, and graceful in her follies, obtained wider worship in her decrepitude than in her youth, and sank from the midst of her admirers into the grave.

It is in Venice, therefore, and in Venice only, that effectual blows can be struck at this pestilent art of the Renaissance. Destroy its claims to admiration there, and it can assert them nowhere else. This, therefore, will be the final purpose of the following essay. I shall not devote a section to Palladio, nor weary the reader with successive chapters of vituperation; but I shall, in my account of the earlier architecture, compare the forms of all its leading features with those into which they were corrupted by the Classicalists; and pause, in the close, on the edge of the precipice of decline, so soon as I have made its depth discernible. In doing this I shall depend upon two distinct kinds of evidence:–the first, the testimony borne by particular incidents and facts to a want of thought or of feeling in the builders; from which we may conclude that their architecture must be bad:–the second, the sense, which I doubt not I shall be able to excite in the reader, of a systematic ugliness in the architecture itself. Of the first kind of testimony I shall here give two instances, which may be immediately useful in fixing in the reader's mind the epoch above indicated for the commencement of decline.

I must again refer to the importance which I have above attached to the death of Carlo Zeno and the Doge Tomaso Mocenigo. The tomb of that doge is, as I said, wrought by a Florentine; but it is of the same general type and feeling as all the Venetian tombs of the period, and it is one of the last which retains it. The classical element enters largely into its details, but the feeling of the whole is as yet unaffected. Like all the lovely tombs of Venice and Verona, it is a sarcophagus with a recumbent figure above, and this figure is a faithful but tender portrait, wrought as far as it can be without painfulness, of the doge as he lay in death. He wears his Ducal robe and bonnet—his head is laid slightly aside upon his pillow—his hands are simply crossed as they fall. The face is emaciated, the features large, but so pure and lordly in their natural chiselling, that they must have looked like marble even in their animation. They are deeply worn away by thought and death; the veins on the temples branched and starting; the skin gathered in sharp folds; the brow high-arched and shaggy; the eye-ball magnificently large; the curve of the lips just veiled by the light moustache at the side; the beard short, double, and sharp-pointed: all noble and quiet; the white sepulchral dust marking like light the stern angles of the cheek and brow.

This tomb was sculptured in 1424, and is thus described by one of the most intelligent of the recent writers who represent the popular feeling respecting Venetian art [Pietro Selvatico].

Of the Italian school is also the rich but ugly (ricco ma non bel) sarcophagus in which repose the ashes of Tomaso Mocenigo. It may be called one of the last links which connect the declining art of the Middle Ages with that of the Renaissance, which was in its rise. We will not stay to particularise the defects of each of the seven figures of the front and sides, which represent the cardinal and theological virtues; nor will we make any remarks upon those which stand in the niches above the pavilion, because we consider them unworthy both of the age and reputation of the Florentine school, which was then with reason considered the most notable in Italy.

It is well, indeed, not to pause over these defects; but it might have been better to have paused a moment beside that noble image of a king's mortality.

In the choir of the same church, St. Giov. and Paolo, is another tomb, that of the Doge Andrea Vendramin. This doge died in 1478, after a short reign of two years, the most disastrous in the annals of Venice. He died of a pestilence which followed the ravage of the Turks, carried to the shores of the lagoons. He died, leaving Venice disgraced by sea and land, with the smoke of hostile devastation rising in the blue distances of Friuli; and there was raised to him the most costly tomb ever bestowed on her monarchs.

If the writer above quoted was cold beside the statue of one of the fathers of his country, he atones for it by his eloquence beside the tomb of the Vendramin. There are two pages and a half of closely printed praise; but there is not a word of the statue of the dead from beginning to end. I am myself in the habit of considering this rather an important part of a tomb, and I was especially interested in it here, because Selvatico only echoes the praise of thousands. It is unanimously declared the chef d'œuvre of Renaissance sepulchral work, and pronounced by Cicognara, (also quoted by Selvatico): 'The very culminating point to which the Venetian arts attained by ministry of the chisel.'

To this culminating point, therefore, covered with dust and cobwebs, I attained, as I did to every tomb of importance in Venice, by the ministry of such ancient ladders as were to be found in the sacristan's keeping. I was struck at first by the excessive awkwardness and want of feeling in the fall of the hand towards the spectator, for it is thrown off the middle of the body in order to show its fine cutting. Now the Mocenigo hand, severe and even stiff in its articulations, has its veins finely drawn, its sculptor having justly felt that the delicacy of the veining expresses alike dignity and age and birth. The Vendramin hand is far more laboriously cut, but its blunt and clumsy contour at once makes us feel that all the care has been thrown away, and well it may be, for it has been entirely bestowed in cutting gouty wrinkels about the joints. Such as the hand is, I looked for its fellow. At first I thought it had been broken off, but on clearing away the dust, I saw the wretched effigy had only *one* hand, and was a mere block on the inner side. The face, heavy and disagreeable in its features, is made monstrous by its semi-sculpture. One side of the forehead is wrinkled elaborately, the other left smooth; one side only of the doge's cap is chased; one cheek only is finished, and the other blocked out and distorted besides; finally, the ermine robe, which is elaborately imitated to its utmost lock of hair and of ground hair on the one side, is blocked out only on the other:—it having been supposed throughout the work that the effigy was only to be seen from below, and from one side.

It was indeed to be so seen by nearly every one; and I do not blame—I should, on the contrary, have praised—the sculptor for regulating his treatment of it by its position; if that treatment had not involved, first, dishonesty, in giving only half a face, a monstrous mask, when we demanded true portraiture of the dead; and, secondly, such utter coldness of feeling, as could only consist with an extreme of intellectual and moral degradation: Who, with a heart in his breast, could have stayed his hand as he drew the dim lines of the old man's countenance—unmajestic once, indeed, but at least sanctified by the

Detail from the tomb of Doge Tomaso Mocenigo, a *'noble image of a king's mortality'*.

The tomb of Doge Andrea Vendramin by Tullio Lombardo.
'It is unanimously declared the chef d'oeuvre of Renaissance sepulchral work.'

solemnities of death – could have stayed his hand, as he reached the bend of the grey forehead, and measured out the last veins of it at so much the zecchin?

But now, reader, comes the very gist and point of the whole matter. This lying monument to a dishonoured doge, this culminating pride of the Renaissance art of Venice, is at least veracious, if in nothing else, in its testimony to the character of its sculptor. *He was banished from Venice for forgery* in 1487.

I have more to say about this convict's work hereafter; but I pass, at present, to the second, slighter, but yet more interesting piece of evidence, which I promised.

The Ducal palace has two principal façades; one towards the sea, the other towards the Piazzetta. The seaward side, and, as far as its seventh main arch inclusive, the Piazzetta side, is work of the early part of the fourteenth century, some of it perhaps even earlier; while the rest of the Piazzetta side is of the fifteenth. The difference in age has been gravely disputed by the Venetian antiquaries, who have examined many documents on the subject, and quoted some which they never examined. I have myself collated most of the written documents, and one document more, to which the Venetian antiquaries never thought of referring – the masonry of the palace itself.

That masonry changes at the centre of the eighth arch from the sea angle on the Piazzetta side. It has been of comparatively small stones up to that point; the fifteenth century work instantly begins with larger stones, 'brought from Istria, a hundred miles away.' The ninth shaft from the sea in the lower arcade, and the seventeenth, which is above it, in the upper arcade, commence the series of fifteenth century shafts. These two are somewhat thicker than the others, and carry the party-wall of the Sala del Scrutinio. Now observe, reader. The face of the palace, from this point to the Porta della Carta, was built at the instance of that noble Doge Mocenigo beside whose tomb you have been standing; at his instance, and in the beginning of the reign of his successor, Foscari; that is to say, circa 1424. This is not disputed; it is only disputed that the sea façade is earlier; of which, however, the proofs are as simple as they are incontrovertible: for not only the masonry, but the sculpture, changes at the ninth lower shaft, and that in the capitals of the shafts both of the upper and lower arcade: the costumes of the figures introduced in the sea façade being purely Giottesque, correspondent with those of Giotto's work in the Arena Chapel at Padua, while the costume on the other capitals is Renaissance-Classic: and the lions' heads between the arches change at the same point. And there are a multitude of other evidences in the statues of the angles, with which I shall not at present trouble the reader.

Now, the architect who built under Foscari, in 1424 (remember my date for the decline of Venice, 1418), was obliged to follow the principal forms of the older palace. But he had not the wit to invent new capitals in the same style; he therefore clumsily copied the old ones. The palace has seventeen main arches on the sea façade, eighteen on the Piazzetta side, which in all are of course carried by thirty-six pillars; and these pillars I shall always number from right to left, from the angle of the palace at the Ponte della Paglia to that next the Porta della Carta. I number them in this succession, because I thus have the earliest shafts first numbered. So counted, the 1st, the 18th, and the 36th, are the great supports of the angles of the palace; and the first of the fifteenth century series, being, as above stated, the 9th from the sea on the Piazzetta side, is the 26th of the entire series, and will always in future be so numbered, so that all numbers above twenty-six indicate fifteenth century work, and all below it, fourteenth century, with some exceptional cases of restoration.

Then the copied capitals are: the 28th, copied from the 7th; the 29th, from the 9th; the 30th, from the 10th; the 31st, from the 8th; the 33rd, from the 12th; and the 34th, from the 11th; the others being dull inventions of the 15th century, except the 36th, which is very nobly designed.

The capitals thus selected from the earlier portion of the palace for imitation, together with the rest, will be accurately described hereafter; the point I have here to notice is in the copy of the ninth capital, which was decorated (being, like the rest, octagonal) with figures of the eight Virtues:–Faith, Hope, Charity, Justice, Temperance, Prudence, Humility (the Venetian antiquaries call it Humanity!), and Fortitude. The Virtues of the fourteenth century are somewhat hard-featured; with vivid and living expression, and plain every-day clothes of the time. Charity has her lap full of apples (perhaps loaves), and is giving one to a little child, who stretches his arm for it across a gap in the leafage of the capital. Fortitude tears open a lion's jaws; Faith lays her hand on her breast, as she beholds the Cross; and Hope is praying, while above her a hand is seen emerging from the sunbeams–the hand of God (according to that of Revelations, 'The Lord God giveth them light'); and the inscription above is, 'Spes optima in Deo.'

This design, then, is rudely and with imperfect chiselling, imitated by the fifteenth century workmen: the Virtues have lost their hard features and living expression; they have got Roman noses, and have had their hair curled. Their actions and emblems are, however, preserved until we come to Hope: she is still praying, but she is praying to the sun only; *the hand of God is gone*.

Is not this a curious and striking type of the spirit which had then become

Details from the 9th and 29th capitals of the Ducal Palace.
The 29th is copied from the 9th in which Hope is praying to the hand of God;
in the 29th the hand of God is gone and Hope prays only to the sun.

dominant in the world, forgetting to see God's hand in the light He gave; so that in the issue, when that light opened into the Reformation on the one side, and into full knowledge of ancient literature on the other, the one was arrested and the other perverted?

Such is the nature of the accidental evidence on which I shall depend for the proof of the inferiority of character in the Renaissance workmen. But the proof of the inferiority of the work itself is not so easy, for in this I have to appeal to judgments which the Renaissance work has itself distorted.

And now come with me, for I have kept you too long from your gondola: come with me, on an autumnal morning, to a low wharf or quay at the extremity of a canal, with long steps on each side down to the water, which latter we fancy for an instant has become black with stagnation; another glance undeceives us—it is covered with the black boats of Venice. We enter one of them, rather to try if they be real boats or not, than with any definite purpose, and glide away; at first feeling as if the water were yielding continually beneath the boat and letting her sink into soft vacancy. It is something clearer than any water we have seen lately, and of a pale green; the banks only two or three feet above it, of mud and rank grass, with here and there a stunted tree; gliding swiftly past the small casement of the gondola, as if they were dragged by upon a painted scene.

Stroke by stroke, we count the plunges of the oar, each heaving up the side of the boat slightly as her silver beak shoots forward. We lose patience, and extricate ourselves from the cushions: the sea air blows keenly by, as we stand leaning on the roof of the floating cell. In front, nothing to be seen but long canal and level bank; to the west, the tower of Mestre is lowering fast, and behind it there have risen purple shades, of the colour of dead rose leaves, all round the horizon, feebly defined against the afternoon sky,—the Alps of Bassano. Forward still: the endless canal bends at last, and then breaks into intricate angles about some low bastions, now torn to pieces and staggering in ugly rents towards the water,—the bastions of the fort of Malghera. Another turn, and another perspective of canal; but not interminable. The silver beak cleaves it fast,—it widens: the rank grass of the banks sinks lower, and lower, and at last dies in tawny knots along an expanse of weedy shore. Over it, on the right, but a few years back, we might have seen the lagoon stretching to the horizon, and the warm southern sky bending over Malamocco to the sea. Now we can see nothing but what seems to be a low and monotonous dockyard wall, with flat arches to let the tide through it;—this is the railroad bridge, conspicuous above all things. But at the end of those dismal arches there rises, out of the wide water, a straggling line of low and confused brick buildings. Four or five domes, pale, and apparently at a greater distance, rise over the centre of the line; but the object which first catches the eye is a sullen cloud of black smoke brooding over the northern half of it, and which issues from the belfry of a church.

It is VENICE.

THE THRONE

In the olden days of travelling, in which distance could not be vanquished
without toil, but in which that toil was rewarded, partly by the power of
deliberate survey of the countries through which the journey lay, and
partly by the happiness of the evening hours, when from the top of the last
hill he had surmounted, the traveller beheld the quiet village where he
was to rest, scattered among the meadows beside its valley stream; or, from the
long hoped for turn in the dusty perspective of the causeway, saw, for the first
time, the towers of some famed city, faint in the rays of sunset—hours of
peaceful and thoughtful pleasure, for which the rush of the arrival in the
railway station is perhaps not always, or to all men, an equivalent,—in those
days, I say, when there was something more to be anticipated and remembered in the first aspect of each successive halting-place, than a new arrangement of glass roofing and iron girder, there were few moments of which the
recollection was more fondly cherished by the traveller, than that which, as I
endeavoured to describe in the close of the last chapter, brought him within
sight of Venice, as his gondola shot into the open lagoon from the canal of
Mestre. Not but that the aspect of the city itself was generally the source of
some slight disappointment, for, seen in this direction, its buildings are far less
characteristic than those of the other great towns of Italy; but this inferiority
was partly disguised by distance, and more than atoned for by the strange
rising of its walls and towers out of the midst, as it seemed, of the deep sea, for it
was impossible that the mind or the eye could at once comprehend the
shallowness of the vast sheet of water which stretched away in leagues of
rippling lustre to the north and south, or trace the narrow line of islets
bounding it to the east. The salt breeze, the white moaning sea-birds, the
masses of black weed separating and disappearing gradually, in knots of
heaving shoal, under the advance of the steady tide, all proclaimed it to be
indeed the ocean on whose bosom the great city rested so calmly; not such
blue, soft, lake-like ocean as bathes the Neapolitan promontories, or sleeps
beneath the marble rocks of Genoa, but a sea with the bleak power of our own
northern waves, yet subdued into a strange spacious rest, and changed from
its angry pallor into a field of burnished gold, as the sun declined behind the

belfry tower of the lonely island church, fitly named 'St. George of the Seaweed.' As the boat drew nearer to the city, the coast which the traveller had just left sank behind him into one long, low line, tufted irregularly with brushwood and willows: but, at what seemed its northern extremity, the hills of Arqua rose in a dark cluster of purple pyramids, balanced on the bright mirage of the lagoon; two or three smooth surges of inferior hill extended themselves about their roots, and beyond these, beginning with the craggy peaks above Vicenza, the chain of the Alps girded the whole horizon to the north—a wall of jagged blue, here and there showing through its clefts a wilderness of misty precipices, fading far back into the recesses of Cadore, and itself rising and breaking away eastward, where the sun struck opposite upon its snow, into mighty fragments of peaked light, standing up behind the barred clouds of evening, one after another, countless, the crown of the Adrian Sea, until the eye turned back from pursuing them, to rest upon the nearer burning of the campaniles of Murano, and on the great city, where it magnified itself along the waves, as the quick silent pacing of the gondola drew nearer and nearer. And at last, when its walls were reached, and the outmost of its untrodden streets was entered, not through towered gate or guarded rampart, but as a deep inlet between two rocks of coral in the Indian sea; when first upon the traveller's sight opened the long ranges of columned palaces,—each with its black boat moored at the portal,—each with its image cast down, beneath its feet, upon that green pavement which every breeze broke into new fantasies of rich tessellation; when first, at the extremity of the bright vista, the shadowy Rialto threw its colossal curve slowly forth from behind the palace of the Camerlenghi; that strange curve, so delicate, so adamantine, strong as a mountain cavern, graceful as a bow just bent; when first, before its moonlike circumference was all risen, the gondolier's cry, 'Ah! Stalì,' struck sharp upon the ear, and the prow turned aside under the mighty cornices that half met over the narrow canal, where the splash of the water followed close and loud, ringing along the marble by the boat's side; and when at last that boat darted forth upon the breadth of silver sea, across which the front of the Ducal palace, flushed with its sanguine veins, looks to the snowy dome of Our Lady of Salvation, it was no marvel that the mind should be so deeply entranced by the visionary charm of a scene so beautiful and so strange, as to forget the darker truths of its history and its being. Well might it seem that such a city had owed her existence rather to the rod of the enchanter, than the fear of the fugitive; that the waters which encircled her had been chosen for the mirror of her state, rather than the shelter of her nakedness; and that all which in nature was wild or merciless,—Time and Decay, as well as the waves and tempests,—had been won to adorn her instead of to destroy, and might still spare, for ages to come, that beauty which seemed to have fixed for its throne the sands of the hour-glass as well as of the sea.

They little thought, who first drove the stakes into the sand, and strewed the ocean reeds for their rest, that their children were to be the princes of that ocean, and their palaces its pride; and yet, in the great natural laws that rule that sorrowful wilderness, let it be remembered what strange preparation had been made for the things which no human imagination could have foretold, and how the whole existence and fortune of the Venetian nation were anticipated or compelled, by the setting of those bars and doors to the rivers and the sea. Had deeper currents divided their islands, hostile navies would again and again have reduced the rising city into servitude; had stronger surges beaten their shores, all the richness and refinement of the Venetian architecture must have been exchanged for the walls and bulwarks of an ordinary seaport. Had there been no tide, as in other parts of the Mediterranean, the narrow canals of the city would have become noisome, and the marsh in which it was built pestiferous. Had the tide been only a foot or eighteen inches higher in its rise, the water-access to the doors of the palaces would have been impossible: even as it is, there is sometimes a little difficulty, at the ebb, in landing without setting foot upon the lower and slippery steps; and the highest tides sometimes enter the courtyards, and overflow the entrance halls. Eighteen inches more of difference between the level of the flood and ebb would have rendered the doorsteps of every palace, at low water, a treacherous mass of weeds and limpets, and the entire system of water-carriage for the higher classes, in their easy and daily intercourse, must have been done away with. The streets of the city would have been widened, its network of canals filled up, and all the peculiar character of the place and the people destroyed.

If, two thousand years ago, we had been permitted to watch the slow settling of the slime of those turbid rivers into the polluted sea, and the gaining upon its deep and fresh waters of the lifeless, impassable, unvoyageable plain, how little could we have understood the purpose with which those islands were shaped out of the void, and the torpid waters enclosed with their desolate walls of sand! How little could we have known, any more than of what now seems to us most distressful, dark, and objectless, the glorious aim which was then in the mind of Him in whose hands are all the corners of the earth! how little imagined that in the laws which were stretching forth the gloomy margins of those fruitless banks, and feeding the bitter grass among their shallows, there was indeed a preparation, and *the only preparation possible*, for the founding of a city which was to be set like a golden clasp on the girdle of the earth, to write her history on the white scrolls of the sea-surges, and to word it in their thunder, and to gather and give forth, in world-wide pulsation, the glory of the West and of the East, from the burning heart of her Fortitude and Splendour!

TORCELLO

SEVEN miles to the north of Venice, the banks of sand which near the city rise little above low-water mark, attain by degrees a higher level, and knit themselves at last into fields of salt morass, raised here and there into shapeless mounds, and intercepted by narrow creeks of sea. One of the feeblest of these inlets, after winding for some time among buried fragments of masonry, and knots of sunburnt weeds whitened with webs of fucus stays itself in an utterly stagnant pool beside a plot of greener grass covered with ground ivy and violets. On this mound is built a rude brick campanile, of the commonest Lombardic type, which if we ascend towards evening we may command from it one of the most notable scenes in this wide world of ours. Far as the eye can reach, a waste of wild sea moor, of a lurid ashen grey; not like our northern moors with their jet-black pools and purple heath, but lifeless, the colour of sackcloth, with the corrupted sea-water soaking through the roots of its acrid weeds, and gleaming hither and thither through its snaky channels. No gathering of fantastic mists, nor coursing of clouds across it; but melancholy clearness of space in the warm sunset, oppressive, reaching to the horizon of its level gloom. To the very horizon, on the north-east; but, to the north and west, there is a blue line of higher land along the border of it, and above this, but farther back, a misty band of mountains, touched with snow. To the east, the paleness and roar of the Adriatic, louder at momentary intervals as the surf breaks on the bars of sand; to the south, the widening branches of the calm lagoon, alternately purple and pale green, as they reflect the evening clouds or twilight sky; and almost beneath our feet, on the same field which sustains the tower we gaze from, a group of four buildings, two of them little larger than cottages (though built of stone, and one adorned by a quaint belfry), the third an octagonal chapel, of which we can see but little more than the flat red roof with its rayed tiling, the fourth, a considerable church with nave and aisles, but of which, in like manner, we can see little but the long central ridge and lateral slopes of roof which the sunlight separates in one glowing mass from the green field beneath and grey moor beyond. There are no living creatures near the buildings, nor any vestige of village or city round about them.

The roof of Santa Fosca, which is raised only 'to the height of a cattle shed'.

Then look farther to the south. Beyond the widening branches of the lagoon, and rising out of the bright lake into which they gather, there are a multitude of towers, dark, and scattered among square-set shapes of clustered palaces, a long and irregular line fretting the southern sky.

Mother and daughter, you behold them both in their widowhood,—Tor-cello, and Venice.

Thirteen hundred years ago, the grey moorland looked as it does this day, and the purple mountains stood as radiantly in the deep distances of evening; but on the line of the horizon, there were strange fires mixed with the light of sunset, and the lament of many human voices mixed with the fretting of the waves on their ridges of sand. The flames rose from the ruins of Altinum; the lament from the multitude of its people seeking, like Israel of old, a refuge from the sword in the paths of the sea.

The cattle are feeding and resting upon the site of the city that they left; the mower's scythe swept this day at dawn over the chief street of the city that they built, and the swathes of soft grass are now sending up their scent into the night air, the only incense that fills the temple of their ancient worship. Let us go down into that little space of meadow land.

The inlet which runs nearest to the base of the campanile is not that by which Torcello is commonly approached. Another, somewhat broader, and overhung by alder copse, winds out of the main channel of the lagoon up to the very edge of the little meadow which was once the Piazza of the city, and there, stayed by a few grey stones which present some semblance of a quay, forms its boundary at one extremity. Hardly larger than an ordinary English farmyard, and roughly enclosed on each side by broken palings and hedges of honeysuckle and briar, the narrow field retires from the water's edge, traversed by a scarcely traceable footpath, for some forty or fifty paces, and then expanding into the form of a small square, with buildings on three sides of it, the fourth being that which opens to the water. Two of these, that on our left and that in front of us as we approach from the canal, are so small that they might well be taken for the outhouses of the farm, though the first is a conventual building, and the other aspires to the title of the 'Palazzo publico,' both dating as far back as the beginning of the fourteenth century; the third, the octagonal church of Santa Fosca, is far more ancient than either, yet hardly on a larger scale. Though the pillars of the portico which surrounds it are of pure Greek marble, and their capitals are enriched with delicate sculpture, they, and the arches they sustain, together only raise the roof to the height of a cattle-shed; and the first strong impression which the spectator receives from the whole scene is, that whatever sin it may have been which has on this spot been visited with so utter a desolation, it could not at least have been ambition. Nor will this impression be diminished as we approach, or enter, the larger church, to which the whole group of building is subordinate. It has evidently been built by men in flight and distress, who sought in the hurried erection of their island church such a shelter for their earnest and sorrowful worship as, on the one hand, could not attract the eyes of their enemies by its splendour, and yet, on the other, might not awaken too bitter feelings by its contrast with the churches which they had seen destroyed. There is visible everywhere a simple and tender effort to recover some of the form of the temples which they had loved, and to do honour to God by that which they were erecting, while distress and humiliation prevented the desire, and prudence precluded the admission, either of luxury of ornament or magnificence of plan. The exterior is absolutely devoid of decoration, with the exception only of the western entrance and the lateral door, of which the former has carved sideposts and architrave, and the latter, crosses of rich sculpture; while the massy stone shutters of the windows, turning on huge rings of stone, which answer the double purpose of stanchions and brackets, cause the whole building rather to resemble a refuge from Alpine storm than the cathedral of a populous city; and, internally, the two solemn mosaics of the eastern and western extemities, – one representing the Last Judgment, the other the Madonna, her tears falling as her hands are raised to bless, – and the noble range of pillars which enclose the space between, terminated by the high throne for the pastor and the semicircular raised seats for the superior clergy, are expressive at once of the deep sorrow and the sacred courage of men who had no home left them upon earth, but who looked for one to come, of men 'persecuted but not forsaken, cast down but not destroyed.'

I am not aware of any other early church in Italy which has this peculiar expression in so marked a degree; and it is so consistent with all that Christian architecture ought to express in every age that I would rather fix the mind of the reader on this general character than on the separate details, however interesting, of the architecture itself. I shall therefore examine these only so far as is necessary to give a clear idea of the means by which the peculiar expression of the building is attained.

John Ruskin THE GREAT SQUARE AT TORCELLO
The pillars of the entrance to Santa Fosca (on the right) are of
'pure Greek marble, and their capitals are enriched with delicate sculpture'.

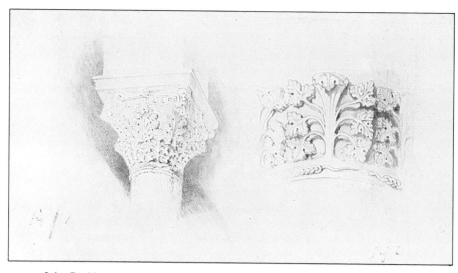

John Ruskin CAPITALS OF TORCELLO CATHEDRAL SHOWING THE SERPENT DESIGN

Opposite is a rude plan of the church. I do not answer for the thickness and external disposition of the walls, which are not to our present purpose, and which I have not carefully examined; but the interior arrangement is given with sufficient accuracy. The church is built on the usual plan of the Basilica, that is to say, its body divided into a nave and aisles by two rows of massive shafts, the roof of the nave being raised high above the aisles by walls sustained on two ranks of pillars, and pierced with small arched windows. At Torcello the aisles are also lighted in the same manner, and the nave is nearly twice their breadth. The capitals of all the great shafts are of white marble, and are among the best I have ever seen, as examples of perfectly calculated effect from every touch of the chisel. Every one of them is different in design, and their variations are as graceful as they are fanciful. I could not, except by an elaborate drawing, give any idea of the sharp, dark, deep penetrations of the chisel into their snowy marble, but a single example is given [above] of the nature of the changes effected in them from the Corinthian type. In this capital, although a kind of acanthus (only with rounded lobes) is indeed used for the upper range of leaves, the lower range is not acanthus at all, but a kind of vine, or at least that species of plant which stands for vine in all early Lombardic and Byzantine work; the leaves are trefoiled, and the stalks cut clear so that they might be grasped with the hand, and cast sharp dark shadows, perpetually changing, across the bell of the capital behind them. I have drawn one of these vine plants larger, that the reader may see how little imitation of the Corinthian there is in them, and how boldly the stems of the leaves are detached from the ground. But there is another circumstance in this ornament still more noticeable. The band which encircles the shaft beneath the spring of the leaves is copied from the common classical wreathed or braided fillet, of which the reader may see examples on almost every building of any pretensions in modern London. But the mediæval builders could not be content with the dead and meaningless scroll: the Gothic energy and love of life, mingled with the early Christian religious sym-

bolism, were struggling daily into more vigorous expression, and they turned the wreathed band into a serpent of three times the length necessary to undulate round the shaft, which, knotting itself into a triple chain, shows at one side of the shaft its tail and head, as if perpetually gliding round it beneath the stalks of the vines. The vine, as is well known, was one of the early symbols of Christ, and the serpent is here typical either of the eternity of his dominion, or of the Satanic power subdued.

It is not, however, to be expected that either the mute language of early Christianity (however important a part of the expression of the building at the time of its erection), or the delicate fancies of the Gothic leafage springing into new life, should be read, or perceived, by the passing traveller who has never been taught to expect anything in architecture except five orders: yet he can hardly fail to be struck by the simplicity and dignity of the great shafts themselves; by the frank diffusion of light, which prevents their serenity from becoming oppressive; by the delicate forms and lovely carving of the pulpit and chancel screen; and, above all, by the peculiar aspect of the eastern extremity of the church, which, instead of being withdrawn, as in later cathedrals, into a chapel dedicated to the Virgin, or contributing by the brilliancy of its windows to the splendour of the altar, and theatrical effect of the ceremonies performed there, is a simple and stern semicircular recess,

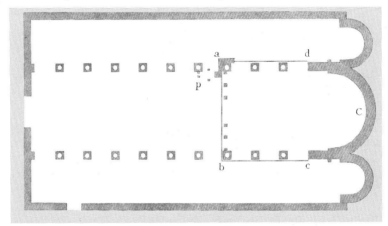

Plan of Torcello Cathedral

filled beneath by three ranks of seats, raised one above the other, for the bishop and presbyters, that they might watch as well as guide the devotions of the people, and discharge literally in the daily service the functions of bishops or *overseers* of the flock of God.

Let us consider a little each of these characters in succession; and first, what is very peculiar to this church, its luminousness. This perhaps strikes the traveller more from its contrast with the excessive gloom of the Church of St. Mark's; but it is remarkable when we compare the Cathedral of Torcello with any of the contemporary basilicas in South Italy or Lombardic churches in the North. St. Ambrogio at Milan, St. Michele at Pavia, St. Zeno at Verona, St. Frediano at Lucca, St. Miniato at Florence, are all like sepulchral caverns compared with Torcello, where the slightest details of the sculptures and mosaics are visible, even when twilight is deepening. And there is something especially touching in our finding the sunshine thus freely admitted into a church built by men in sorrow. They did not need the darkness; they could not perhaps bear it. There was fear and depression upon them enough, without a material gloom. They sought for comfort in their religion, for tangible hopes and promises, not for threatenings or mysteries; and though the subjects chosen for the mosaics on the walls are of the most solemn character, there are no artificial shadows cast upon them, nor dark colours used in them: all is fair and bright, and intended to be regarded in hopefulness, and not with terror.

For observe this choice of subjects. It is indeed possible that the walls of the nave and aisles, which are now whitewashed, may have been covered with fresco or mosaic, and thus have supplied a series of subjects, on the choice of which we cannot speculate. I do not, however, find record of the destruction of any such works; and I am rather inclined to believe that at any rate the central division of the building was originally decorated, as it is now, simply by mosaics representing Christ, the Virgin and the Apostles, at one extremity, and Christ coming to judgment at the other. And if so, I repeat, observe the significance of this choice. Most other early churches are covered with imagery sufficiently suggestive of the vivid interest of the builders in the history and occupations of the world. Symbols or representations of political events, portraits of living persons, and sculptures of satirical, grotesque, or trivial subjects are of constant occurrence, mingled with the more strictly appointed representations of scriptural or ecclesiastical history; but at Torcello even these usual, and one should have thought almost necessary, successions of Bible events do not appear. The mind of the worshipper was fixed entirely upon two great facts, to him the most precious of all facts, – the present mercy of Christ to His Church, and His future coming to judge the world. That Christ's mercy was, at this period, supposed chiefly to be attainable through the pleading of the Virgin, and that therefore beneath the figure of the Redeemer is seen that of the weeping Madonna in the act of intercession, may indeed be matter of sorrow to the Protestant beholder, but ought not to blind him to the earnestness and singleness of the faith with which these men sought their sea-solitudes; not in hope of founding new dynasties, or entering upon new epochs of prosperity, but only to humble themselves before God, and to pray that in His infinite mercy He would hasten the time when the sea should give up the dead which were in it, and Death and Hell give up the dead which were in them, and when they might enter into the better kingdom, 'where the wicked cease from troubling and the weary are at rest.'

Nor were the strength and elasticity of their minds, even in the least matters, diminished by thus looking forward to the close of all things. On the contrary, nothing is more remarkable than the finish and beauty of all the portions of the building, which seem to have been actually executed for the place they occupy in the present structure; the rudest are those which they brought with them from the mainland, the best and most beautiful, those which appear to have been carved for their island church: of these, the new capitals already noticed, and the exquisite panel ornaments of the chancel screen, are the most conspicuous; the latter form a low wall across the church between the six small shafts whose places are seen in the plan, and serve to enclose a space raised two steps above the level of the nave, destined for the singers, and indicated also in the plan by an open line *a b c d*. The bas-reliefs on this low screen are groups of peacocks and lions, two face to face on each panel, rich and fantastic beyond description, though not expressive of very accurate knowledge either of leonine or pavonine forms. And it is not until we pass to the back of the stair of the pulpit, which is connected with the northern extremity of this screen, that we find evidence of the haste with which the church was constructed.

The pulpit, however, is not among the least noticeable of its features. It is sustained on the four small detached shafts marked at *p* in the plan, between the two pillars at the north side of the screen; both pillars and pulpit studiously plain, while the staircase which ascends to it is a compact mass of masonry (shaded in the plan), faced by carved slabs of marble; the parapet of the staircase being also formed of solid blocks like paving-stones, lightened by rich, but not deep exterior carving. Now these blocks, or at least those which adorn the staircase towards the aisle, have been brought from the mainland; and, being of size and shape not easily to be adjusted to the proportions of the stair, the architect has cut out of them pieces of the size he needed, utterly regardless of the subject or symmetry of the original design. The pulpit is not the only place where this rough procedure has been permitted; at the lateral door of the church are two crosses, cut out of slabs of marble, formerly covered with rich sculpture over their whole surfaces, of which portions are left on the surface of the crosses; the lines of the original design being, of course, just as arbitrarily cut by the incisions between the arms, as the patterns upon a piece of silk which has been shaped anew. The fact is, that in all early Romanesque work, large surfaces are covered with sculpture for the sake of enrichment only; sculpture which indeed had always meaning, because it was easier for the sculptor to work with some chain of thought to guide his chisel, than without any; but it was not always intended, or at least not always hoped, that this chain of thought might be traced by the spectator. All that was proposed appears to have been the enrichment of surface, so as to make it delightful to the eye; and this being once understood, a decorated piece of marble became to the architect just what a piece of lace or embroidery is to a dressmaker, who takes of it such portions as she may require, with little regard to the places where the patterns are divided. And though it may appear, at first sight, that the procedure is indicative of bluntness and rudeness of feeling, we may perceive, upon reflection, that it may also indicate the redundance of power which sets little price upon its own exertion. When a barbarous nation builds its fortress-walls out of fragments of the refined architecture it has overthrown, we can read nothing but its savageness in the vestiges of art which may thus chance to have been preserved; but when the new work is equal, if not superior, in execution, to the pieces of the older art which are associated with it, we may justly conclude that the rough treatment to which the latter have been subjected is rather a sign of the hope of doing better things, than of want of feeling for those already accomplished. And, in general, this careless fitting of ornament is, in very truth, an evidence of life in the school of builders, and of their making a due distinction between work which is to be used for architectural effect, and work which is to possess an abstract perfection; and it commonly shows also that the exertion of design is so easy to them, and their

Above: Torcello Cathedral: '. . . *there is something especially touching in our finding the sunshine thus freely admitted into a Church built by men in sorrow.*'
Below: Twelfth-century mosaic of the weeping Madonna.

fertility so inexhaustible, that they feel no remorse in using somewhat injuriously what they can replace with so slight an effort.

It appears, however, questionable in the present instance whether, if the marbles had not been carved to his hand, the architect would have taken the trouble to enrich them. For the execution of the rest of the pulpit is studiously simple, and it is in this respect that its design possesses, it seems to me, an interest to the religious spectator greater than he will take in any other portion of the building. It is supported, as I said, on a group of four slender shafts; itself of a slightly oval form, extending nearly from one pillar of the nave to the next, so as to give the preacher free room for the action of the entire person, which always gives an unaffected impressiveness to the eloquence of the southern nations. In the centre of its curved front, a small bracket and detached shaft sustain the projection of a narrow marble desk (occupying the place of a cushion in a modern pulpit), which is hollowed out into a shallow curve on the upper surface, leaving a ledge at the bottom of the slab, so that a book laid upon it, or rather into it, settles itself there, opening as if by instinct, but without the least chance of slipping to the side, or in any way moving beneath the preacher's hands. Six balls, or rather almonds, of purple marble veined with white are set round the edge of the pulpit, and form its only decoration. Perfectly graceful, but severe and almost cold in its simplicity, built for permanence and service, so that no single member, no stone of it, could be spared, and yet all are firm and uninjured as when they were first set together, it stands in venerable contrast both with the fantastic pulpits of mediæval cathedrals and with the rich furniture of those of our modern churches.

The severity is still more striking in the raised seats and episcopal throne which occupy the curve of the apse. The arrangement at first somewhat recalls to the mind that of the Roman amphitheatres; the flight of steps which lead up to the central throne divides the curve of the continuous steps or seats (it appears in the first three ranges questionable which were intended, for they seem too high for the one, and too low and close for the other), exactly as in an amphitheatre the stairs for access intersect the sweeping ranges of seats. But in the very rudeness of this arrangement, and especially in the want of all appliances of comfort (for the whole is of marble, and the arms of the central throne are not for convenience, but for distinction, and to separate it more conspicuously from the undivided seats), there is a dignity which no furniture of stalls nor carving of canopies ever could attain, and well worth the contemplation of the Protestant, both as sternly significative of an episcopal authority which in the early days of the Church was never disputed, and as dependent for all its impressiveness on the utter absence of any expression either of pride or self-indulgence.

But there is one more circumstance which we ought to remember as giving peculiar significance to the position which the episcopal throne occupies in this island church, namely, that in the minds of all early Christians the Church itself was most frequently symbolized under the image of a ship, of which the bishop was the pilot. Consider the force which this symbol would assume in the imaginations of men to whom the spiritual Church had become an ark of refuge in the midst of a destruction hardly less terrible than that from which the eight souls were saved of old, a destruction in which the wrath of man had become as broad as the earth and as merciless as the sea, and who saw the actual and literal edifice of the Church raised up, itself like an ark in the midst of the waters. No marvel if with the surf of the Adriatic rolling between them and the shores of their birth, from which they were separated for ever, they should have looked upon each other as the disciples did when the storm came down on the Tiberias Lake, and have yielded ready and loving obedience to those who ruled them in His name, who had there rebuked the winds and commanded stillness to the sea. And if the stranger would yet learn in what spirit it was that the dominion of Venice was begun, and in what strength she went forth conquering and to conquer, let him not seek to estimate the wealth of her arsenals or number of her armies, nor look upon the pageantry of her palaces, nor enter into the secrets of her councils; but let him ascend the highest tier of the stern ledges that sweep round the altar of Torcello, and then, looking as the pilot did of old along the marble ribs of the goodly temple-ship, let him repeople its veined deck with the shadows of its dead mariners, and strive to feel in himself the strengh of heart that was kindled within them, when first, after the pillars of it had settled in the sand, and the roof of it had been closed against the angry sky that was still reddened by the fires of their homesteads, – first, within the shelter of its knitted walls, amidst the murmur of the waste of waves and the beating of the wings of the sea-birds round the rock that was strange to them, – rose that ancient hymn, in the power of their gathered voices:

> THE SEA IS HIS, AND HE MADE IT;
> AND HIS HANDS PREPARED THE DRY LAND.

MURANO

IT is morning now: we have a hard day's work to do at Murano.

The Church of San Donato, the 'Matrice' or 'Mother' Church of Murano, stands in a small triangular field of somewhat fresher grass than is usual near Venice, traversed by a paved walk with green mosaic of short grass between the rude squares of its stones, bounded on one side by ruinous garden walls, on another by a line of low cottages, on the third, the base of the triangle, by the shallow canal from which we have just landed. Near the point of the triangular space is a simple well, bearing date 1502.

The cathedral itself occupies the northern angle of the field, encumbered with modern buildings, small outhouse-like chapels, and wastes of white wall with blank square windows, and itself utterly defaced in the whole body of it, nothing but the apse having been spared; the original plan is only discoverable by careful examination, and even then but partially. The whole impression and effect of the building are lost, but the fragments of it are still most precious.

Of the body of the church, unhappily, they are few and obscure; but the general form and extent of the building, as shown in the plan, are determined, first, by the breadth of the uninjured east end D E; secondly, by some remains of the original brickwork of the clerestory, and in all probability of the side walls also, though those have been refaced; and finally by the series of nave shafts, which are still perfect. The doors A and B may or may not be in their original positions; there must of course have been always, as now, a principal entrance at the west end. The ground plan is composed, like that of Torcello, of nave and aisles only, but the clerestory has transepts extending as far as the outer wall of the aisles. The semicircular apse, thrown out in the centre of the east end, is now the chief feature of interest in the church, though the nave shafts and the eastern extremities of the aisles, outside, are also portions of the original building; the latter having been modernised in the interior, it cannot now be ascertained whether, as is probable, the aisles had once round ends as well as the choir. The spaces F G form small chapels, of which G has a straight terminal wall behind its altar, and F a curved one, marked by the dotted line; the partitions which divide these chapels from the presbytery are also indicated by dotted lines, being modern work.

The plan is drawn carefully to scale, but the relation in which its proportions are disposed can hardly be appreciated by the eye. The width of the nave from shaft to opposite shaft is 32 feet 8 inches; of the aisles, from the shaft to the wall, 16 feet 2 inches, or allowing 2 inches for the thickness of the modern wainscot, 16 feet 4 inches, half the breadth of the nave exactly. The intervals between the shafts are exactly one-fourth of the width of the nave, or 8 feet 2 inches, and the distance between the great piers which form the pseudo-transept is 24 feet 6 inches, exactly three times the interval of the shafts. So the four distances are accurately in arithmetical proportion; *i.e.* –

	Ft.	In.
Interval of shafts	8	2
Width of aisle	16	4
Width of transept	24	6
Width of nave	32	8

The shafts average 5 feet 4 inches in circumference, as near the base as they can be got at, being covered with wood; and the broadest sides of the main piers are 4 feet 7 inches wide, their narrowest sides 3 feet 6 inches. The distance A C from the outmost angle of these piers to the beginning of the curve of the apse is 25 feet, and from that point the apse is nearly semicircular, but it is so encumbered with Renaissance fittings that its form cannot be ascertained with perfect accuracy. It is roofed by a concha, or semi-dome; and the external arrangement of its walls provides for the security of this dome by what is, in fact, a system of buttresses as effective and definite as that of any of the northern churches, although the buttresses are obtained entirely by adaptations of the Roman shaft and arch, the lower story being formed by a thick mass of wall lightened by ordinary semicircular round-headed niches, like those used so extensively afterwards in Renaissance architecture, each niche flanked by a pair of shafts standing clear of the wall, and bearing deeply moulded arches thrown over the niche. The wall with its pillars thus forms a series of massy buttresses (as seen in the ground plan), on the top of which is an open gallery, backed by a thinner wall, and roofed by arches whose shafts are set above the pairs of shafts below. On the heads of these arches rests the roof. We have, therefore, externally a heptagonal apse, chiefly of rough and common brick, only with marble shafts and a few marble ornaments; but for that very reason all the more interesting, because in its proportions, and in the use of the few ornaments it possesses, it displays a delicacy of feeling rendered doubly notable by the roughness of the work in which laws so subtle are observed, and with which so thoughtful ornamentation is associated.

First, for its proportions: I shall have occasion in Chapter 6 to dwell at some length on the peculiar subtlety of the early Venetian perception for ratios of magnitude; the relations of the sides of this heptagonal apse supply one of the first and most curious instances of it. The proportions above given of the nave and aisles might have been dictated by a mere love of mathematical precision; but those of the apse could only have resulted from a true love of harmony.

The plan of this part of the church is given on a large scale, showing that its seven external sides are arranged on a line less than a semicircle, so that if the figure were completed, it would have sixteen sides; and it will be observed also,

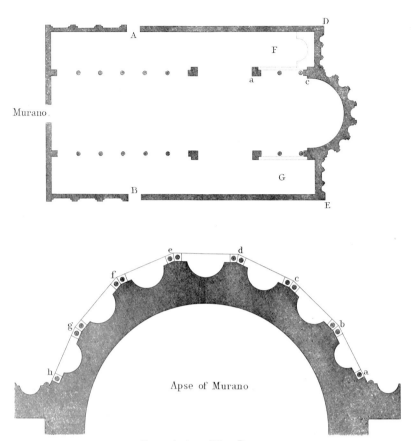

Ground plan of San Donato

that the seven sides are arranged in four magnitudes, the widest being the central one. The brickwork is so much worn away, that the measures of the arches are not easily ascertainable, but those of the plinth on which they stand, which is nearly uninjured, may be obtained accurately. This plinth is indicated by the open line in the ground plan, and its sides measure respectively:

	Ft.	In.
1st, *a b* in plan	6	7
2nd, *b c*	7	7
3rd, *c d*	7	5
4th, *d e* (central)	7	10
5th, *e f*	7	5
6th, *f g*	7	8
7th, *g h*	6	10

Now observe what subtle feeling is indicated by this delicacy of proportion. How fine must the perceptions of grace have been in those builders who could not be content without *some* change between the second and third, the fifth and sixth terms of proportion, such as should oppose the general direction of its cadence, and yet *were* content with a diminution of two inches on a breadth of seven feet and a half! The relations of the numbers are not easily comprehended in the form of feet and inches, but if we reduce the first four of them

The Church of San Donato, Murano.

into inches, and then subtract some constant number, suppose 75, from them all, the remainders 4, 16, 14, 19, will exhibit the ratio of proportion in a clearer, though exaggerated form.

The pairs of circular spots at b, c, d, etc., on the ground plan represent the bearing shafts, which are all of solid marble as well as their capitals. I wish the reader to note the colouring of their capitals. Those of the two single shafts in the angles (a, h) are both of deep purple marble; the two next pairs, b and g, are of white marble; the pairs c and f are of purple, and d and e are of white: thus alternating with each other on each side; two white meeting in the centre. Now observe, *the purple capitals are all left plain; the white are all sculptured.* For the old builders knew that by carving the purple capitals they would have injured them in two ways: first, they would have mixed a certain quantity of grey shadow with the surface hue, and so adulterated the purity of the colour; secondly, they would have drawn away the thoughts from the colour, and prevented the mind from fixing upon it or enjoying it, by the degree of attention which the sculpture would have required. So they left their purple capitals full broad masses of colour; and sculptured the white ones, which would otherwise have been devoid of interest.

But the feature which is most to be noted in this apse is a band of ornament, which runs round it like a silver girdle, composed of sharp wedges of marble, preciously inlaid, and set like jewels into the brickwork; above it there is

Sculptures of Murano.

another band of triangular recesses in the bricks, of nearly similar shape, and it seems equally strange that all the marble should have fallen from it, or that it should have been originally destitute of them. The reader may choose his hypothesis; but there is quite enough left to interest us in the lower band, which is fortunately left in its original state, as is sufficiently proved by the curious niceties in the arrangement of its colours, which are assuredly to be attributed to the care of the first builder.

Above the first story of the apse runs a gallery under open arches, protected by a light balustrade. This balustrade is worked on the *outside* with mouldings, of which I shall only say that they are of exactly the same school as the greater part of the work of the existing church. But the great horizontal pieces of stone which form the top of this balustrade are fragments of an older building turned inside out. They are covered with sculptures on the back, only to be seen by mounting into the gallery. They have once had an arcade of low wide arches traced on their surface, the spandrils filled with leafage, and archivolts enriched with studded chainwork and with crosses in their centres. These pieces have been used as waste marble by the architect of the existing apse. The small arches of the present balustrade are cut mercilessly through the old work, and the profile of the balustrade is cut out of what was once the back of the stone: only some respect is shown for the crosses in the old design, the blocks are cut so that these shall be not only left uninjured, but come in the centre of the balustrades.

Now let the reader observe carefully that this balustrade of Murano is a fence of other things than the low gallery round the deserted apse. It is a barrier between two great schools of early architecture. On one side it was cut by Romanesque workmen of the early Christian ages, and furnishes us with a distinct type of a kind of ornament which, as we meet with other examples of it, we shall be able to describe in generic terms, and to throw back behind this balustrade, out of our way. The *front* of the balustrade presents us with a totally different condition of design, less rich, more graceful, and here shown in its simplest possible form. From the outside of this bar of marble we shall commence our progress in the study of existing Venetian architecture.

I have not space to give any farther account of the exterior of the building, though one half of what is remarkable in it remains untold. We must now see what is left of interest within the walls.

All hope is taken away by our first glance; for it falls on a range of shafts whose bases are concealed by wooden panelling, and which sustain arches decorated in the most approved style of Renaissance upholstery, with stucco roses in squares under the soffits, and egg and arrow mouldings on the architraves, gilded, on a ground of spotty black and green, with a small pink-faced and black-eyed cherub on every keystone; the rest of the church being for the most part concealed either by dirty hangings, or dirtier white-wash, or dim pictures on warped and wasting canvas; all vulgar, vain, and foul. Yet let us not turn back, for in the shadow of the apse our more careful glance shows us a Greek Madonna, pictured on a field of gold; and we feel giddy at the first step we make on the pavement, for it, also, is of Greek mosaic, waved like the sea, and dyed like a dove's neck.

The pavement is of infinite interest, although grievously distorted and

John Ruskin THE GALLERY OF SAN DONATO, MURANO

defaced. For whenever a new chapel has been built, or a new altar erected, the pavement has been broken up and readjusted so as to surround the newly inserted steps or stones with some appearance of symmetry; portions of it either covered or carried away, others mercilessly shattered or replaced by modern imitations, and those of very different periods, with pieces of the old floor left here and there in the midst of them, and worked round so as to deceive the eye into acceptance of the whole as ancient. The portion, however, which occupies the western extremity of the nave, and the parts immediately adjoining it in the aisles, are, I believe, in their original positions, and very little injured: they are composed chiefly of groups of peacocks, lions, stags, and griffins,—two of each in a group, drinking out of the same vase, or shaking claws together,—enclosed by interlacing bands, and alternating with chequer or star patterns, and here and there an attempt at representation of architecture, all worked in marble mosaic. The floors of Torcello and of St. Mark's are executed in the same manner; but what remains at Murano is finer than either, in the extraordinary play of colour obtained by the use of variegated marbles. At St. Mark's the patterns are more intricate, and the pieces far more skilfully set together; but each piece is there commonly of one colour: at Murano every fragment is itself variegated, and all are arranged with a skill and feeling not to be taught, and to be observed with deep reverence, for that pavement is not dateless, like the rest of the church; it bears its date on one of its central circles, 1140, and is, in my mind, one of the most precious monuments in Italy, showing thus early, and in those rude chequers which the bared knee of the Murano fisher wears in its daily bending, the beginning of that mighty spirit of Venetian colour, which was to be consummated in Titian.

ST. MARK'S

'AND so Barnabas took Mark, and sailed unto Cyprus.' If as the shores of Asia lessened upon his sight, the spirit of prophecy had entered into the heart of the weak disciple who had turned back when his hand was on the plough, and who had been judged, by the chiefest of Christ's captains, unworthy thenceforward to go forth with him to the work, how wonderful would he have thought it, that by the lion symbol in future ages he was to be represented among men!

That the Venetians possessed themselves of his body in the ninth century, there appears no sufficient reason to doubt, nor that it was principally in consequence of their having done so, that they chose him for their patron saint. There exists, however, a tradition that before he went into Egypt he had founded the church at Aquileia, and was thus in some sort the first bishop of the Venetian isles and people. But whether St. Mark was first bishop of Aquileia or not, St. Theodore was the first patron of the city; nor can he yet be considered as having entirely abdicated his early right, as his statue, standing on a crocodile, still companions the winged lion on the opposing pillar of the piazzetta. A church erected to this Saint is said to have occupied, before the ninth century, the site of St. Mark's; and the traveller, dazzled by the brilliancy of the great square, ought not to leave it without endeavouring to imagine its aspect in that early time, when it was a green field, cloister-like and quiet, divided by a small canal, with a line of trees on each side; and extending between the two churches of St. Theodore and St. Gemanium, as the little piazza of Torcello lies between its 'palazzo' and cathedral.

But in the year 813, when the seat of government was finally removed to the Rialto, a Ducal Palace, built on the spot where the present one stands, with a Ducal Chapel beside it, gave a very different character to the Square of St. Mark; and fifteen years later, the acquisition of the body of the Saint, and its deposition in the Ducal Chapel, perhaps not yet completed, occasioned the investiture of that Chapel with all possible splendour. St. Theodore was deposed from his patronship, and his church destroyed, to make room for the aggrandizement of the one attached to the Ducal Palace, and thenceforward known as 'St. Mark's'.

The roofs of St. Mark's:
*'a vision out of the earth . . . a treasureheap it seems, partly of gold,
and partly of opal and mother of pearl.'*

This first church was however destroyed by fire, when the Ducal Palace was burned in the revolt against Candiano, in 976. It was partly rebuilt by his successor, Pietro Orseolo, on a larger scale; and, with the assistance of Byzantine architects, the fabric was carried on under successive Doges for nearly a hundred years; the main building being completed in 1071, but its incrustation with marble not till considerably later. It was consecrated between 1084 and 1096. It was again injured by fire in 1106, but repaired; and from that time to the fall of Venice there was probably no Doge who did not in some slight degree embellish or alter the fabric, so that few parts of it can be pronounced boldly to be of any given date. Two periods of interference are, however, notable above the rest: the first, that in which the Gothic school had superseded the Byzantine towards the close of the fourteenth century, when the pinnacles, upper archivolts, and window traceries were added to the exterior, and the great screen, with various chapels and tabernacle-work, to the interior; the second, when the Renaissance school superseded the Gothic, and the pupils of Titian and Tintoret substituted, over one half of the church, their own compositions for the Greek mosaics with which it was originally decorated; happily, though with no good-will, having left enough to enable us to imagine and lament what they destroyed.

We have seen that the main body of the church may be broadly stated to be of the eleventh century, the Gothic additions of the fourteenth, and the restored mosaics of the seventeenth. There is no difficulty in distinguishing at a glance the Gothic portions from the Byzantine; but there is considerable difficulty in ascertaining how long, during the course of the twelfth and thirteenth centuries, additions were made to the Byzantine church, which cannot be easily distinguished from the work of the eleventh century, being purposely executed in the same manner. Two of the most important pieces of evidence on this point are, a mosaic in the south transept, and another over the northern door of the façade; the first representing the interior, the second the exterior, of the ancient church.

The existing building was consecrated by the Doge Vital Falier. A peculiar solemnity was given to that of consecration, in the minds of the Venetian people, by what appears to have been one of the best arranged and most successful impostures ever attempted by the clergy of the Romish Church. The body of St. Mark had, without doubt, perished in the conflagration of 976; but the revenues of the church depended too much upon the devotion excited by these relics to permit the confession of their loss. The following is the account given by Corner, and believed to this day by the Venetians, of the pretended miracle by which it was concealed.

After the repairs undertaken by the Doge Orseolo, the place in which the body of the holy Evangelist rested had been altogether forgotten; so that the Doge Vital Falier was entirely ignorant of the place of the venerable deposit. This was no light affliction, not only to the pious Doge, but to all the citizens and people; so that at last, moved by confidence in the Divine mercy, they determined to implore, with prayer and fasting, the manifestation of so great a treasure, which did not now depend upon any human effort. A general fast

The daguerreotype of St. Mark's that Ruskin used for his watercolour
of the South Side of St. Mark's from the Loggia of the Ducal Palace.

being therefore proclaimed, and a solemn procession appointed for the 25th day of June, while the people assembled in the church interceded with God in fervent prayers for the desired boon, they beheld, with as much amazement as joy, a slight shaking in the marbles of a pillar (near the place where the altar of the Cross is now), which, presently falling to the earth, exposed to the view of the rejoicing people the chest of bronze in which the body of the Evangelist was laid.

Of the main facts of this tale there is no doubt. They were embellished afterwards, as usual, by many fanciful traditions; but the fast and the discovery of the coffin, by whatever means effected, are facts; and they are recorded in one of the best-preserved mosaics of the north transept, executed very certainly not long after the event had taken place, and showing, in a conventional manner, the interior of the church, as it then was, filled by the people, first in prayer, then in thanksgiving, the pillar standing open before them, and the Doge, in the midst of them, distinguished by his crimson bonnet embroidered with gold, but more unmistakably by the inscription 'Dux' over his head.

For all our purposes, it will be enough for the reader to remember that the earliest parts of the building belong to the eleventh, twelfth, and first part of the thirteenth century; the Gothic portions to the fourteenth; some of the altars and embellishments to the fifteenth and sixteenth; and the modern portion of the mosaics to the seventeenth.

This, however, I only wish him to recollect in order that I may speak generally of the Byzantine architecture of St. Mark's, without leading him to suppose the whole church to have been built and decorated by Greek artists. Its later portions, with the single exception of the seventeenth century mosaics, have been so dexterously accommodated to the original fabric that the general effect is still that of a Byzantine building; and I shall not, except when it is absolutely necessary, direct attention to the discordant points, or weary the reader with anatomical criticism. Whatever in St. Mark's arrests the eye, or affects the feelings, is either Byzantine, or has been modified by Byzantine influence; and our inquiry into its architectural merits need not therefore be disturbed by the anxieties of antiquarianism, or arrested by the obscurities of chronology.

And now I wish that the reader would imagine himself at the entrance into St. Mark's Place, called the Bocca di Piazza (mouth of the square). We will push fast through into the shadow of the pillars at the end of the 'Bocca di Piazza.' Between those pillars there opens a great light, and, in the midst of it, as we advance slowly, the vast tower of St. Mark seems to lift itself visibly forth from the level field of chequered stones; and, on each side, the countless arches prolong themselves into ranged symmetry, as if the rugged and irregular houses that pressed together above the dark alley had been struck back into sudden obedience and lovely order, and all their rude casements and broken walls had been transformed into arches charged with goodly sculpture, and fluted shafts of delicate stone.

And well may they fall back, for beyond those troops of ordered arches there rises a vision out of the earth, and all the great square seems to have opened from it in a kind of awe, that we may see it far away;—a multitude of pillars and

Above: Detail from the mosaic in the south transept of St. Mark's, showing the
interior of the eleventh-century basilica.
Below: Mosaic from the northern door of the facade of St. Mark's,
showing the exterior of the eleventh-century basilica.

white domes, clustered into a long low pyramid of coloured light; a treasure-heap, it seems, partly of gold, and partly of opal and mother-of-pearl, hollowed beneath into five great vaulted porches, ceiled with fair mosaic, and beset with sculpture of alabaster, clear as amber and delicate as ivory, –sculpture fantastic and involved, of palm leaves and lilies, and grapes and pomegranates, and birds clinging and fluttering among the branches, all twined together into an endless network of buds and plumes; and in the midst of it, the solemn forms of angels, sceptred, and robed to the feet, and leaning to each other across the gates, their figures indistinct among the gleaming of the golden ground through the leaves beside them, interrupted and dim, like the morning light as it faded back among the branches of Eden, when first its gates were angel-guarded long ago. And round the walls of the porches there are set pillars of variegated stones, jasper and porphyry, and deep-green serpentine spotted with flakes of snow, and marbles, that half refuse and half yield to the sunshine, Cleopatra-like, 'their bluest veins to kiss' – the shadow, as it steals back from them, revealing line after line of azure undulation, as a receding tide leaves the waved sand; their capitals rich with interwoven tracery, rooted knots of herbage, and drifting leaves of acanthus and vine, and mystical signs, all beginning and ending in the Cross; and above them, in the broad archivolts, a continuous chain of language and of life – angels, and the signs of heaven, and the labours of men, each in its appointed season upon the earth; and above these, another range of glittering pinnacles, mixed with white arches edged with scarlet flowers, –a confusion of delight, amidst which the breasts of the Greek horses are seen blazing in their breadth of golden strength, and the St. Mark's lion, lifted on a blue field covered with stars, until at last, as if in ecstasy, the crests of the arches break into a marble foam, and toss themselves far into the blue sky in flashes and wreaths of sculptured spray, as if the breakers on the Lido shore had been frost-bound before they fell, and the sea-nymphs had inlaid them with coral and amethyst.

Let us turn aside under the portico which looks towards the sea, and passing round within the two massive pillars brought from St. Jean d'Acre, we shall find the gate of the Baptistery; let us enter there. The heavy door closes behind us instantly, and the light and the turbulence of the Piazzetta are together shut out by it.

We are in a low vaulted room; vaulted, not with arches but with small cupolas starred with gold, and chequered with gloomy figures: in the centre is a bronze font charged with rich bas-reliefs, a small figure of the Baptist standing above it in a single ray of light that glances across the narrow room, dying as it falls from a window high in the wall, and the first thing that it strikes, and the only thing that it strikes brightly, is a tomb. We hardly know if it be a tomb indeed; for it is like a narrow couch set beside the window, above the pavement, to have been drawn towards the window, that the sleeper might be wakened early;–Only there are two angels, who have drawn the curtain back, and are looking down upon him. Let us look also, and thank that gentle light that rests upon his forehead for ever, and dies away upon his breast.

The face is of a man in middle life, but there are two deep furrows right across the forehead, dividing it like the foundations of a tower: the height of it above is bound by the fillet of the ducal cap. The rest of the features are singularly small and delicate, the lips sharp, perhaps the sharpness of death being added to that of the natural lines; but there is a sweet smile upon them, and a deep serenity upon the whole countenance. The roof of the canopy above has been blue, filled with stars; beneath, in the centre of the tomb on which the figure rests, is a seated figure of the Virgin, and the border of it is of flowers and soft leaves, growing rich and deep, as if in a field in summer.

It is the Doge Andrea Dandolo, a man early great among the great of Venice; and early lost. She chose him for her king in his 36th year; he died ten years later, leaving behind him that history to which we owe half of what we know of her former fortunes.

Look around at the room in which he lies. The floor of it is of rich mosaic, encompassed by a low seat of red marble, and its walls are of alabaster, but worn and shattered, and darkly stained with age, almost a ruin, – in places the slabs of marble have fallen away altogether, and the rugged brickwork is seen through the rents, but all beautiful; the ravaging fissures fretting their way among the islands and channelled zones of the alabaster, and the time-stains on its translucent masses darkened into fields of rich golden brown, like the colour of seaweed when the sun strikes on it through deep sea. The light fades away into the recess of the chamber towards the altar, and the eye can hardly trace the lines of the bas-relief behind it of the baptism of Christ: but on the vaulting of the roof the figures are distinct, and there are seen upon it two great circles, one surrounded by the 'Principalities and powers in heavenly places,' and around the other, the Apostles; Christ the centre of both: and upon the walls, again and again repeated, the gaunt figure of the Baptist, in every circumstance of his life and death; and the streams of the Jordan running down between their cloven rocks; the axe laid to the root of a fruitless tree that springs up on their shore. 'Every tree that bringeth not forth good fruit shall be hewn down, and cast into the fire.' Yes, verily: to be baptized with fire, or to be cast therein; it is the choice set before all men. The march-notes still murmur through the grated window, and mingle with the sounding in our ears of the sentence of judgment, which the old Greek has written on that Baptistery wall. Venice has made her choice.

He who lies under that stony canopy would have taught her another choice, in his day, if she would have listened to him; but he and his counsels have long been forgotten by her, and the dust lies upon his lips.

Through the heavy door whose bronze network closes the place of his rest, let us enter the church itself. It is lost in still deeper twilight, to which the eye must be accustomed for some moments before the form of the building can be traced; and then there opens before us a vast cave, hewn out into the form of a Cross, and divided into shadowy aisles by many pillars. Round the domes of its roof the light enters only through narrow apertures like large stars; and here and there a ray or two from some far-away casement wanders into the darkness, and casts a narrow phosphoric stream upon the waves of marble that heave and fall in a thousand colours along the floor. What else there is of

Overleaf: John Ruskin THE NORTH WEST PORCH OF ST. MARK'S
'St. Mark's is the purest example in Italy of the great school of architecture in which the ruling principle is the incrustation of brick with more precious materials.'

light is from torches, or silver lamps, burning ceaselessly in the recesses of the chapels; the roof sheeted with gold, and the polished walls covered with alabaster, give back at every curve and angle some feeble gleaming to the flames; and the glories round the heads of the sculptured saints flash out upon us as we pass them, and sink again into the gloom. Under foot and over head, a continual succession of crowded imagery, one picture passing into another, as in a dream; forms beautiful and terrible mixed together; dragons and serpents, and ravening beasts of prey, and graceful birds that in the midst of them drink from running fountains and feed from vases of crystal; the passions and the pleasures of human life symbolized together, and the mystery of its redemption; for the mazes of interwoven lines and changeful pictures lead always at last to the Cross, lifted and carved in every place and upon every stone; sometimes with the serpent of eternity wrapt round it, sometimes with doves beneath its arms, and sweet herbage growing forth from its feet; but conspicuous most of all on the great rood that crosses the church before the altar, raised in bright blazonry against the shadow of the apse. And although in the recesses of the aisles and chapels, when the mist of the incense hangs heavily, we may see continually a figure traced in faint lines upon their marble, a woman standing with her eyes raised to heaven, and the inscription above her, 'Mother of God', she is not here the presiding deity. It is the Cross that is first seen, and always burning in the centre of the temple; and every dome and hollow of its roof has the figure of Christ in the utmost height of it, raised in power, or returning in judgment.

It must be altogether without reference to its present usefulness, that we pursue our inquiry into the merits and meaning of the architecture of this marvellous building; and it can only be after we have terminated that inquiry, conducting it carefully on abstract grounds, that we can pronounce with any certainty how far this church is to be considered as the relic of a barbarous age, incapable of attracing the admiration, or influencing the feelings of a civilized community.

In the succeeding sections of this work, devoted to the examination of the Gothic and Renaissance buildings in Venice, I have endeavoured to analyze, and state, as briefly as possible, the true nature of each school, – first in Spirit, then in Form. I wished to have given a similar analysis, in this section, of the nature of Byzantine architecture; but could not make my statements general, because I have never seen this kind of building on its native soil. Nevertheless, in the following sketch of the principles exemplified in St. Mark's, I believe that most of the leading features and motives of the style will be found clearly enough distinguished to enable the reader to judge of it with tolerable fairness, as compared with the better known systems of European architecture in the middle ages.

Now the first broad characteristic of the building, and the root nearly of every other important peculiarity in it, is its confessed *incrustation*. It is the purest example in Italy of the great school of architecture in which the ruling principle is the incrustation of brick with more precious materials; and it is necessary, before we proceed to criticise any one of its arrangements, that the reader should consider the principles which are likely to have influenced, or might legitimately influence the architects of such a school, as distinguished from those whose designs are to be executed in massive materials.

First, consider the natural circumstances which give rise to such a style. Suppose a nation of builders, placed far from any quarries of available stone, and having precarious access to the mainland where they exist; compelled therefore either to build entirely with brick, or to import whatever stone they use from great distances, in ships of small tonnage, and, for the most part, dependent for speed on the oar rather than the sail. The labour and cost of carriage are just as great, whether they import common or precious stone, and therefore the natural tendency would always be to make each shipload as valuable as possible. But in proportion to the preciousness of the stone, is the limitation of its possible supply; limitation not determined merely by cost, but by the physical conditions of the material, for of many marbles pieces above a certain size are not to be had for money. There would also be a tendency in such circumstances to import as much stone as possible ready sculptured, in order to save weight; and therefore, if the traffic of their merchants led them to places where there were ruins of ancient edifices, to ship the available fragments of them home. Out of this supply of marble, partly composed of pieces of so precious a quality that only a few tons of them could be on any terms obtained, and partly of shafts, capitals, and other portions of foreign buildings, the island architect has to fashion, as best he may, the anatomy of his edifice. It is at his choice either to lodge his few blocks of precious marble here and there among his masses of brick, and to cut out of the sculptured fragments such new forms as may be necessary for the observance of fixed proportions in the new building; or else to cut the coloured stones into thin pieces, of extent sufficient to face the whole surface of the walls, and to adopt a method of construction irregular enough to admit the insertion of fragmentary sculptures; rather with a view of displaying their intrinsic beauty, than of setting them to any regular service in the support of the building.

An architect who cared only to display his own skill, and had no respect for the works of others, would assuredly have chosen the former alternative, and would have sawn the old marbles into fragments in order to prevent all interference with his own designs. But an architect who cared for the preservation of noble work, whether his own or others', and more regarded the beauty of his building than his own fame, would have done what those old builders of St. Mark's did for us, and saved every relic with which he was entrusted.

But these were not the only motives which influenced the Venetians in the adoption of their method of architecture. It might, under all the circumstances above stated, have been a question with other builders, whether to import one shipload of costly jaspers, or twenty of chalk flints; and whether to build a small church faced with porphyry and paved with agate, or to raise a vast cathedral in freestone. But with the Venetians it could not be a question for an instant; they were exiles from ancient and beautiful cities, and had been accustomed to build with their ruins, not less in affection than in admiration: they had thus not only grown familiar with the practice of inserting older fragments in modern buildings, but they owed to that practice a great part of the splendour of their city, and whatever charm of association might aid its change from a Refuge into a Home. The practice which began in the affections of a fugitive nation, was prolonged in the pride of a conquering one; and besides the memorials of departed happiness, were elevated the trophies of returning victory. The ship of war brought home more marble in triumph than the merchant vessel in speculation; and the front of St. Mark's became rather a shrine at which to dedicate the splendour of miscellaneous spoil, than the organized expression of any fixed architectural law or religious emotion.

Thus far, however, the justification of the style of this church depends on circumstances peculiar to the time of its erection, and to the spot where it arose. The merit of its method, considered in the abstract, rests on far broader grounds.

The perception of colour is a gift just as definitely granted to one person, and denied to another, as an ear for music; and the very first requisite for true judgment of St. Mark's, is the perfection of that colour-faculty which few people ever set themselves seriously to find out whether they possess or not. For it is on its value as a piece of perfect and unchangeable colouring, that the claims of this edifice to our respect are finally rested; and a deaf man might as well pretend to pronounce judgment on the merits of a full orchestra, as an architect trained in the composition of form only, to discern the beauty of St. Mark's. It possesses the charm of colour in common with the greater part of the architecture, as well as of the manufacturers, of the East; but the Venetians deserve especial note as the only European people who appear to have sympathized to the full with the great instinct of the Eastern races. They indeed were compelled to bring artists from Constantinople to design the mosaics of the vaults of St. Mark's, and to group the colours of its porches; but they rapidly took up and developed, under more masculine conditions, the system of which the Greeks had shown them the example: while the burghers and barons of the North were building their dark streets and grisly castles of oak and sandstone, the merchants of Venice were covering their palaces with porphyry and gold; and at last, when her mighty painters had created for her a colour more priceless than gold or porphyry, even this, the richest of her treasures, she lavished upon walls whose foundations were beaten by the sea; and the strong tide, as it runs beneath the Rialto, is reddened to this day by the reflection of the frescoes of Giorgione.

If, therefore, the reader does not care for colour, I must protest against his endeavour to form any judgment whatever of this church of St. Mark's. But, if he both cares for and loves it, let him remember that the school of incrusted architecture is *the only one in which perfect and permanent chromatic decoration is possible*; and let him look upon every piece of jasper and alabaster given to the architect as a cake of very hard colour, of which a certain portion is to be ground down or cut off, to paint the walls with. Once understand this thoroughly, and accept the condition that the body and availing strength of the edifice are to be in brick, and that this under muscular power of brickwork is to be clothed with the defence of the brightness of the marble, as the body of an animal is protected and adorned by its scales or its skin, and all the consequent fitnesses and laws of the structure will be easily discernible: These I shall state in their natural order.

The Cupola of the Pentecost, showing
'the majesty of the colossal images of the apostles . . . that look down from the darkening gold of the domes of Venice'.

The Lily Capital of St. Mark's.

Law I. *That the plinths and cornices used for binding the armour are to be light and delicate.* They must be delicate, slight, and visibly incapable of severer work than that assigned to them.

Law II. *Science of inner structure is to be abandoned.* As the body of the structure is confessedly of inferior, and comparatively incoherent materials, it would be absurd to attempt in it any expression of the higher refinements of construction.

Law III. *All shafts are to be solid.* Wherever, by the smallness of the parts, we may be driven to abandon the incrusted structure at all, it must be abandoned altogether. The eye must never be left in the least doubt as to what is solid and what is coated. Whatever appears *probably* solid must be *assuredly* so, and therefore it becomes an inviolable law that no shaft shall ever be incrusted.

Law IV. *The shafts may sometimes be independent of the construction.* Exactly in proportion to the importance which the shaft assumes as a large jewel, is the diminution of its importance as a sustaining member; for the delight which we receive in abstract bulk, and beauty of colour, is altogether independent of any perception of adaptation to mechanical necessities.

Law V. *The shafts may be of variable size.* Since the value of each shaft depends upon its bulk, and diminishes with the diminution of its mass in a greater ratio than the size itself diminishes, as in the case of all other jewellery, it is evident that we must not in general expect perfect symmetry and equality among the series of shafts, any more than definiteness of application.

Law VI. *The decoration must be shallow in cutting.* The method of construction being thus systematized, it is evident that a certain style of decoration must arise out of it, based on the primal condition that over the greater part of the edifice there can be *no deep cutting*. The thin sheets of covering stones do not admit of it; we must not cut them through to the bricks; and whatever ornaments we engrave upon them cannot, therefore, be more than an inch deep at the utmost.

Exactly in proportion to the degree in which the force of sculpture is subdued, will be the importance attached to colour as a means of effect or constituent of beauty. I have above stated that the incrusted style was the only one in which perfect or permanent colour decoration was *possible*. It is also the only one in which a true system of colour decoration was ever likely to be invented. In order to understand this, the reader must permit me to review with some care the nature of the principles of colouring adopted by the Northern and Southern nations.

I believe that from the beginning of the world there has never been a true or fine school of art in which colour was despised. It has often been imperfectly attained and injudiciously applied, but I believe it to be one of the essential signs of life in a school of art that it loves colour; and I know it to be one of the first signs of death in the Renaissance schools, that they despised colour.

Observe, it is not the question whether our Northern cathedrals are better with colour or without. Perhaps the great monotone grey of Nature and of Time is a better colour than any that the human hand can give; but that is nothing to our present business. The simple fact is, that the builders of those cathedrals laid upon them the brightest colours they could obtain, and that there is not, as far as I am aware, in Europe, any monument of a truly noble school which has not been either painted all over, or vigorously touched with paint, mosaic, and gilding in its prominent parts. Thus far, Egyptians, Greeks, Goths, Arabs, and mediæval Christians all agree: none of them, when in their right senses, ever think of doing without paint; and, therefore, when I said above that the Venetians were the only people who had thoroughly sympathized with the Arabs in this respect, I referred, first to their intense love of colour, which led them to lavish the most expensive decorations on ordinary dwelling-houses; and, secondly, to that perfection of the colour-instinct in them, which enabled them to render whatever they did, in this kind, as just in principle as it was gorgeous in appliance. It is this principle of theirs, as distinguished from that of the Northern builders, which we have finally to examine.

LAW VII. *That the impression of the architecture is not to be dependent on size.* And now there is but one final consequence to be deduced. The reader understands, I trust, by this time, that the claims of these several parts of the building upon his attention will depend upon their delicacy of design, their perfection of colour, their preciousness of material, and their legendary interest. All these qualities are independent of size, and partly inconsistent with it. Neither delicacy of surface sculpture, nor subtle gradations of colour, can be appreciated by the eye at a distance; and since we have seen that our sculpture is generally to be only an inch or two in depth, and that our colouring is in great part to be produced with the soft tints and veins of natural stones, it will follow necessarily that none of the parts of the building can be removed far from the eye, and therefore that the whole mass of it cannot be large. It is not even desirable that it should be so; for the temper in which the mind addresses itself to contemplate minute and beautiful details is altogether different from that in which it submits itself to vague impressions of space and size. And therefore we must not be disappointed, but grateful, when we find all the best work of the building concentrated within a space comparatively small; and that, for the great cliff-like buttresses and mighty piers of the North shooting up into indiscernible height, we have here low walls spread before us like the pages of a book, and shafts whose capitals we may touch with our hand.

Now there is one circumstance to which I must direct the reader's special attention, as forming a notable distinction between ancient and modern days. Our eyes are now familiar and wearied with writing; and if an inscription is put upon a building, unless it be large and clear, it is ten to one whether we ever trouble ourselves to decipher it. But the old architect was sure of readers. He knew that every one would be glad to decipher all that he wrote; that they would rejoice in possessing the vaulted leaves of his stone manuscript; and that the more he gave them, the more grateful would the people be. We must take some pains, therefore, when we enter St. Mark's, to read all that is inscribed, or we shall not penetrate into the feeling either of the builder or of his times.

A large atrium or portico is attached to two sides of the church, a space which was especially reserved for unbaptized persons and new converts. It was though right that, before their baptism, these persons should be led to contemplate the great facts of the Old Testament history; the history of the Fall of Man, and of the lives of Patriarchs up to the period of the covenant by

Detail from the mosaic of the first cupola of St. Mark's, showing the great
facts of Old Testament history.

Moses; significantly closing with the Fall of the Manna in order to mark to the catechumen the insufficiency of the Mosaic covenant for salvation, – 'Our fathers did eat manna in the wilderness, and are dead,' – and to turn his thoughts to the true Bread of which that manna was the type.

Then, when after his baptism he was permitted to enter the church, over its main entrance he saw, on looking back, a mosaic of Christ enthroned, with the Virgin on one side and St. Mark on the other, in attitudes of adoration. Christ is represented as holding a book open upon His knee, on which is written: I AM THE DOOR; BY ME IF ANY MAN ENTER IN, HE SHALL BE SAVED. On the red marble moulding which surrounds the mosaic is written: I AM THE GATE OF LIFE; LET THOSE WHO ARE MINE ENTER BY ME. Above, on the red marble fillet which forms the cornice of the west end of the church, is written, with reference to the figure of Christ below: WHO HE WAS, AND FROM WHOM HE CAME, AND AT WHAT PRICE HE REDEEMED THEE, AND WHY HE MADE THEE, AND GAVE THEE ALL THINGS, DO THOU CONSIDER.

Now observe, this was not to be seen and read only by the catechumen when he first entered the church; every one who at any time entered was supposed to look back and to read this writing; their daily entrance into the church was thus made a daily memorial of their first entrance into the spiritual church; and we shall find that the rest of the book which was open for them upon its walls continually led them in the same manner to regard the visible temple as in every part a type of the invisible Church of God.

Therefore the mosaic of the first dome, which is over the head of the spectator as soon as he has entered by the great door (that door being the type of baptism), represents the effusion of the Holy Spirit, as the first consequence and seal of the entrance into the church of God. In the centre of the cupola is the Dove, enthroned in the Greek manner, as the Lamb is enthroned, when the Divinity of the Second and Third Persons is to be insisted upon, together with their peculiar offices. From the central symbol of the Holy Spirit twelve streams of fire descend upon the heads of the twelve apostles, who are represented standing around the dome; and below them, between the windows which are pierced in its walls, are represented, by groups of two figures for each separate people, the various nations who heard the apostles speak, at Pentecost, every man in his own tongue. Finally, on the vaults, at the four angles which support the cupola, are pictured four angels each bearing a tablet upon the end of a rod in his hand: on each of the tablets of the three first angels is inscribed the word 'Holy'; on that of the fourth is written 'Lord'; and the beginning of the hymn being thus put into the mouths of the four angels, the words of it are continued around the border of the dome, uniting praise to God for the gift of the Spirit, with welcome to the redeemed soul received into His Church:

> HOLY, HOLY, HOLY, LORD GOD OF SABAOTH:
> HEAVEN AND EARTH ARE FULL OF THY GLORY.
> HOSANNA IN THE HIGHEST:
> BLESSED IS HE THAT COMETH IN THE NAME OF THE LORD.

And observe in this writing that the convert is required to regard the outpouring of the Holy Spirit especially as a work of *satisfaction*. It is the *holiness*

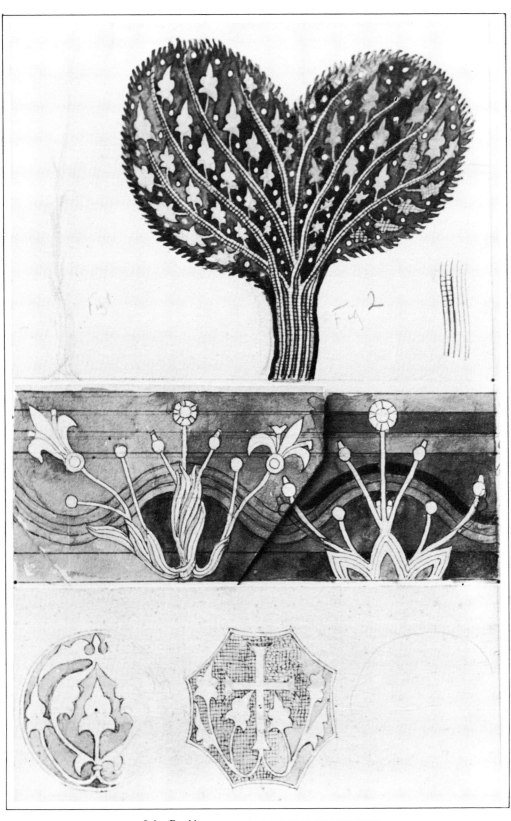

John Ruskin MOSAICS OF OLIVETREE AND FLOWERS
Overleaf: Detail from the mosaic of the first cupola of St. Mark's,
showing the fifth day of the Creation.

of God manifested in the giving of His Spirit to sanctify those who had become His children, which the four angels celebrate in their ceaseless praise; and it is on account of this holiness that the heaven and earth are said to be full of His glory.

After thus hearing praise rendered to God by the angels for the salvation of the newly-entered soul, it was thought fittest that the worshipper should be led to contemplate, in the most comprehensive forms possible, the past evidence and the future hopes of Christianity, as summed up in the three facts without assurance of which all faith is vain; namely, that Christ died, that He rose again, and that He ascended into heaven, there to prepare a place for His elect. On the vault between the first and second cupolas are represented the crucifixion and resurrection of Christ, with the usual series of intermediate scenes, – the treason of Judas, the judgment of Pilate, the crowning with thorns, the descent into Hades, the visit of the women to the Sepulchre, and the apparition to Mary Magdalene. The second cupola itself, which is the central and principal one of the church, is entirely occupied by the subject of the Ascension. At the highest point of it Christ is represented as rising into the blue heaven, borne up by four angels, and throned upon a rainbow, the type of reconciliation. Beneath Him, the twelve apostles are seen upon the Mount of Olives, with the Madonna, and, in the midst of them, the two men in white apparel who appeared at the moment of the Ascension.

The third cupola, that over the altar, represents the witness of the Old Testament to Christ; showing Him enthroned in its centre, and surrounded by the patriarchs and prophets. But this dome was little seen by the people; their contemplation was intended to be chiefly drawn to that of the centre of the church, and thus the mind of the worshipper was at once fixed on the main groundwork and hope of Christianity, – 'Christ is risen', and 'Christ shall come.' If he had time to explore the minor lateral chapels and cupolas, he could find in them the whole series of New Testament history, the events of the life of Christ, and the Apostolic miracles in their order, and finally the scenery of the Book of Revelation; but if he only entered, as often the common people do to this hour, snatching a few moments before beginning the labour of the day to offer up an ejaculatory prayer, and advanced but from the main entrance as far as the altar screen, all the splendour of the glittering nave and variegated dome, if they smote upon his heart, as they might often, in strange contrast with his reed cabin among the shallows of the lagoon, smote upon it only that they might proclaim the two great messages; – 'Christ is risen', and 'Christ shall come.' Daily, as the white cupolas rose like wreaths of sea-foam in the dawn, while the shadowy campanile and frowning palace were still withdrawn into the night, they rose with the Easter Voice of Triumph, – 'Christ is risen'; and daily, as they looked down upon the tumult of the people, deepening and eddying in the wide square that opened from their feet to the sea, they uttered above them the sentence of warning, – 'Christ shall come.'

And this thought may surely dispose the reader to look with some change of temper upon the gorgeous building and wild blazonry of that shrine of St. Mark's. He now perceives that it was in the hearts of the old Venetian people far more than a place of worship. It was at once a type of the Redeemed

Church of God, and a scroll for the written word of God. It was to be to them, both an image of the Bride, all glorious within, her clothing of wrought gold; and the actual Table of the Law and the Testimony, written within and without. And whether honoured as the Church or as the Bible, was it not fitting that neither the gold nor the crystal should be spared in the adornment of it; that, as the symbol of the Bride, the building of the wall thereof should be of jasper, and the foundations of it garnished with all manner of precious stones; and that, as the channel of the Word, that triumphant utterance of the Psalmist should be true of it, – 'I have rejoiced in the way of Thy testimonies, as much as in all riches'? And shall we not look with changed temper down the long perspective of St. Mark's Place towards the sevenfold gates and glowing domes of its temple, when we know with what solemn purpose the shafts of it were lifted above the pavement of the populous square? Men met there from all countries of the earth, for traffic or for pleasure; but, above the crowd swaying for ever to and fro in the restlessness of avarice or thirst of delight, was seen perpetually the glory of the temple, attesting to them, whether they would hear or whether they would forbear, that there was one treasure which the merchantmen might buy without a price, and one delight better than all others, in the word and the statutes of God. Not in the wantonness of wealth, not in vain ministry to the desire of the eyes or the pride of life, were those marbles hewn into transparent strength, and those arches arrayed in the colours of the iris. There is a message written in the dyes of them, that once was written in blood; and a sound in the echoes of their vaults, that one day shall fill the vault of heaven; – 'He shall return to do judgment and justice.' The strength of Venice was given her, so long as she remembered this: her destruction found her when she had forgotten this; and it found her irrevocably, because she forgot it without excuse. Never had a city a more glorious Bible. Among the nations of the North, a rude and shadowy sculpture filled their temples with confused and hardly legible imagery; but, for her, the skill and the treasures of the East had gilded every letter, and illumined every page, till the Book-Temple shone from afar off like the star of the Magi. In other cities, the meetings of the people were often in places withdrawn from religious association, subject to violence and to change; and on the grass of the dangerous rampart, and in the dust of the troubled street, there were deeds done and counsels taken, which, if we cannot justify, we may sometimes forgive. But the sins of Venice, whether in her palace or in her piazza, were done with the Bible at her right hand. The walls on which its testimony was written were separated but by a few inches of marble from those which guarded the secrets of her councils, or confined the victims of her policy. And when in her last hours she threw off all shame and all restraint, and the great square of the city became filled with the madness of the whole earth, be it remembered how much her sin was greater, because it was done in the face of the House of God, burning with the letters of His Law. Mountebank and masquer laughed their laugh and went their way; and a silence has followed them, not unforetold; for amidst them all, through century after century of gathering vanity and festering guilt, that dome of St. Mark's had uttered in the dead ear of Venice, 'Know thou, that for all these things God will bring thee into judgment.'

John Ruskin CAPITALS: CONVEX GROUP
The two in the centre are from the southern portico of St. Mark's.
*'The zigzagged capital is highly curious, and in its place
very effective and beautiful.'*

sculpture, and fragments of the bases of small pillars, entangled among festoons of the Erba della Madonna. In what references I have to make to it here, I shall speak of it as the Rio Foscari House.

We have now to reascend the Grand Canal, and approach the Rialto. As soon as we have passed the Casa Grimani, the traveller will recognise, on his right, two rich and extensive masses of building, which form important objects in almost every picturesque view of the noble bridge. Of these, the first, that farthest from the Rialto, retains great part of its ancient materials in a dislocated form. It has been entirely modernised in its upper stories, but the ground floor and first floor have nearly all their original shafts and capitals, only they have been shifted hither and thither to give room for the introduction of various small apartments, and present, in consequence, marvellous anomalies in proportion. This building is known in Venice as the Casa Farsetti.

The one next to it, though not conspicuous, and often passed with neglect, will, I believe, be felt at last, by all who examine it carefully, to be the most beautiful palace in the whole extent of the Grand Canal. It has been restored often, once in the Gothic, once in the Renaissance times,—some writers say even rebuilt; but, if so, rebuilt in its old form. The Gothic additions harmonise exquisitely with its Byzantine work, and it is easy, as we examine its lovely central arcade, to forget the Renaissance additions which encumber it above. It is known as the Casa Loredan.

They all agree in being round-arched and incrusted with marble, but there are only six in which the original disposition of the parts is anywise traceable; namely the Fondaco de' Turchi, Casa Loredan, Casa Farsetti, Rio-Foscari House, Terraced House, and Madonnetta House: and these six agree farther in having continuous arcades along their entire fronts from one angle to the other, and in having their arcades divided, in each case, into a centre and wings; both by greater size in the midmost arches, and by the alternation of shafts in the centre, with pilasters, or with small shafts, at the flanks.

So far as their structure can be traced, they agree also in having tall and few arches in their lower stories, and shorter and more numerous arches above: but it happens most unfortunately that in the only two cases in which the second stories are left the ground floors are modernized, and in the others where the sea stories are left the second stories are modernized; so that we never have more than two tiers of the Byzantine arches, one above the other. These, however, are quite enough to show the first main point on which I wish to insist, namely, the subtlety of the feeling for proportion in the Greek architects: and I hope that even the general reader will not allow himself to be frightened by the look of a few measurements, for, if he will only take the little pains necessary to compare them, he will, I am almost certain, find the result not devoid of interest.

The Fondaco de' Turchi has sixteen arches in its sea story, and twenty-six above them in its first story, the whole based on a magnificent foundation, built of blocks of red marble, some of them seven feet long by a foot and a half thick, and raised to a height of about five feet above high-water mark. At this level, the elevation of one half of the building, from its flank to the central pillars of its arcades, is rudely given to show the arrangement of the parts, as the sculptures which are indicated by the circles and upright oblongs between the arches are too delicate to be shown in a sketch three times the size of this. The building once was crowned with an Arabian parapet; but it was taken down some years since, and I am aware of no authentic representation of its details. The greater part of the sculptures between the arches, indicated only by blank circles, have also fallen, or been removed, but enough remain on the two flanks to justify the representation given in the diagram of their original arrangement.

And now observe the dimensions. The small arches of the wings in the ground story, *a, a, a*, measure, in breadth, from

	Ft.	In.
shaft to shaft	4	5
interval *b*	7	6½
interval *c*	7	11
intervals *d, e, f*, etc.	8	1

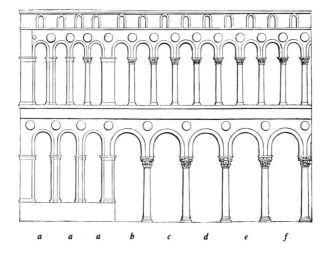

The difference between the width of the arches *b* and *c* is necessitated by the small recess of the cornice on the left hand as compared with that of the great capitals; but this sudden difference of half a foot between the two extreme arches of the centre offended the builder's eye, so he diminished the next one, *unnecessarily*, two inches, and thus obtained the gradual cadence to the flanks, from eight feet down to four and a half in a series of continually increasing steps. Of course the effect cannot be shown in the diagram, as the first difference is less than the thickness of its lines. In the upper story the capitals are all nearly of the same height, and there was no occasion for the difference between the extreme arches. Its twenty-six arches are placed, four small ones above each lateral three of the lower arcade, and eighteen larger above its central ten; thus throwing the shafts into all manner of relative positions, and completely confusing the eye in any effort to count them: but there is an exquisite symmetry running through their apparent confusion; for it will be seen that the four arches in each flank are arranged in two groups, of which one has a large single shaft in the centre, and the other a pilaster and two small shafts. The way in which the large shaft is used as an echo of those in the

The Fondaco de' Turchi.
Engraving from a drawing by Ruskin for *Examples of the Architecture of Venice*.

central arcade, dovetailing them, as it were, into the system of the pilasters, is highly characteristic of the Byzantine care in composition. There are other evidences of it in the arrangement of the capitals, which will be noticed below in the seventh chapter. The lateral arches of this upper arcade measure 3 ft. 2 in. across, and the central 3 ft. 11 in., so that the arches in the building are altogether of six magnitudes.

Next let us take the Casa Loredan. The mode of arrangement of its pillars is precisely like that of the Fondaco de' Turchi, so that I shall merely indicate them by vertical lines in order to be able to letter the intervals. It has five arches in the centre of the lower story, and two in each of its wings.

	Ft.	In.
The midmost interval, *a*, of the central five, is	6	1
The two on each side, *b, b*	5	2
The two extremes, *c, c*	4	9
Inner arches of the wings, *d, d*	4	4
Outer arches of the wings, *e, e*	4	6

e	*d*	*c*	*b*	*a*	*b*	*c*	*d*	*e*

The gradation of these dimensions is visible at a glance; the boldest step being here taken nearest the centre, while in the Fondaco it is farthest from the centre. The first loss here is of eleven inches, the second of five, the third of five, and then there is a most subtle increase of two inches in the extreme arches, as if to contradict the principle of diminution, and stop the falling away of the building by firm resistance at its flanks.

I could not get the measures of the upper story accurately, the palace having been closed all the time I was in Venice; but it has seven central arches above the five below, and three at the flanks above the two below, the groups being separated by double shafts.

Again in the Casa Farsetti, the lower story has a centre of five arches, and wings of two. Referring, therefore, to the last figure, which will answer for this palace also, the measures of the intervals are:

	Ft.	In.
a	8	0
b	5	10
c	5	4
d and e	5	3

It is, however, possible that the interval c and the wing arches may have been intended to be similar; for one of the wing arches measures 5 ft. 4 in. We have thus a simpler proportion than any we have hitherto met with; only two losses taking place, the first of 2 ft. 2 in., the second of 6 inches.

The upper story has a central group of seven arches, whose widths are 4 ft. 1 in.

	Ft.	In.
The next arch on each side	3	5
The three arches of each wing	3	6

Here again we have a most curious instance of the subtlety of eye which was not satisfied without a third dimension, but *could* be satisfied with a difference of an inch on three feet and a half.

In the Terraced House, the ground floor is modernized, but the first story is composed of a centre of five arches with wings of two, measuring as follows:

	Ft.	In.
Three midmost arches of the central group	4	0
Outermost arch of the central group	4	6
Innermost arch of the wing	4	10
Outermost arch of the wing	5	0

Here the greatest step is toward the centre; but the increase, which is unusual, is towards the outside, the gain being successively six, four, and two inches.

I could not obtain the measure of the second story, in which only the central group is left; but the two outermost arches are visibly larger than the others, thus beginning a correspondent proportion to the one below, of which the lateral quantities have been destroyed by restorations.

Finally, in the Rio-Foscari House, the central arch is the principal feature, and the four lateral ones form one magnificent wing; the dimensions being from the centre to the side:

	Ft.	In.
Central arch	9	9
Second ,,	3	8
Third ,,	3	10
Fourth ,,	3	10
Fifth ,,	3	8

The difference of two inches on nearly three feet in the two midmost arches being all that was necessary to satisfy the builder's eye.

I need not point out to the reader that these singular and minute harmonies of proportion indicate, beyond all dispute, not only that the buildings in which they are found are of one school, but (so far as these subtle coincidences of measurement can still be traced in them) in their original form. No modern builder has any idea of connecting his arches in this manner, and restorations in Venice are carried on with too violent hands to admit of the supposition that such refinements would be even noticed in the progress of demolition, much less imitated in heedless reproduction. And as if to direct our attention especially to this character, as indicative of Byzantine workmanship, the most interesting example of all will be found in the arches of the front of St. Mark's itself, whose proportions I have not noticed before, in order that they might here be compared with those of the contemporary palaces.

The doors actually employed for entrance in the western façade are as usual five, arranged as at *a*, but the Byzantine builder could not be satisfied with so simple a group, and he therefore introduced two minor arches at the extremities, as at *b*, by adding two small porticos which are of *no use whatever* except to consummate  the proportions of the façade, and themselves to exhibit the most exquisite proportions in arrangements of shaft and archivolt with which I am acquainted in the entire range of European architecture.

If the reader will be at the pains to compare the whole evidence now laid before him, with that deduced above from Murano, he cannot but confess that it amounts to an irrefragable proof of an intense perception of harmony in the relation of quantities, on the part of the Byzantine architects; a perception which we have at present lost so utterly as hardly to be able even to conceive it. And let it not be said, as it was of the late discoveries of subtle curvature in the Parthenon, that what is not to be demonstrated without laborious measurement, cannot have influence on the beauty of the design. The eye is continually influenced by what it cannot detect; nay, it is not going too far to say, that it is most influenced by what it detects least. Indeed, there is nothing truly noble either in colour or in form, but its power depends on circumstances infinitely too intricate to be explained, and almost too subtle to be traced. And as for these Byzantine buildings, we only do not feel them because we do not *watch* them; otherwise we should as much enjoy the variety of proportion in their arches, as we do at present that of the natural architecture of flowers and leaves. Nature is often far more subtle in her proportions. In looking at some lilies, full in the front of the flower, we may fancy for a moment that they form a symmetrical six-petaled star; but on examining them more closely, we shall find that they are thrown into a group of three magnitudes by the expansion of two of the inner petals above the stamens to a breadth greater than any of the four others; while the third inner petal, on which the stamens rest, contracts itself into the narrowest of the six, and the three under petals remain of one intermediate magnitude, as seen in the annexed figure.

I must not, however, weary the reader with this subject, which has always been a favourite one with me, and is apt to lead me too far; we will return to the palaces on the Grand Canal. Admitting, then, that their fragments are proved, by the minute correspondence of their arrangement, to be still in their original positions, they indicate to us a form, whether of palace or dwelling-house, in which there were, universally, central galleries or loggias, opening into apartments on each wing, the amount of light admitted being immense; and the general proportions of the building, slender, light, and graceful in the utmost degree, it being in fact little more than an aggregate of shafts and arches. Of the interior disposition of these palaces there is in no one instance the slightest trace left, nor am I well enough acquainted with the existing architecture of the East to risk any conjecture on this subject. I pursue the statement of the facts which are still ascertainable respecting their external forms.

In every one of the buildings above mentioned, except the Rio-Foscari House (which has only one great entrance between its wings), the central arcades are sustained, at least in one story, and generally in both, on bold detached cylindrical shafts, with rich capitals, while the arches of the wings are carried on smaller shafts assisted by portions of wall, which become pilasters of greater or less width.

And now I must remind the reader that there are two great orders of capitals in the world; that one of these is convex in its contour, the other concave; and that richness of ornament, with all freedom of fancy, is for the most part found in the one, and severity of ornament, with stern discipline of the fancy, in the other.

Of these two families of capitals, both occur in the Byzantine period, but the concave group is the longest-lived, and extends itself into the Gothic times. We must investigate their characters in detail; and these may be best generally represented by considering both families as formed upon the types of flowers,—the one upon that of the water-lily, the other upon that of the convolvulus. There was no intention in the Byzantine architects to imitate either one or other of these flowers; but all beautiful works of art must either intentionally imitate or accidentally resemble natural forms; and the direct comparison with the natural forms which these capitals most resemble, is the likeliest mode of fixing their distinctions in the reader's mind.

The Four Venetian Flower Orders.

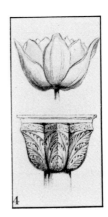

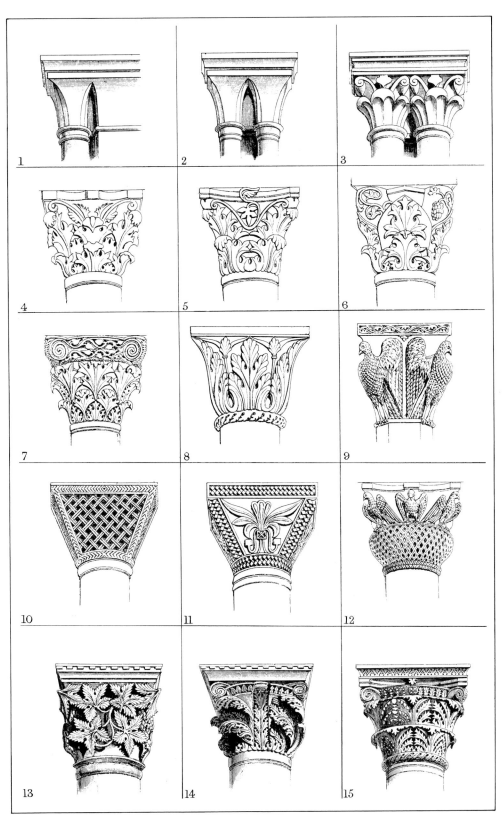

Byzantine Capitals. Concave Group.

The one then, the convex family, is modelled according to the commonest shapes of that great group of flowers which form rounded cups, like that of the water-lily, the leaves springing horizontally from the stalk, and closing together upwards. The rose is of this family, but her cup is filled with the luxuriance of her leaves; the crocus, campanula, ranunculus, anemone, and almost all the loveliest children of the field, are formed upon the same type.

The other family resembles the convolvulus, trumpet-flower, and such others, in which the lower part of the bell is slender, and the lip curves outward at the top. There are fewer flowers constructed on this than on the convex model; but in the organization of trees and of clusters of herbage it is seen continually. Of course, both of these conditions are modified, when applied to capitals, by the enormously greater thickness of the stalk or shaft, but in other respects the parallelism is close and accurate; and the reader had better at once fix the flower outlines in his mind, and remember them as representing the only two orders of capitals that the world has ever seen, or can see.

The examples of the concave family in the Byzantine times are found principally either in large capitals founded on the Greek Corinthian, used chiefly for the nave pillars of churches, or in the small lateral shafts of the palaces. It appears somewhat singular that the pure Corinthian form should have been reserved almost exclusively for nave pillars, as at Torcello, Murano, and St. Mark's; it occurs, indeed, together with almost every other form, on the exterior of St. Mark's also, but never so definitely as in the nave and transept shafts. Of the conditions assumed by it at Torcello enough has been said; and one of the most delicate of the varieties occurring in St. Mark's is given on page 107, remarkable for the cutting of the sharp thistle-like leaves into open relief, so that the light sometimes shines through them from behind, and for the beautiful curling of the extremities of the leaves outwards, joining each other at the top, as in an undivided flower.

The other characteristic examples of the concave groups in the Byzantine times are as simple as those resulting from the Corinthian are rich. They occur on the *small* shafts at the flanks of the Fondaco de' Turchi, the Casa Farsetti, Casa Loredan, Terraced House, and upper story of the Madonnetta House, in forms so exactly similar that the two figures 1 and 2 on page 107 may sufficiently represent them all. They consist merely of portions cut out of the plinths or string-courses which run along all the faces of these palaces, by four truncations in the form of arrowy leaves (fig. 1, Fondaco de' Turchi), and the whole rounded a little at the bottom so as to fit the shaft. When they occur between two arches they assume the form of the group fig. 2 (Terraced House). Fig. 3 is from the central arches of the Casa Farsetti, and is only given because either it is a later restoration or a form absolutely unique in the Byzantine period.

The concave group, however, was not naturally pleasing to the Byzantine mind. Its own favourite capital was of the bold convex or cushion shape, so conspicuous in all the buildings of the period, that I have devoted the plate opposite, entirely to its illustration. The form in which it is first used is practically obtained from a square block laid on the head of the shaft (fig. 1, page 109), by first cutting off the lower corners, as in fig. 2, and then rounding the edges, as in fig. 3; this gives us the bell stone; on which is laid a simple

Byzantine Capitals. Convex Group.

abacus, as seen in fig. 4, which is the actual form used in the upper arcade of Murano, and the framework of the capital is complete. Fig. 5 shows the general manner and effect of its decoration on the same scale; the other figures, 6 and 7 both from the apse of Murano, 8 from the Terraced House, and 9 from the Baptistery of St. Mark's, show the method of chiselling the surfaces in capitals of average richness, such as occur everywhere, for there is no limit to the fantasy and beauty of the more elaborate examples.

In consequence of the peculiar affection entertained for these massy forms by the Byzantines, they were apt, when they used any condition of capital founded on the Corinthian, to modify the concave profile by making it bulge out at the bottom. Fig 1 on page 106, is a capital of the pure concave family; and observe, it needs a fillet or cord round the neck of the capital to show where it separates from the shaft. Fig. 4, on the other hand, is of the pure convex group, which not only needs no such projecting fillet, but would be encumbered by it; while fig. 2 is one of the Byzantine capitals (Fondaco de' Turchi, lower arcade) founded on Corinthian, of which the main sweep is concave, but which bends below into the convex bell-shape, where it joints the shaft. And lastly fig. 3 is the profile of the nave shafts of St. Mark's, where, though very delicately granted, the concession to the Byzantine temper is twofold; first at the spring of the curve from the base, and secondly at the top, where it again becomes convex, though the expression of the Corinthian bell is still given to it by the bold concave leaves.

These, then, being the general modifications of Byzantine profiles, I have thrown together on page 107, some of the most characteristic examples of the decoration of the concave and transitional types.

In all the capitals hitherto spoken of, the form of the head of the bell has been square, and its varieties of outline have been obtained in the transition from the square of the abacus to the circular outline of the shafts. A far more complex series of forms results from the division of the bell by recesses into separate lobes or leaves, like those of a rose or tulip, which are each in their turn covered with flowerwork or hollowed into reticulation. The example (fig.

John Ruskin STILTED ARCHIVOLTS FROM A RUIN IN THE RIO DI CA' FOSCARI
'It was a beautifully picturesque fragment; the archivolt sculptures being executed in marble . . .'

10, page 109) from St. Mark's will give some idea of the simplest of these conditions: perhaps the most exquisite in Venice, on the whole, is the central capital of the upper arcade of the Fondaco de' Turchi.

Such are the principal generic conditions of the Byzantine capital; but the reader must always remember that the examples given are single instances, and those not the most beautiful but the most intelligible, chosen out of thousands: the designs of the capitals of St. Mark's alone would form a volume.

Of the archivolts which these capitals generally sustain, details are given in the notice of Venetian doors in Chapter 8. In the private palaces, the ranges of archivolt are for the most part very simple, with dentilled mouldings; and all the ornamental effect is entrusted to pieces of sculpture set in the wall above or between the arches, in the manner shown in [the Rio-Foscari house]. These pieces of sculpture are either crosses, upright oblongs, or circles: of all the three forms an example is given on page 113 overleaf. The cross was apparently an invariable ornament, placed either in the centre of the archivolt of the door-way, or in the centre of the first story above the windows; on each side of it the circular and oblong ornaments were used in various alternation. In too many instances the wall marbles have been torn away from the earliest Byzantine palaces, so that the crosses are left on their archivolts only. The best examples of the cross set above the windows are found in houses of the transitional period: one in the Campo St^a M. Formosa; another, in which a cross is placed between every window, is still well preserved in the Campo St^a Maria Mater Domini; another, on the Grand Canal, in the parish of the Apostoli, has two crosses, one on each side of the first story, and a bas-relief of Christ enthroned in the centre; and finally, that from which the larger cross in the Plate was taken is the house once belonging to Marco Polo, at San Giovanni Grisostomo.

This habit of placing the symbol of the Christian faith in the centres of their palaces was universal in early Venice; it does not cease till about the middle of the fourteenth century. The other sculptures, which were set above or between the arches, consist almost invariably of groups of birds or beasts; either standing opposite to each other with a small pillar of spray of leafage between them, or else tearing and devouring each other. The multitude of these sculptures, especially of the small ones enclosed in circles, as figs. 5 and 6, page 113, which are now scattered through the city of Venice, is enormous, but they are seldom to be seen in their original positions. When the Byzantine palaces were destroyed, these fragments were generally preserved, and inserted again in the walls of the new buildings, with more or less attempt at symmetry; fragments of friezes and mouldings being often used in the same manner; so that the mode of their original employment can only be seen in St. Mark's, the Fondaco de' Turchi, Braided House, and one or two others. The most remarkable point about them is, that the groups of beasts or birds on each side of the small pillars bear the closest possible resemblance to the group of Lions over the gate of Mycenæ; and the whole of the ornamentation of that gate as far as I can judge of it from drawings, is so like Byzantine sculpture, that I cannot help sometimes suspecting the original conjecture of the French anti-quarians, that it was a work of the middle ages, to be not altogether indefensible. By far the best among the sculptures at Venice are those consisting of groups thus arranged; the first figure on page 113 is one of those used on St. Mark's, and, with its chain of wreathen work round it, is very characteristic of the finest kind, except that the intermediate trunk or pillar often branches into luxuriant leafage, usually of the vine.

The groups of contending and devouring animals are always much ruder in cutting, and take somewhat the place in Byzantine sculpture which the lower grotesques do in the Gothic: true, though clumsy, grotesques being sometimes mingled among them, as four bodies joined to one head in the centre; but never showing any attempt at variety of invention, except only in the effective disposition of the light and shade, and in the vigour and thoughtfulness of the touches which indicate the plumes of the birds, or foldings of the leaves. Care, however, is always taken to secure variety enough to keep the eye entertained, no two sides of these Byzantine ornaments being in all respects the same: for instance, in the chainwork round the first figure on page 113 there are two circles enclosing squares on the left-hand side of the arch at the top, but two smaller circles and a diamond on the other, enclosing one square, and two small circular spots or bosses; and in the line of chain at the bottom there is a circle on the right, and a diamond on the left, and so down to the working of the smallest details. I have represented this upper sculpture as dark, in order to give some idea of the general effect of these ornaments when seen in shadow against light; an effect much calculated upon by their designer, and obtained by the use of a golden ground, formed of glass mosaic inserted in the hollow of the marble. Each square of glass has the leaf gold upon its surface protected by another thin film of glass above it, so that no time or weather can affect its lustre, until the pieces of glass are bodily torn from their setting. The smooth glazed surface of the golden ground is washed by every shower of rain, but the marble usually darkens into an amber colour in process of time; and when the whole ornament is cast into shadow, the golden surface, being perfectly reflective, refuses the darkness, and shows itself in bright and burnished light behind the dark traceries of the ornament. Where the marble has retained its perfect whiteness, on the other hand, and is seen in sunshine, it is shown as a snowy tracery on a golden ground; and the alternations and intermingling of these two effects form one of the chief enchantments of Byzantine ornamentation.

How far the system of grounding with gold and colour, universal in St. Mark's, was carried out in the sculptures of the private palaces, it is now impossible to say. The wrecks of them which remain, as above noticed, show few of their ornamental sculptures in their original position: and from those marbles which were employed in succeeding buildings, during the Gothic period, the fragments of their mosaic grounds would naturally rather have been removed than restored. Mosaic, while the most secure of all decorations if carefully watched and refastened when it loosens, may, if neglected and exposed to weather, in process of time disappear so as to leave no vestige of its existence. However this may have been, the assured facts are that both the shafts of the pillars and the facing of the whole building were of veined or variously coloured marble: the capitals and sculptures were either, as they now appear, of pure white marble, relieved upon the veined ground; or, which

John Ruskin BYZANTINE SCULPTURE

is infinitely the more probable, grounded in the richer palaces with mosaic of gold, in the inferior ones with blue colour, and only the leaves and edges of the sculpture gilded. These brighter hues were opposed by bands of deeper colour, generally alternate russet and green in the archivolts,—bands which still remain in the Casa Loredan and Fondaco de' Turchi, and in a house in the Corte del Remer near the Rialto, as well as in St. Mark's; and by circular disks of green serpentine and porphyry, which, together with the circular sculptures, appear to have been an ornament peculiarly grateful to the Eastern mind, derived probably in the first instance from the suspension of shields upon the wall, as in the majesty of ancient Tyre. The sweet and solemn harmony of purple with various green remained a favourite chord of colour with the Venetians, and was constantly used even in the later palaces; but never could have been seen in so great perfection as when opposed to the pale and delicate sculpture of the Byzantine time.

Such, then, was that first and fairest Venice which rose out of the barrenness of the lagoon, and the sorrow of her people, a city of graceful arcades and gleaming walls, veined with azure and warm with gold, and fretted with white sculpture like frost upon forest branches turned to marble. And yet, in this beauty of her youth, she was no city of thoughtless pleasure. There was still a sadness of heart upon her, and a depth of devotion, in which lay all her strength. I do not insist upon the probable religious signification of many of the sculptures which are now difficult of interpretation; but the temper which made the cross the principal ornament of every building is not to be misunderstood, nor can we fail to perceive, in many of the minor sculptural subjects, meanings perfectly familiar to the mind of early Christianity. The principal circumstance which marks the seriousness of the early Venetian mind is perhaps the last in which the reader would suppose it was traceable;—that love of bright and pure colour which, in a modified form, was afterwards the root of all the triumph of the Venetian schools of painting, but which, in its utmost simplicity, was characteristic of the Byzantine period only; and of which, therefore, in the close of our review of that period, it will be well that we should truly estimate the significance. The fact is, we none of us enough appreciate the nobleness and sacredness of colour. Nothing is more common than to hear it spoken of as a subordinate beauty,—nay, even as the mere source of a sensual pleasure. But it is not so. Such expressions are used for the most part in thoughtlessness; and if the speakers would only take the pains to imagine what the world and their own existence would become, if the blue were taken from the sky, and the gold from the sunshine, and the verdure from the leaves, and the crimson from the blood which is the life of man, the flush from the cheek, the darkness from the eye, the radiance from the hair—if they could but see, for an instant, white human creatures living in a white world—they would soon feel what they owe to colour. The fact is, that, of all God's gifts to the sight of man, colour is the holiest, the most divine, the most solemn. We speak rashly of gay colour and sad colour, for colour cannot at once be good and gay. All good colour is in some degree pensive, the loveliest is melancholy, and the

John Ruskin STUDY OF THE MARBLE INLAYING ON THE FRONT OF THE CASA LOREDAN
'*The Gothic additions harmonise exquisitely with the Byzantine work . . .*'

Casa Loredan.

purest and most thoughtful minds are those which love colour the most.

I know that this will sound strange in many ears, and will be especially startling to those who have considered the subject chiefly with reference to painting: for the great Venetian schools of colour are not usually understood to be either pure or pensive, and the idea of its pre-eminence is associated in nearly every mind with the coarseness of Rubens, and the sensualities of Correggio and Titian. But a more comprehensive view of art will soon correct this impression. It will be discovered, in the first place, that the more faithful and earnest the religion of the painter, the more pure and prevalent is the system of his colour. It will be found, in the second place, that where colour becomes a primal intention with a painter otherwise mean or sensual, it instantly elevates him, and becomes the one sacred and saving element in his work. The very depth of the stoop to which the Venetian painters and Rubens sometimes condescend, is a consequence of their feeling confidence in the power of their colour to keep them from falling. They hold on by it, as by a chain let down from heaven, with one hand, though they may sometimes seem to gather dust and ashes with the other. And, in the last place, it will be found that so surely as a painter is irreligious, thoughtless, or obscene in disposition, so surely is his colouring cold, gloomy, and valueless. The opposite poles of art in this respect are Frà Angelico and Salvator Rosa; of whom the one was a man who smiled seldom, wept often, prayed constantly, and never harboured an impure thought. His pictures are simply so many pieces of jewellery, the colours of the draperies being perfectly pure, as various as those of a painted window, chastened only by paleness, and relieved upon a gold ground. Salvator was a dissipated jester and satirist, a man who spent his life in masquing and revelry. But his pictures are full of horror, and their colour is for the most part gloomy grey. It would seem as if art had so much of eternity in it, that it must take its dye from the close rather than the course of life.

These are no singular instances. I know no law more severely without exception than this of the connexion of pure colour with profound and noble thought. The late Flemish pictures, shallow in conception and obscene in subject, are always sober in colour. But the early religious painting of the Flemings is as brilliant in hue as it is holy in thought. The Bellinis, Francias, Peruginos painted in crimson, and blue, and gold. The Caraccis, Guidos, and Rembrandts in brown and grey. The builders of our great cathedrals veiled their casements and wrapped their pillars with one robe of purple splendour. The builders of the luxurious Renaissance left their palaces filled only with cold white light, and in the paleness of their native stone.

Observe how in the Oriental mind a peculiar seriousness is associated with this attribute of the love of colour; a seriousness rising out of repose, and out of the depth and breadth of the imagination, as contrasted with the activity, and consequent capability of surprise, and of laughter, characteristic of the Western mind: as a man on a journey must look to his steps always, and view things narrowly and quickly; while one at rest may command a wider view, though an unchanging one, from which the pleasure he receives must be one of contemplation, rather than of amusement or surprise. Wherever the pure Oriental spirit manifests itself definitely, I believe its work is serious; and the meeting of the influences of the Eastern and Western races is perhaps marked in Europe more by the dying away of the grotesque laughter of the Goth than by any other sign. The point I wish to impress upon the reader is, that the bright hues of the early architecture of Venice were no sign of gaiety of heart, and that the investiture with the mantle of many colours by which she is known above all other cities of Italy and of Europe, was not granted to her in the fever of her festivity, but in the solemnity of her early and earnest religion. She became in after times the revel of the earth, the masque of Italy; and *therefore* is she now desolate: but her glorious robe of gold and purple was given her when first she rose a vestal from the sea, not when she became drunk with the wine of her fornication.

And we have never yet looked with enough reverence upon the separate gift which was thus bestowed upon her; we have never enough considered what an inheritance she has left us, in the works of those mighty painters who were the chief of her children. That inheritance is indeed less than it ought to have been, and other than it ought to have been; but before Titian and Tintoret arose, – the men in whom her work and her glory should have been together consummated, – she had already ceased to lead her sons in the way of truth, and they erred much, and fell short of that which was appointed for them.

The power with which this Venice had been entrusted was perverted, when at its highest, in a thousand miserable ways: still, it was possessed by her alone; to her all hearts have turned which could be moved by its manifestation, and none without being made stronger and nobler by what her hand had wrought. That mighty Landscape, of dark mountains that guard the horizon with their purple towers, and solemn forests that gather their weight of leaves, bronzed with sunshine, not with age, into those gloomy masses fixed in heaven, which storm and frost have power no more to shake or shed; – that mighty Humanity, so perfect and so proud, that hides no weakness beneath the mantle, and gains no greatness from the diadem; the majesty of thoughtful form, on which the dust of gold and flame of jewels are dashed as the sea-spray upon the rock, and still the great Manhood seems to stand bare against the blue sky; – that mighty Mythology, which fills the daily walks of men with spiritual companionship, and beholds the protecting angels break with their burning presence through the arrow-flights of battle: – measure the compass of that field of creation, weigh the value of the inheritance that Venice thus left to the nations of Europe, and then judge if so vast, so beneficent a power could indeed have been rooted in dissipation or decay. It was when she wore the ephod of the priest, not the motley of the masquer, that the fire fell upon her from heaven; and she saw the first rays of it through the rain of her own tears, when, as the barbaric deluge ebbed from the hills of Italy, the circuit of her palaces, and the orb of her fortunes, rose together, like the Iris, painted upon the Cloud.

THE NATURE OF
GOTHIC

I F the reader will look back to the division of our subject which was made in the first chapter, he will find that we are now about to enter upon the examination of that school of Venetian architecture which forms an intermediate step between the Byzantine and Gothic forms; but which I find may be conveniently considered in its connexion with the latter style. In order that we may discern the tendency of each step of this change, it will be wise in the outset to endeavour to form some general idea of its final result. We know already what the Byzantine architecture is from which the transition was made, but we ought to know something of the Gothic architecture into which it led. I shall endeavour therefore to give the reader in this chapter an idea, at once broad and definite, of the true nature of *Gothic* architecture, properly so called; not of that of Venice only, but of universal Gothic.

The principal difficulty in doing this arises from the fact that every building of the Gothic period differs in some important respect from every other; and many include features which, if they occurred in other buildings, would not be considered Gothic at all; so that all we have to reason upon is merely a greater or less degree of *Gothicness* in each building we examine. We all have some notion, most of us of us a very determined one, of the meaning of the term Gothic; but I know that many persons have this idea in their minds without being able to define it: that is to say, understanding generally that Westminster Abbey is Gothic, and St. Paul's is not, that Strasburg Cathedral is Gothic, and St. Peter's is not, they have, nevertheless, no clear notion of what it is that they recognize in the one or miss in the other, such as would enable them to say how far the work at Westminster or Strasburg is good and pure of its kind. And I believe this inquiry to be a pleasant and profitable one; and that there will be found something more than usually interesting in tracing out this grey, shadowy, many-pinnacled image of the Gothic spirit within us; and discerning what fellowship there is between it and our Northern hearts.

We have, then, the Gothic character submitted to our analysis, just as the rough mineral is submitted to that of the chemist, entangled with many other foreign substances, itself perhaps in no place pure, or ever to be obtained or seen in purity for more than an instant; but nevertheless a thing of definite and separate nature; however inextricable or confused in appearance. Now observe: the chemist defines his mineral by two separate kinds of character; one external, its crystalline form, hardness, lustre, etc.; the other internal, the proportions and nature of its constituent atoms. Exactly in the same manner, we shall find that Gothic architecture has external forms and internal elements. Its elements are certain mental tendencies of the builders, legibly expressed in it; as fancifulness, love of variety, love of richness, and such others. Its external forms are pointed arches, vaulted roofs, etc. And unless both the elements and the forms are there, we have no right to call the style Gothic. It is not enough that it has the Form, if it have not also the power and life. It is not enough that it has the Power, if it have not the form. We must therefore inquire into each of these characters successively; and determine first, what is the Mental Expression, and secondly, what the Material Form of Gothic architecture, properly so called.

1st. Mental Power or Expression. What characters, we have to discover, did the Gothic builders love, or instinctively express in their work, as distinguished from all other builders?

I believe that the characteristic or moral elements of Gothic are the following, placed in the order of their importance: 1. Savageness. 2. Changefulness. 3. Naturalism. 4. Grotesqueness. 5. Rigidity. 6. Redundance.

These characters are here expressed as belonging to the building; as belonging to the builder, they would be expressed thus:—1. Savageness or Rudeness. 2. Love of Change. 3. Love of Nature. 4. Disturbed Imagination. 5. Obstinacy. 6. Generosity. The withdrawal of any one, or any two, will not at once destroy the Gothic character of a building, but the removal of a majority of them will. I shall proceed to examine them in their order.

I. SAVAGENESS. I am not sure when the word 'Gothic' was first generically applied to the architecture of the North; but I presume that it was intended to imply reproach, and express the barbaric character of the nations among whom that architecture arose. It never implied that they were literally of Gothic lineage, far less that their architecture had been originally invented by the Goths themselves; but it did imply that they and their buildings together exhibited a degree of sternness and rudeness, which, in contradiction to the character of Southern and Eastern nations, appeared like a perpetual reflection of the contrast between the Goth and the Roman in their first encounter. As far as the epithet was used scornfully, it was used falsely; but there is no reproach in the word, rightly understood; on the contrary, there is a profound truth, which the instinct of mankind almost unconsciously recognizes. It is true, greatly and deeply true, that the architecture of the North is rude and wild; but it is not true, that, for this reason, we are to condemn it, or despise. Far otherwise: I believe it is in this very character that it deserves our profoundest reverence.

There is, I repeat, no degradation, no reproach in this, but all dignity and honourableness: and we should err grievously in refusing either to recognize as an essential character of the existing architecture of the North, or to admit as a desirable character in that which it yet may be, this wildness of thought, and roughness of work; this look of mountain brotherhood between the cathedral and the Alp; this magnificence of sturdy power, put forth only the more energetically because the fine finger-touch was chilled away by the frosty wind, and the eye dimmed by the moor-mist, or blinded by the hail; this outspeaking of the strong spirit of men who may not gather redundant fruitage from the earth, not bask in dreamy benignity of sunshine, but must break the rock for bread, and cleave the forest for fire, and show, even in what they did for their delight, some of the hard habits of the arm and heart that grew on them as they swung the axe or pressed the plough.

If, however, the savageness of Gothic architecture, merely as an expression of its origin among Northern nations, may be considered, in some sort, a noble character, it possesses a higher nobility still, when considered as an index, not of climate, but of religious principle.

The systems of architectural ornament, properly so called, may be divided into three:–1. Servile ornament, in which the execution or power of the inferior workman is entirely subjected to the intellect of the higher;–2. Constitutional ornament, in which the executive inferior power is, to a certain point, emancipated and independent, having a will of its own, yet confessing its inferiority and rendering obedience to higher powers;–and 3. Revolutionary ornament, in which no executive inferiority is admitted at all.

Of Servile ornament, the principal schools are the Greek, Ninevite, and Egyptian; but their servility is of different kinds. The Greek master-workman was far advanced in knowledge and power above the Assyrian or Egyptian. Neither he nor those for whom he worked could endure the appearance of imperfection in anything; and, therefore, what ornament he appointed to be done by those beneath him was composed of mere geometrical forms;–balls, ridges, and perfectly symmetrical foliage,–which could be executed with absolute precision by line and rule, and were as perfect in their way, when completed, as his own figure sculpture. The Assyrian and Egyptian, on the contrary, less cognisant of accurate form in anything, were content to allow their figure sculpture to be executed by inferior workmen, but lowered the method of its treatment to a standard which every workman could reach, and then trained him by discipline so rigid, that there was no chance of his falling beneath the standard appointed. The Greek gave to the lower workman no subject which he could not perfectly execute. The Assyrian gave him subjects which he could only execute imperfectly, but fixed a legal standard for his imperfection. The workman was, in both systems, a slave.

But in the mediæval, or especially Christian, system of ornament, this slavery is done away with altogether; Christianity having recognized, in small things as well as great, the individual value of every soul. But it not only recognizes its value; it confesses its imperfection, in only bestowing dignity upon the acknowledgment of unworthiness. Therefore, to every spirit which Christianity summons to her service, her exhortation is: Do what you can, and confess frankly what you are unable to do; neither let your effort be shortened for fear of failure, nor your confession silenced for fear of shame. And it is, perhaps, the principal admirableness of the Gothic schools of architecture, that they thus receive the results of the labour of inferior minds; and out of fragments full of imperfection, and betraying that imperfection in every touch, indulgently raise up a stately and unaccusable whole.

It seems a fantastic paradox, but it is nevertheless a most important truth, that no architecture can be truly noble which is *not* imperfect. And this is easily demonstrable. For since the architect, whom we will suppose capable of doing all in perfection, cannot execute the whole with his own hands, he must either make slaves of his workmen in the old Greek, and present English fashion, and level his work to a slave's capacities, which is to degrade it; or else he must take his workmen as he finds them, and let them show their weaknesses together with their strength, which will involve the Gothic imperfection, but render the whole work as noble as the intellect of the age can make it.

But the principle may be stated more broadly still. I have confined the illustration of it to architecture, but I must not leave it as if true of architecture only. Hitherto I have used the words imperfect and perfect merely to distinguish between work grossly unskilful, and work executed with average precision and science; and I have been pleading that any degree of unskilfulness should be admitted, so only that the labourer's mind had room for expression. But, accurately speaking, no good work whatever can be perfect, and *the demand for perfection is always a sign of a misunderstanding of the ends of art.*

This for two reasons, both based on everlasting laws. The first, that no great man ever stops working till he has reached his point of failure: that is to say, his mind is always far in advance of his powers of execution, and the latter will now and then give way in trying to follow it; besides that he will always give to the inferior portions of his work only such inferior attention as they require; and according to his greatness he becomes so accustomed to the feeling of dissatisfaction with the best he can do, that in moments of lassitude or anger with himself he will not care though the beholder be dissatisfied also. I believe there has only been one man who would not acknowledge this necessity, and strove always to reach perfection, Leonardo; the end of his vain effort being merely that he would take ten years to a picture and leave it unfinished. And therefore, if we are to have great men working at all, or less men doing their best, the work will be imperfect, however beautiful. Of human work none but what is bad can be perfect, in its own bad way.

The second reason is, that imperfection is in some sort essential to all that we know of life. It is the sign of life in a mortal body, that is to say, of a state of progress and change. Nothing that lives is, or can be, rigidly perfect; part of it is decaying, part nascent. The foxglove blossom,—a third part bud, a third part past, a third part in full bloom,—is a type of the life of this world. And in all things that live there are certain irregularities and deficiencies which are not only signs of life, but sources of beauty. All admit irregularity as they imply change; and to banish imperfection is to destroy expression, to check exertion, to paralyze vitality.

Accept this then for a universal law, that neither architecture nor any other noble work of man can be good unless it be imperfect; and let us be prepared for the otherwise strange fact, which we shall discern clearly as we approach the period of the Renaissance, that the first cause of the fall of the arts of Europe was a relentless requirement of perfection, incapable alike either of being silenced by veneration for greatness, or softened into forgiveness of simplicity.

Thus far then of the Rudeness or Savageness, which is the first mental element of Gothic architecture. It is an element in many other healthy architectures also, as the Byzantine and Romanesque; but true Gothic cannot exist without it.

The second mental element above named was CHANGEFULNESS, or Variety.

Wherever the workman is utterly enslaved, the parts of the building must of course be absolutely like each other; for the perfection of his execution can only be reached by exercising him in doing one thing, and giving him nothing else to do. The degree in which the workman is degraded may be thus known at a glance, by observing whether the several parts of the building are similar or not; and if, as in Greek work, all the capitals are alike, and all the mouldings unvaried, then the degradation is complete; if, as in Egyptian or Ninevite work, though the manner of executing certain figures is always the same, the order of design is perpetually varied, the degradation is less total; if, as in Gothic work, there is perpetual change both in design and execution, the workman must have been altogether set free.

The Gothic spirit not only dared, but delighted in, the infringement of every servile principle; and invented a series of forms of which the merit was, not merely that they were new, but that they were *capable of perpetual novelty*. The pointed arch was not merely a bold variation from the round, but it admitted of millions of variations in itself; for the proportions of a pointed arch are changeable to infinity, while a circular arch is always the same. The grouped shaft was not merely a bold variation from the single one, but it admitted of millions of variations in its grouping, and in the proportions resultant from its grouping. The introduction of tracery was not only a startling change in the treatment of window lights, but admitted endless changes in the interlacement of the tracery bars themselves. So that, while in all living Christian architecture the love of variety exists, the Gothic schools exhibited that love in culminating energy; and their influence, wherever it extended itself, may be sooner and farther traced by this character than by any other: the tendency to the adoption of Gothic types being always first shown by greater irregularity and richer variation in the forms of architecture it is about to supersede, long before the appearance of the pointed arch or of any other recognizable *outward* sign of the Gothic mind.

We must, however, herein note carefully what distinction there is between a healthy and a diseased love of change; for as it was in healthy love of change that the Gothic architecture rose, it was partly in consequence of diseased love of change that it was destroyed. In order to understand this clearly, it will be necessary to consider the different ways in which change and monotony are presented to us in nature; both having their use, like darkness and light, and the one incapable of being enjoyed without the other: change being most delightful after some prolongation of monotony, as light appears most brilliant after the eyes have been for some time closed.

Monotony is, and ought to be, in itself painful to us, just as darkness is; an architecture which is altogether monotonous is a dark or dead architecture; and of those who love it, it may be truly said, 'they love darkness rather than light.' But monotony in certain measure, used in order to give value to change, and above all, that *transparent* monotony, which, like the shadows of a great painter, suffers all manner of dimly suggested form to be seen through the body of it, is an essential in architectural as in all other composition; and the endurance of monotony has about the same place in a healthy mind that the endurance of darkness has: that is to say, as a strong intellect will have pleasure in the solemnities of storm and twilight, and in the broken and mysterious lights that gleam among them, rather than in mere brilliancy and glare, while a frivolous mind will dread the shadow and the storm; and as a great man will be ready to endure much darkness of fortune in order to reach greater eminence of power or felicity, while an inferior man will not pay the price; exactly in like manner a great mind will accept, or even delight in, monotony which would be wearisome to an inferior intellect, because it has more patience and power of expectation, and is ready to pay the full price for the great future pleasure of change. But in all cases it is not that the noble nature loves monotony, any more than it loves darkness or pain. But it can bear with it, and receive a high pleasure in the endurance or patience, a pleasure necessary to the well-being of this world; while those who will not submit to the temporary sameness, but rush from one change to another, gradually dull the edge of change itself, and bring a shadow and weariness over the whole world from which there is no more escape.

From these general uses of variety in the economy of the world, we may at once understand its use and abuse in architecture. The variety of the Gothic schools is the more healthy and beautiful, because in many cases it is entirely unstudied, and results, not from mere love of change, but from practical necessities. For in one point of view Gothic is not only the best, but the *only rational* architecture, as being that which can fit itself most easily to all services, vulgar or noble. Undefined in its slope of roof, height of shaft, breadth of arch, or disposition of ground plan, it can shrink into a turret, expand into a hall, coil into a staircase, or spring into a spire, with undegraded grace and unexhausted energy; and whenever it finds occasion for change in its form or purpose, it submits to it without the slightest sense of loss either to its unity or majesty—subtle and flexible like a fiery serpent, but ever attentive to the voice of the charmer. And it is one of the chief virtues of the Gothic builders, that they never suffered ideas of outside symmetries and consistencies to interfere with the real use and value of what they did. If they wanted a window, they opened one; a room, they added one; a buttress, they built one; utterly regardless of any established conventionalities of external appearance. So that, in the best times of Gothic, a useless window would rather have been opened in an unexpected place for the sake of the surprise, than a useful one forbidden for the sake of symmetry. In the ninth chapter we shall see a remarkable instance of this sacrifice of symmetry to convenience in the arrangement of the windows of the Ducal Palace.

The third constituent element of the Gothic mind was stated to be NATURALISM; that is to say, the love of natural objects for their own sake, and the effort to represent them frankly, unconstrained by artistical laws.

This characteristic of the style partly follows in necessary connection with those named above. For, so soon as the workman is left free to represent what subjects he chooses, he must look to the nature that is round him for material, and will endeavour to represent it as he sees it, with more or less accuracy according to the skill he possesses, and with much play of fancy, but with small respect for law. There is, however, a marked distinction between the imaginations of the Western and Eastern races, even when both are left free; the Western, or Gothic, delighting most in the representation of facts, and the Eastern (Arabian, Persian, and Chinese) in the harmony of colours and forms. Each of these intellectual dispositions has its particular forms of error and abuse, which, though I have often before stated, I must here again briefly explain; and this the rather, because the word Naturalism is, in one of its senses, justly used as a term of reproach, and the questions respecting the real relations of art and nature are so many and so confused throughout all the schools of Europe at this day, that I cannot clearly enunciate any single truth without appearing to admit, in fellowship with it, some kind of error, unless the reader will bear with me in entering into such an analysis of the subject as will serve us for general guidance.

We are to remember, in the first place, that the arrangement of colours and lines is an art analogous to the composition of music, and entirely independent of the representation of facts. Good colouring does not necessarily convey the image of anything but itself. It consists in certain proportions and arrangements of rays of light, but not in likenesses to anything. A few touches of certain greys and purples laid by a master's hand on white paper will be good colouring; as more touches are added beside them, we may find out that they were intended to represent a dove's neck, and we may praise, as the drawing advances, the perfect imitation of the dove's neck. But the good colouring does not consist in that imitation, but in the abstract qualities and relations of the grey and purple.

Now the noblest art is an exact unison of the abstract value, with the imitative power, of forms and colours. It is the noblest composition, used to express the noblest facts. But the human mind cannot in general unite the two perfections: it either pursues the fact to the neglect of the composition, or pursues the composition to the neglect of the fact.

Men are universally divided, as respects their artistical qualifications, into three great classes; a right, a left, and a centre. On the right side are the men of facts, on the left the men of design, in the centre the men of both. The three classes of course pass into each other by imperceptible gradations. The men of facts are hardly ever altogether without powers of design; the men of design are always in some measure cognizant of facts; and as each class possesses more or less of the powers of the opposite one, it approaches to the character of the central class. Now each of these classes has, as I above said, a healthy function in the world, and correlative diseases or unhealthy functions; and, when the work of either of them is seen in its morbid condition, we are apt to find fault with the class of workmen, instead of finding fault only with the particular abuse which has perverted their action.

Let us take an instance of the healthy action of the three classes on a simple subject, so as fully to understand the distinction between them, and then we shall more easily examine the corruptions to which they are liable. Fig. 1 on page 125 is a spray of vine with a bough of cherry-tree, which I have outlined from nature as accurately as I could, without in the least endeavouring to compose or arrange the form. It is a simple piece of fact-work, healthy and good as such, and useful to any one who wanted to know plain truths about tendrils of vines, but there is no attempt at design in it. Page 127 represents a

The Vine, Free and in Service.

branch of vine used to decorate the angle of the Ducal Palace. It is faithful as a representation of vine, and yet so designed that every leaf serves an architectural purpose, and could not be spared from its place without harm. This is central work; fact and design together. Fig. 2 on page 125 is a spandril from St. Mark's, in which the forms of the vine are dimly suggested, the object of the design being merely to obtain graceful lines and well-proportioned masses upon the gold ground. There is not the least attempt to inform the spectator of any facts about the growth of the vine; there are no stalks or tendrils, – merely running bands with leaves emergent from them, of which nothing but the outline is taken from the vine, and even that imperfectly. This is design, unregardful of facts.

Now the work is, in all these three cases, perfectly healthy. Fig. 1 is not bad work because it has not design, nor Fig. 2 bad work because it has not facts. The object of the one is to give pleasure through truth, and of the other to give pleasure through composition. And both are right.

What, then, are the diseased operations to which the three classes of workmen are liable?

Primarily, two; affecting the two inferior classes;

1st, When either of those two classes Despises the other;

2nd, When either of the two classes Envies the other;

producing, therefore, four forms of dangerous error.

First, when the men of facts despise design. This is the error of the common Dutch painters, of merely imitative painters of still life, flowers, etc., and other men who, having either the gift of accurate imitation or strong sympathies with nature, suppose that all is done when the imitation is perfected or sympathy expressed.

The second form of error is when the men of design despise facts. All noble design must deal with facts to a certain extent, for there is no food for it but in nature. The best colourist invents best by taking hints from natural colours; from birds, skies, or groups of figures. And if, in the delight of inventing fantastic colour and form, the truths of nature are wilfully neglected, the intellect becomes comparatively decrepit, and that state of art results which we find among the Chinese. The Greek designers delighted in the facts of the human form, and became great in consequence; but the facts of lower nature were disregarded by them, and their inferior ornament became, therefore, dead and valueless.

The third form of error is when the men of facts envy design; that is to say, when, having only imitative powers, they refuse to employ those powers upon the visible world around them; but, having been taught that composition is the end of art, strive to obtain the inventive powers which nature has denied them, study nothing but the works of reputed designers, and perish in a fungous growth of plagiarism and laws of art.

The fourth form of error is when the men of design envy facts; that is to say, when the temptation of closely imitating nature leads them to forget their own proper ornamental function, and when they lose the power of the composition for the sake of graphic truth.

So much, then, of the diseases of the inferior classes, caused by their envying or despising each other. It is evident that the men of the central class cannot be liable to any morbid operation of this kind, they possessing the powers of both.

The reader may be somewhat wearied with a statement which has led us apparently so far from our immediate subject. But the digression was necessary, in order that I might clearly define the sense in which I use the word Naturalism when I state it to be the third most essential characteristic of Gothic architecture. I mean that the Gothic builders belong to the central or greatest rank of artists.

The Gothic builders were of that central class; but the part of the work which was more especially their own was the truthfulness. Their power of artistical invention or arrangement was not greater than that of Romanesque and Byzantine workmen: by those workmen they were taught the principles, and from them received their models, of design; but to the ornamental feeling and rich fancy of the Byzantine the Gothic builder added a love of *fact* which is never found in the South. Both Greek and Roman used conventional foliage in their ornament, passing into something that was not foliage at all, knotting itself into strange cup-like buds or clusters, and growing out of lifeless rods instead of stems; the Gothic sculptor received these types, at first, as things that ought to be, just as we have a second time received them; but he could not rest in them. He saw there was no veracity in them, no knowledge, no vitality. Do what he would, he could not help liking the true leaves better; and cautiously, a little at a time, he put more of nature into his work, until at

Leafage of the Vine Angle of the Ducal Palace.

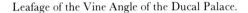

last it was all true, retaining, nevertheless, every valuable character of the original well-disciplined and designed arrangement.

Nor is it only in external and visible subject that the Gothic workman wrought for truth: he is as firm in his rendering of imaginative as of actual truth; that is to say, when an idea would have been by a Roman, or Byzantine, symbolically represented, the Gothic mind realizes it to the utmost. For instance, the purgatorial fire is represented in the mosaic of Torcello (Romanesque) as a red stream, longitudinally striped like a riband, descending out of the throne of Christ, and gradually extending itself to envelope the wicked. When we are once informed what this means, it is enough for its purpose; but the Gothic inventor does not leave the sign in need of interpretation. He makes the fire as like real fire as he can; and in the porch of St. Maclou at Rouen the sculptured flames burst out of the Hades gate, and flicker up, in writhing tongues of stone, through the interstices of the niches, as if the church itself were on fire. This is an extreme instance, but it is all the more illustrative of the entire difference in temper and thought between the two schools of art, and of the intense love of veracity which influenced the Gothic design.

I do not say that this love of veracity is always healthy in its operation. I have above noticed the errors into which it falls from despising design; and there is another kind of error noticeable in the instance just given, in which the love of truth is too hasty, and seizes on a surface truth instead of an inner one. For in representing the Hades fire, it is not the mere *form* of the flame which needs most to be told, but its unquenchableness, its Divine ordainment and limitation, and its inner fierceness, not physical and material, but in being the expression of the wrath of God. And these things are not to be told by imitating the fire that flashes out of a bundle of sticks. If we think over his symbol a little, we shall perhaps find that the Romanesque builder told more truth in that likeness of a blood-red stream, flowing between definite shores, and out of God's throne, and expanding, as if fed by a perpetual current, into the lake wherein the wicked are cast, than the Gothic builder in those torch-flickerings about his niches. But this is not to our immediate purpose; I am not at present to insist upon the faults into which the love of truth was led in the later Gothic times, but on the feeling itself, as a glorious and peculiar characteristic of the Northern builders. For, observe, it is not, even in the above instance, love of truth, but want of thought, which *causes* the fault. The love of truth, as such, is good, but when it is misdirected by thoughtfulness or over-excited by vanity, and either seizes on facts of small value, or gathers them chiefly that it may boast of its grasp and apprehension, its work may well become dull or offensive. Yet let us not, therefore, blame the inherent love of facts, but the incautiousness of their selection, and impertinence of their statement.

There is one direction in which the Naturalism of the Gothic workmen is peculiarly manifested; and this direction is even more characteristic of the school than the Naturalism itself; I mean their peculiar fondness for the forms of Vegetation. In rendering the various circumstances of daily life, Egyptian and Ninevite sculpture is as frank and as diffuse as the Gothic. From the highest pomps of state or triumphs of battle, to the most trivial domestic arts

Detail from the twelfth-century mosaic of the Universal Judgment at Torcello.

and amusements, all is taken advantage of to fill the field of granite with the perpetual interest of a crowded drama; and the early Lombardic and Romanesque sculpture is equally copious in its description of the familiar circumstances of war and the chase. But in all the scenes portrayed by the workmen of these nations, vegetation occurs only as an explanatory accessary; the reed is introduced to mark the course of the river, or the tree to mark the covert of the wild beast, or the ambush of the enemy, but there is no especial interest in the forms of the vegetation strong enough to induce them to make it a subject of separate and accurate study. Again, among the nations who followed the arts of design exclusively, the forms of foliage introduced were meagre and general, and their real intricacy and life were neither admired nor expressed. But to the Gothic workman the living foliage became a subject of intense affection, and he struggled to render all its characters with as much accuracy as was compatible with the laws of his design and the nature of his material, not unfrequently tempted in his enthusiasm to transgress the one and disguise the other.

There is a peculiar significance in this, indicative both of higher civilization and gentler temperament, than had before been manifested in architecture. Rudeness, and the love of change, which we have insisted upon as the first elements of Gothic, are also elements common to all healthy schools. But here is a softer element mingled with them, peculiar to the Gothic itself. The rudeness or ignorance which would have been painfully exposed in the treatment of the human form, are still not so great as to prevent the successful rendering of the wayside herbage; and the love of change, which becomes morbid and feverish in following the haste of the hunter and the rage of the combatant, is at once soothed and satisfied as it watches the wandering of the tendril, and the budding of the flower. Nor is this all: the new direction of mental interest marks an infinite change in the means and the habits of life. The nations whose chief support was in the chase, whose chief interest was in the battle, whose chief pleasure was in the banquet, would take small care respecting the shapes of leaves and flowers; and notice little in the forms of the forest trees which sheltered them, except the signs indicative of the wood which would make the toughest lance, the closest roof, or the clearest fire. The affectionate observation of the grace and outward character of vegetation is the sure sign of a more tranquil and gentle existence, sustained by the gifts, and gladdened by the splendour, of the earth. In that careful distinction of species, and richness of delicate and undisturbed organization, which characterize the Gothic design, there is the history of rural and thoughtful life, influenced by habitual tenderness, and devoted to subtle inquiry; and every discriminating and delicate touch of the chisel, as it rounds the petal or guides the branch, is a prophecy of the development of the natural sciences, beginning with that of medicine, of the recovery of literature, and the establishment of the most necessary principles of domestic wisdom and national peace.

The fourth essential element of the Gothic mind was above stated to be the sense of the GROTESQUE; every reader familiar with Gothic architecture must understand what I mean, and will, I believe, have no hesitation in admitting that the tendency to delight in fantastic and ludicrous, as well as in sublime, images, is a universal instinct of the Gothic imagination.

The fifth element above named was RIGIDITY; and this character I must endeavour carefully to define, for neither the word I have used, nor any other that I can think of, will express it accurately. For I mean, not merely stable, but *active* rigidity; the peculiar energy which gives tension to movement, and stiffness to resistance, which makes the fiercest lightning forked rather than curved, and the stoutest oak-branch angular rather than bending, and is as much seen in the quivering of the lance as in the glittering of the icicle. It shows itself throughout the whole structure and decoration of Gothic work. Egyptian and Greek buildings stand, for the most part, by their own weight and mass, one stone passively incumbent on another; but in the Gothic vaults and traceries there is a stiffness analogous to that of the bones of a limb, or fibres of a tree; an elastic tension and communication of force from part to part, and also a studious expression of this throughout every visible line of the building. And, in like manner, the Greek and Egyptian ornament is either mere surface engraving, as if the face of the wall had been stamped with a seal, or its lines are flowing, lithe, and luxuriant; in either case, there is no expression of energy in the framework of the ornament itself. But the Gothic ornament stands out in prickly independence, and frosty fortitude, jutting into crockets, and freezing into pinnacles; here starting up into a monster, there germinating into a blossom, anon knitting itself into a branch, alternately thorny, bossy, and bristly, or writhed into every form of nervous entanglement; but, even when most graceful, never for an instant languid, always quickset: erring, if at all, ever on the side of brusquerie.

The feelings or habits in the workman which give rise to this character in the work, are more complicated and various than those indicated by any other sculptural expression hitherto named. There is, first, the habit of hard and rapid working; the industry of the tribes of the North, quickened by the coldness of the climate, and giving an expression of sharp energy to all they do, as opposed to the languor of the Southern tribes, however much of fire there may be in the heart of that languor, for lava itself may flow languidly. There is also the habit of finding enjoyment in the signs of cold, which is never found, I believe, in the inhabitants of countries south of the Alps. Cold is to them an unredeemed evil, to be suffered and forgotten as soon as may be; but the long winter of the North forces the Goth (I mean the Englishman, Frenchman, Dane, or German), if he would lead a happy life at all, to find sources of happiness in foul weather as well as fair, and to rejoice in the leafless as well as in the shady forest.

There are many subtle sympathies and affections which join to confirm the Gothic mind in this peculiar choice of subject; and when we add to the influence of these, the necessities consequent upon the employment of a rougher material, compelling the workman to seek for vigour of effect, rather than refinement of texture or accuracy of form, we have direct and manifest causes for much of the difference between the northern and southern cast of conception: but there are indirect causes holding a far more important place in the Gothic heart, though less immediate in their influence on design. Strength of will, independence of character, resoluteness of purpose, impatience of undue control, and that general tendency to set the individual reason against authority, and the individual deed against destiny, which, in the Northern tribes, has opposed itself throughout all ages to the languid submission, in the Southern, of thought to tradition, and purpose to fatality, are all more or less traceable in the rigid lines, vigorous and various masses, and daringly projecting and independent structure of the Northern Gothic ornament: while the opposite feelings are in like manner legible in the graceful and softly guided waves and wreathed bands, in which Southern decoration is constantly disposed; in its tendency to lose its independence, and fuse itself into the surface of the masses upon which it is traced; and in the expression seen so often, in the arrangement of those masses themselves, of an abandonment of their strength to an inevitable necessity, or a listless repose.

There is virtue in the measure, and error in the excess, of both these characters of mind, and in both of the styles which they have created; the best architecture, and the best temper, are those which unite them both; and this fifth impulse of the Gothic heart is therefore that which needs most caution in its indulgence. It is more definitely Gothic than any other, but the best Gothic building is not that which is *most* Gothic: it can hardly be too frank in its confession of rudeness, hardly too rich in its changefulness, hardly too faithful in its naturalism; but it may go too far in its rigidity, and, like the great Puritan spirit in its extreme, lose itself either in frivolity of division, or perversity of purpose.

Last, because the least essential, of the constituent elements of this noble school, was placed that of REDUNDANCE,—the uncalculating bestowal of the wealth of its labour. There is, indeed, much Gothic, and that of the best period, in which this element is hardly traceable, and which depends for its effect almost exclusively on loveliness of simple design and grace of uninvolved proportion: still, in the most characteristic buildings, a certain portion of their effect depends upon accumulation of ornament; and many of those which have most influence on the minds of men, have attained it by means of this attribute alone. And although, by careful study of the school, it is possible to arrive at a condition of taste which shall be better contented by a few perfect lines than by a whole façade covered with fretwork, the building which only satisfies such a taste is not to be considered the best. For the very first requirement of Gothic architecture being, as we saw above, that it shall both admit the aid, and appeal to the admiration, of the rudest as well as the most refined minds, the richness of the work is, paradoxical as the statement may appear, a part of its humility. No architecture is so haughty as that which is simple; which refuses to address the eye, except in a few clear and forceful lines; which implies, in offering so little to our regards, that all it has offered is perfect; and disdains, either by the complexity or the attractiveness of its features, to embarrass our investigation, or betray us into delight. That humility, which is the very life of the Gothic school, is shown not only in the imperfection, but in the accumulation, of ornament. The inferior rank of the workman is often shown as much in the richness, as the roughness, of his work; and if the co-operation of every hand, and the sympathy of every heart, are to be received, we must be content to allow the redundance which disguises the failure of the feeble, and wins the regard of the inattentive. There are, however, far nobler interests mingling, in the Gothic heart, with the rude love of decorative accumulation: a magnificent enthusiasm, which feels as if it never could do enough to reach the fulness of its ideal; an unselfishness of sacrifice, which would rather cast fruitless labour before the altar than stand idle in the market; and, finally, a profound sympathy with the fulness and wealth of the material universe, rising out of that Naturalism whose operation we have already endeavoured to define. The sculptor who sought for his models among the forest leaves, could not but quickly and deeply feel that complexity need not involve the loss of grace, nor richness that of repose; and every hour which he spent in the study of the minute and various work of Nature, made him feel more forcibly the barrenness of what was best in that of man: nor is it to be wondered at, that, seeing her perfect and exquisite creations poured forth in a profusion which conception could not grasp nor calculation sum, he should think that it ill became him to be niggardly of his own rude craftsmanship; and where he saw throughout the universe a faultless beauty lavished on measureless spaces of broidered field and blooming mountain, to grudge his poor and imperfect labour to the few stones that he had raised one upon another, for habitation or memorial. The years of his life passed away before his task was accomplished; but generation succeeded generation with unwearied enthusiasm, and the cathedral front was at last lost in the tapestry of its traceries, like a rock among the thickets and herbage of spring.

We have now, I believe, obtained a view approaching to completeness of the various moral or imaginative elements which composed the inner spirit of Gothic architecture. We have, in the second place, to define its outward form.

Now, as the Gothic spirit is made up of several elements, some of which may, in particular examples, be wanting, so the Gothic form is made up of minor conditions of form, some of which may, in particular examples, be imperfectly developed.

We cannot say, therefore, that a building is either Gothic or not Gothic in form, any more than we can in spirit. We can only say that it is more or less Gothic, in proportion to the number of Gothic forms which it unites.

There have been made lately many subtle and ingenious endeavours to base the definition of Gothic form entirely upon the roof-vaulting; endeavours which are both forced and futile: for many of the best Gothic buildings in the world have roofs of timber, which have no more connexion with the main structure of the walls of the edifice than a hat has with that of the head it protects; and other Gothic buildings are merely enclosures of spaces, as ramparts and walls, or enclosures of gardens or cloisters, and have no roofs at all, in the sense in which the word 'roof' is commonly accepted. But every reader who has ever taken the slightest interest in architecture must know that there is a great popular impression on this matter, which maintains itself stiffly in its old form, in spite of all ratiocination and definition; namely, that a flat lintel from pillar to pillar is Grecian, a round arch Norman or Romanesque, and a pointed arch Gothic.

And the old popular notion, as far as it goes, is perfectly right, and can never be bettered. The most striking outward feature in all Gothic architecture is, that it is composed of pointed arches, as in Romanesque that it is in like manner composed of round; and this distinction would be quite as clear, though the roofs were taken off every cathedral in Europe. And yet if we examine carefully into the real force and meaning of the term 'roof,' we shall perhaps be able to retain the old popular idea in a definition of Gothic architecture which shall also express whatever dependence that architecture has upon true forms of roofing.

Roofs were generally divided into two parts: the roof proper, that is to say, the shell, vault, or ceiling, internally visible; and the roof mask, which protects this lower roof from the weather. In some buildings these are united in one framework; but, in most, they are more or less independent of each other, and in nearly all Gothic buildings there is a considerable interval between them.

Now it will often happen that owing to the nature of the apartments required, or the materials at hand, the roof proper may be flat, coved, or domed, in buildings which in their walls employ pointed arches, and are, in the straitest sense of the word, Gothic in all other respects. Yet so far forth as the roofing alone is concerned, they are not Gothic unless the pointed arch be the principal form adopted either in the stone vaulting or the timbers of the roof proper.

I shall say then, in the first place, that 'Gothic architecture is that which uses, if possible, the pointed arch in the roof proper.' This is the first step in our definition.

Secondly, although there may be many advisable or necessary forms for the lower roof or ceiling, there is, in cold countries exposed to rain and snow, only one advisable form for the roof-mask, and that is the gable, for this alone will throw off both rain and snow from all parts of its surface as speedily as possible. Snow can lodge on the top of a dome, not on the ridge of a gable. And thus, as far as roofing is concerned, the gable is a far more essential feature of Northern architecture than the pointed vault, for the one is a thorough necessity, the other often a graceful conventionality; the gable occurs in the timber roof of every dwelling-house and every cottage, but not the vault; and the gable built on a polygonal or circular plan, is the origin of the turret and spire; and all the so-called aspiration of Gothic architecture is nothing more than its development. So that we must add to our definition another clause, which will be, at present, by far the most important, and it will stand thus: 'Gothic architecture is that which uses the pointed arch for the roof proper, and the gable for the roof-mask.'

Now there are three good architectures in the world, and there never can be more, correspondent to each of three simple ways of covering in a space, which is the original function of all architectures. And those three architectures are *pure* exactly in proportion to the simplicity and directness with which they express the condition of roofing on which they are founded. They have many interesting varieties, according to their scale, manner of decoration, and character of the nations by whom they are practised, but all their varieties are finally referable to the three great heads:

A Greek: Architecture of the Lintel.
B Romanesque: Architecture of the Round Arch.
C Gothic: Architecture of the Gable.

The three names, Greek, Romanesque, and Gothic, are indeed inaccurate when used in this vast sense, because they imply national limitations; but the three architectures may nevertheless not unfitly receive their names from those nations by whom they were carried to the highest perfection. We may thus briefly state their existing varieties.

A. GREEK: Lintel Architecture. The worst of the three; and, considered with reference to stone construction, always in some measure barbarous. Its simplest type is Stonehenge; its most refined, the Parthenon; its noblest, the Temple of Karnak.

In the hands of the Egyptian, it is sublime; in those of the Greek, pure; in those of the Roman, rich; and in those of the Renaissance builder, effeminate.

B. ROMANESQUE: Round-arch Architecture. Never thoroughly developed until Christian times. It falls into two great branches, Eastern and Western, or Byzantine and Lombardic; changing respectively in process of time, with certain helps from each other, into Arabian Gothic, and Teutonic Gothic. Its most perfect Lombardic type is the Duomo of Pisa; its most perfect Byzantine type (I believe), St. Mark's at Venice. Its highest glory is, that it has no corruption. It perishes in giving birth to another architecture as noble as itself.

C. GOTHIC: Architecture of the Gable. The daughter of the Romanesque; and, like the Romanesque, divided into two great branches, Western and Eastern, or Pure Gothic and Arabian Gothic; of which the latter is called Gothic, only because it has many Gothic forms, pointed arches, vaults, etc., but its spirit remains Byzantine, more especially in the form of the roof-mask, of which, with respect to these three great families, we have next to determine the typical form.

For, observe, the distinctions we have hitherto been stating depend on the form of the stones first laid from pier to pier; that is to say, of the simplest condition of roofs proper. Adding the relations of the roof-mask to these lines, we shall have the perfect type of form for each school.

In the Greek, the Western Romanesque, and Western Gothic, the roof-mask is the gable; in the Eastern Romanesque, and Eastern Gothic, it is the dome: but I have not studied the roofing of either of these last two groups, and shall not venture to generalise them in a diagram. But the three groups, in the hands of the Western builders, may be thus simply represented: a, Greek; b, Western Romanesque; c, Western, or true, Gothic.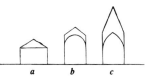

Now, observe, first, that the relation of the roof-mask to the roof proper, in the Greek type, forms that pediment which gives its most striking character to the temple, and is the principal recipient of its sculptural decoration. The relation of these lines, therefore, is just as important in the Greek as in the Gothic schools.

Secondly, the reader must observe the difference of steepness in the Romanesque and Gothic gables. This is not an unimportant distinction, nor an undecided one. The Romanesque gable does not pass gradually into the more elevated form; there is a great gulf between the two; the whole effect of all Southern architecture being dependent upon the use of the flat gable, and of all Northern upon that of the acute. I need not here dwell upon the difference between the lines of an Italian village, or the flat tops of most Italian towers, and the peaked gables and spires of the North, attaining their most fantastic development, I believe, in Belgium: but it may be well to state the law of separation, namely, that a Gothic gable *must* have all its angles acute, and a

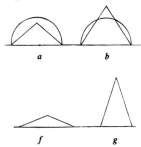

Romanesque one *must* have the upper one obtuse; or, to give the reader a simple practical rule, take any gable, *a* or *b*, and strike a semicircle on its base; if its top rises above the semicircle, as at *b*, it is a Gothic gable; if it falls beneath it, a Romanesque one; but the best forms in each group are those which are distinctly steep, or distinctly low. In the figure, *f* is, perhaps, the average of Romanesque slope, and *g* of Gothic.

But although we do not find a transition from one school into the other in the slope of the gable, there is often a confusion between the two schools in the association of the gable with the arch below it. It has been stated that the pure Romanesque condition is the round arch under the low gable, *a*, and the pure Gothic condition is the pointed arch under the high gable, *b*. But in the passage from one style to the other, we sometimes find the conditions reversed: the pointed arch under a low gable, as *d*, or the round arch under a high gable, as *c*. The form *d* occurs in the tombs of Verona, and *c* in the doors of Venice.

We have thus determined the relation of Gothic to the other architectures of the world, as far as regards the main lines of its construction; but there is still one word which needs to be added to our definition of its form, with respect to a part of its decoration, which rises out of that construction. We have seen that

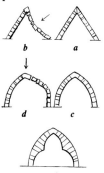

the first condition of its form is, that it shall have pointed arches. When Gothic is perfect, therefore, it will follow that the pointed arches must be built in the strongest possible manner. The weakness of the pointed arch is in its flanks, and by merely thickening them gradually at this point all chance of fracture is removed. Or, perhaps, more simply still: suppose a gable built of stone, as at *a*, and pressed upon from without by a weight in the direction of the arrow, clearly it would be liable to fall in, as at *b*. To prevent this, we make a pointed arch of it, as at *c*; and now it cannot fall inwards, but if pressed upon from above may give way outwards, as at *d*. But at last we build it as at *e*, and now it can neither fall out nor in.

The forms of arch thus obtained, with a pointed projection called a cusp on each side, must for ever be delightful to the human mind, as being expressive of the utmost strength and permanency obtainable with a given mass of material. But it was not by any such process of reasoning that the cusp was invented. It is merely the special application to the arch of the great ornamental system of FOLIATION; or the adaptation of the forms of leafage which has been above insisted upon as the principal characteristic of Gothic Naturalism. This love of foliage was exactly proportioned, in its intensity, to the increase of strength in the Gothic spirit: in the Southern Gothic it is *soft* leafage that is most loved; in the Northern, *thorny* leafage. And if we take up any Northern illuminated manuscript of the great Gothic time, we shall find every one of its leaf ornaments surrounded by a thorny structure laid round it in gold or in colour; sometimes apparently copied faithfully from the prickly development of the root of the leaf in the thistle, running along the stems and branches exactly as the thistle leaf does along its own stem, and with sharp spines proceeding from the points. At other times, and for the most part in work of the thirteenth century, the golden ground takes the form of pure and severe cusps, sometimes enclosing the leaves, sometimes filling up the forks of the branches, passing imperceptibly from the distinctly vegetable condition (in which it is just as certainly representative of the thorn, as other parts of the design are of the bud, leaf, and fruit) into the crests on the necks, or the membranous sails of the wings, of serpents, dragons, and other grotesques, and into rich and vague fantasies of curvature; among which, however, the pure cusped system of the pointed arch is continually discernible, not accidentally, but designedly indicated, and connecting itself with the literally architectural portions of the design.

It is evident that the structural advantage of the cusp is available only in the case of arches on a comparatively small scale. If the arch becomes very large, the projections under the flanks must become too ponderous to be secure; the suspended weight of stone would be liable to break off, and such arches are therefore never constructed with heavy cusps, but rendered secure by general mass of masonry; and what additional *appearance* of support may be thought necessary (sometimes a considerable degree of *actual* support) is given by means of tracery.

The term 'foliated' is equally descriptive of the most perfect conditions both of the simple arch and of the traceries by which in later Gothic it is filled; and this foliation is an essential character of the style. No Gothic is either good or characteristic, which is not foliated either in its arches or apertures. Sometimes the bearing arches are foliated, and the ornamentation above composed of figure sculpture; sometimes the bearing arches are plain, and the ornamentation above them is composed of foliated apertures. But the element of foliation *must* enter somewhere, or the style is imperfect. And our final definition of Gothic will, therefore, stand thus:

'*Foliated* Architecture, which uses the pointed arch for the roof proper, and the gable for the roof-mask.'

Now there is but one point more to be examined, and we have done.

Foliation, while it is the most distinctive and peculiar, is also the easiest method of decoration which Gothic architecture possesses; and, although in the disposition of the proportions and forms of foils, the most noble imagination may be shown, yet a builder without imagination at all, or any other faculty of design, can produce some effect upon the mass of his work by merely covering it with foolish foliation. But floral decoration, and the disposition of mouldings, require some skill and thought; and, if they are to be agreeable at all, must be verily invented, or accurately copied. They cannot be drawn altogether at random, without becoming so commonplace as to involve detection: and although the noblest imagination may be shown in the disposition of traceries, there is far more room for its play and power when those traceries are associated with floral or animal ornament; and it is probable, *a priori*, that, wherever true invention exists, such ornament will be employed in profusion.

Now, all Gothic may be divided into two vast schools, one early, the other late; of which the former, noble, inventive, and progressive, uses the element of foliation moderately, that of floral and figure-sculpture decoration profusely; the latter, ignoble, uninventive, and declining, uses foliation immoderately, floral and figure sculpture subordinately.

We have now, I believe, obtained a sufficiently accurate knowledge both of the spirit and form of Gothic architecture; but it may, perhaps, be useful to the general reader, if, in conclusion, I set down a few plain and practical rules for determining, in every instance, whether a given building be good Gothic or not, and, if not Gothic, whether its architecture is of a kind which will probably reward the pains of careful examination.

First, Look if the roof rises in a steep gable, high above the walls. If it does not do this, the building is not quite pure Gothic, or has been altered.

Secondly, Look if the principal windows and doors have pointed arches with gables over them. If not, the building is not Gothic; if they have not any gables over them, it is either not pure, or not first-rate.

If, however, it has the steep roof, the pointed arch, and gable all united, it is nearly certain to be a Gothic building of a very fine time.

Thirdly, Look if the arches are cusped, or apertures foliated. If the building has met the first two conditions, it is sure to be foliated somewhere; but, if not everywhere, the parts which are unfoliated are imperfect, unless they are large bearing arches, or small and sharp arches in groups, forming a kind of foliation by their own multiplicity, and relieved by sculpture and rich mouldings. If there be no foliation anywhere, the building is assuredly imperfect Gothic.

Fourthly, If the building meets all the first three conditions, look if its arches in general, whether of windows and doors, or of minor ornamentation, are carried on *true shafts with bases and capitals*. If they are, then the building is assuredly of the finest Gothic style. It may still, perhaps, be an imitation, a feeble copy, or a bad example, of a noble style; but the manner of it, having met all these four conditions, is assuredly first-rate.

If its apertures have not shafts and capitals, look if they are plain openings in the walls, studiously simple, and unmoulded at the sides. If so, the building may still be of the finest Gothic adapted to some domestic or military service. But if the sides of the window be moulded, and yet there are no capitals at the spring of the arch, it is assuredly of an inferior school.

This is all that is necessary to determine whether the building be of a fine Gothic style. The next tests to be applied are in order to discover whether it be good architecture or not; for it may be very impure Gothic, and yet very noble architecture; or it may be very pure Gothic, and yet if a copy, or originally raised by an ungifted builder, very bad architecture.

If it belong to any of the great schools of colour, its criticism becomes as complicated, and needs as much care, as that of a piece of music, and no general rules for it can be given; but if not—

First, See if it looks as if it had been built by strong men; if it has the sort of roughness, and largeness, and nonchalance, mixed in places with the exquisite tenderness which seems always to be the sign-manual of the broad vision, and massy power of men who can see *past* the work they are doing, and betray here and there something like disdain for it. If the building has this character, it is much already in its favour; it will go hard but it proves a noble one. If it has not this, but is altogether accurate, minute, and scrupulous in its workmanship, it must belong to either the very best or very worst of schools: the very best, in which exquisite design is wrought out with untiring and conscientious care, as in the Giottesque Gothic; or the very worst, in which mechanism has taken the place of design.

Secondly, Observe if it be irregular, its different parts fitting themselves to different purposes, no one caring what becomes of them, so that they do their work. If one part always answers accurately to another part, it is sure to be a bad building; and the greater and more conspicuous the irregularities, the greater the chances are that it is a good one. For instance, in the Ducal Palace, the general idea is sternly symmetrical; but two windows are lower than the rest of the six; and if the reader will count the arches of the small arcade as far as to the great balcony, he will find it is not in the centre, but set to the right-hand side by the whole width of one of those arches. We may be pretty sure that the building is a good one; none but a master of his craft would have ventured to do this.

Thirdly, Observe if all the traceries, capitals, and other ornaments are of perpetually varied design. If not, the work is assuredly bad.

Lastly, *Read* the sculpture. Preparatory to reading it, you will have to discover whether it is legible (and, if legible, it is nearly certain to be worth reading). On a good building, the sculpture is *always* so set, and on such a scale, that at the ordinary distance from which the edifice is seen, the sculpture shall be thoroughly intelligible and interesting. In order to accomplish this, the uppermost statues will be ten or twelve feet high, and the upper ornamentation will be colossal, increasing in fineness as it descends, till on the foundation it will often be wrought as if for a precious cabinet in a king's chamber; but the spectator will not notice that the upper sculptures are colossal. He will merely feel that he can see them plainly, and make them all out at his ease.

And having ascertained this, let him set himself to read them. Thenceforward the criticism of the building is to be conducted precisely on the same principles as that of a book; and it must depend on the knowledge, feeling, and not a little on the industry and perseverance of the reader, whether, even in the case of the best works, he either perceive them to be great, or feel them to be entertaining.

GOTHIC PALACES

THE buildings out of the remnants of which we have endeavoured to recover some conception of the appearance of Venice during the Byzantine period, contribute hardly anything at this day to the effect of the streets of the city. They are too few and too much defaced to attract the eye or influence the feelings. The charm which Venice still possesses, and which for the last fifty years has rendered it the favourite haunt of all the painters of picturesque subject, is owing to the effect of the palaces belonging to the period we have now to examine, mingled with those of the Renaissance.

This effect is produced in two different ways. The Renaissance palaces are not more picturesque in themselves than the club-houses of Pall Mall; but they become delightful by the contrast of their severity and refinement with the rich and rude confusion of the sea-life beneath them, and of their white and solid masonry with the green waves. Remove from beneath them the orange sails of the fishing-boats, the black gliding of the gondolas, the cumbered decks and rough crews of the barges of traffic, and the fretfulness of the green water along their foundations, and the Renaissance palaces possess no more interest than those of London or Paris. But the Gothic palaces are picturesque in themselves, and wield over us an independent power. Sea and sky, and every other accessory, might be taken away from them, and still they would be beautiful and strange. They are not less striking in the loneliest streets of Padua and Vicenza (where many were built during the period of the Venetian authority in those cities) than in the most crowded thoroughfares of Venice itself; and if they could be transported into the midst of London, they would still not altogether lose their power over the feelings.

The best proof of this is in the perpetual attractiveness of all pictures, however poor in skill, which have taken for their subject the principal of these Gothic buildings, the Ducal Palace. And the Ducal Palace itself owes the peculiar charm which we have hitherto felt, not so much to its greater size as compared with other Gothic buildings, or nobler design (for it never yet has been rightly drawn), as to its comparative isolation. The other Gothic structures are as much injured by the continual juxtaposition of the Renaissance palaces, as the latter are aided by it; they exhaust their own life by breathing it

John Ruskin CASA CONTARINI FASAN
The Casa Contarini-Fasan (second from the right) shows
*'how much beauty and dignity may be bestowed on a very small and
unimportant dwelling-house by Gothic sculpture'.*

into the Renaissance coldness: but the Ducal Palace stands comparatively alone, and fully expresses the Gothic power.

And it is just that it should be so seen, for it is the original of nearly all the rest. It is not the elaborate and more studied development of a national style, but the great and sudden invention of one man, instantly forming a national style, and becoming the model for the imitation of every architect in Venice for upwards of a century. I do not mean that there was no Gothic in Venice before the Ducal Palace, but that the mode of its application to domestic architecture had not been determined. The real root of the Ducal Palace is the apse of the Church of the Frari. The traceries of that apse, though earlier and ruder in workmanship, are nearly the same in mouldings, and precisely the same in treatment (especially in the placing of the lions' heads), as those of the great Ducal Arcade; and the originality of thought in the architect of the Ducal Palace consists in his having adapted those traceries, in a more highly developed and finished form, to civil uses. In the apse of the church they form narrow and tall window lights, somewhat more massive than those of Northern Gothic, but similar in application: the thing to be done was to adapt these traceries to the forms of domestic building necessitated by national usage. The early palaces consisted, as we have seen, of arcades sustaining walls faced with marble, rather broad and long than elevated. This form was kept for the Ducal Palace; but instead of round arches from shaft to shaft, the Frari traceries were substituted, with two essential modifications. Besides being enormously increased in scale and thickness, that they might better bear the superincum-

bent weight, the quatrefoil, which in the Frari windows is above the arch, as at *a*, was in the Ducal Palace put between the arches, as at *b*; the main reason for this alteration being that the bearing power of the arches, which was now to be trusted with the weight of a wall forty feet high, was thus thrown *between* the quatrefoils, instead of under them, and thereby applied at far

a   *b*

better advantage. And, in the second place, the joints of the masonry were changed. In the Frari (as often also in St. John and Paul's) the tracery is formed of two simple cross bars or slabs of stone, pierced into the requisite forms, and separated by a horizontal joint, just on a level with the lowest cusp of the quatrefoils, as seen in *a*. But at the Ducal Palace the horizontal joint is in the centre of the quatrefoils, and two others are introduced beneath it at right angles to the run of the mouldings, as seen in *b*.

The ascertaining the formation of the Ducal Palace traceries from those of the Frari, and its priority to all other buildings which resemble it in Venice, rewarded me for a great deal of very uninteresting labour in the examination of mouldings and other minor features of the Gothic palaces, in which alone the internal evidence of their date was to be discovered, there being no historical records whatever respecting them. But the accumulation of details on which the complete proof of the fact depends, could not either be brought within the compass of this volume, or be made in anywise interesting to the general reader. I shall therefore, without involving myself in any discussion, give a brief account of the development of Gothic design in Venice, as I believe it to have taken place.

The Gothic architecture of Venice is divided into two great periods: one, in which, while various irregular Gothic tendencies are exhibited, no consistent type of domestic building was developed; the other, in which a formed and consistent school of domestic architecture resulted from the direct imitation of the great design of the Ducal Palace. We must deal with these two periods separately; the first of them being that which has been often alluded to under the name of the transitional period.

We shall consider in succession the general form, the windows, doors, balconies, and parapets, of the Gothic palaces belonging to each of these periods. We have seen that the wrecks of the Byzantine palaces consisted merely of upper and lower arcades surrounding cortiles; the disposition of the interiors being now entirely changed, and their original condition untraceable. The entrances to these early buildings are, for the most part, merely large circular arches, the central features of their continuous arcades: they do not present us with definitely separated windows and doors.

But a great change takes place in the Gothic period. These long arcades break, as it were, into pieces, and coagulate into central and lateral windows, and small arched doors, pierced in great surfaces of brick wall. The sea story of a Byzantine palace consists of seven, nine, or more arches in a continuous line; but the sea story of a Gothic palace consists of a door and one or two windows on each side, as in a modern house. The first story of a Byzantine palace consists of, perhaps, eighteen or twenty arches, reaching from one side of the house to the other; the first story of a Gothic palace consists of a window of four or five lights in the centre, and one or two single windows on each side. The germ, however, of the Gothic arrangement is already found in the Byzantine, where, as we have seen, the arcades, though continuous, are always composed of a central mass and two wings of smaller arches. The central group becomes the door or the middle light of the Gothic palace, and the wings break into its lateral windows.

But the most essential difference in the entire arrangement, is the loss of the unity of conception which regulated Byzantine composition. How subtle the sense of gradation which disposed the magnitudes of the early palaces we have seen already, but I have not hitherto noticed that the Byzantine work was centralised in its ornamentation as much as in its proportions. Not only were the lateral capitals and archivolts kept comparatively plain, while the central ones were sculptured, but the midmost piece of sculpture, whatever it might be, – capital, inlaid circle, or architrave – was always made superior to the rest.

Now, long after the Byzantine arcades had been contracted into windows, this system of centralization was more or less maintained; and in all the early groups of windows of five lights the midmost capital is different from the two on each side of it, which always correspond. So strictly is this the case, that whenever the capitals of any group of windows are not centralised in this

Overleaf: John Ruskin THE CASA D'ORO
Even as Ruskin was painting this watercolour in 1845, workmen
were destroying part of the building.

Casa d'Oro

Ca' d'Oro.
Ruskin. 1845.

manner, but are either entirely like each other, or all different, so as to show no correspondence, it is a certain proof, even if no other should exist, of the comparative lateness of the building.

In every group of windows in Venice which I was able to examine, and which were centralised in this manner, I found evidence in their mouldings of their being *anterior* to the Ducal Palace. That palace did away with the subtle proportion and centralisation of the Byzantine. Its arches are of equal width and its capitals are all different and ungrouped; some, indeed, are larger than the rest, but this is not for the sake of proportion, only for particular service, when more weight is to be borne. But, among other evidences of the early date of the sea façade of that building, is one subtle and delicate concession to the system of centralisation which it finally closed. The capitals of the upper arcade are, as I said, all different, and show no arranged correspondence with each other; but *the central one is of pure Parian marble*, while all the others are of Istrian stone.

The bold decoration of the central window and balcony above, in the Ducal Palace, is only a peculiar expression of the principality of the central window, which was characteristic of the Gothic period not less than of the Byzantine. In the private palaces the central windows become of importance by their number of lights; in the Ducal Palace such an arrangement was, for various reasons, inconvenient, and the central window, which, so far from being more important than the others, is every way inferior in design to the two at the eastern extremity of the façade, was nevertheless made the leading feature by its noble canopy and balcony.

Such being the principal differences in the general conception of the Byzantine and Gothic palaces, the particulars in the treatment of the latter are easily stated. The marble facings are gradually removed from the walls; and the bare brick either stands forth confessed boldly, contrasted with the marble shafts and archivolts of the windows, or it is covered with stucco painted in fresco, of which more hereafter. The Ducal Palace, as in all other respects, is an exact expression of the middle point in the change. It still retains marble facing; but instead of being disposed in slabs as in the Byzantine times, it is applied in solid bricks or blocks of marble, $11\frac{1}{2}$ inches long, by 6 inches high.

The stories of the Gothic palaces are divided by string courses, considerably bolder in projection than those of the Byzantines, and more highly decorated; and while the angles of the Byzantine palaces are quite sharp and pure, those of the Gothic palaces are wrought into a chamfer, filled by small twisted shafts which have capitals under the cornice of each story.

These capitals are little observed in the general effect, but the shafts are of essential importance in giving an aspect of firmness to the angle; a point of peculiar necessity in Venice, where, owing to the various convolutions of the canals, the angles of the palaces are not only frequent, but often necessarily *acute*, every inch of ground being valuable. In other cities, the appearance as well as the assurance of stability can always be secured by the use of massy stones, as in the fortress palaces of Florence; but it must have been always desirable at Venice to build as lightly as possible, in consequence of the comparative insecurity of the foundations. The early palaces were, as we have seen, perfect models of grace and lightness, and the Gothic, which followed, though much more massive in the style of its details, never admitted more weight into its structure than was absolutely necessary for its strength. Hence, every Gothic palace has the appearance of enclosing as many rooms, and attaining as much strength, as is possible, with a minimum quantity of brick and stone. The traceries of the windows, which in Northern Gothic only support the *glass*, at Venice support the *building*; and thus the greater ponderousness of the *traceries* is only an indication of the greater lightness of the *structure*.

And so in all the palaces built at the time, consummate strength was joined with a lightness of form and sparingness of material which rendered it eminently desirable that the eye should be convinced, by every possible expedient, of the stability of the building; and these twisted pillars at the angles are not among the least important means adopted for this purpose, for they seem to bind the walls together as a cable binds a chest. In the Ducal Palace, where they are carried up the angle of an unbroken wall forty feet high, they are divided into portions, gradually diminishing in length towards the top, by circular bands or rings, set with the nail-head or dog-tooth ornament, vigorously projecting, and giving the column nearly the aspect of the stalk of a reed; its diminishing proportions being exactly arranged as they are by Nature in all jointed plants. At the top of the palace, like the wheat-stalk branching into the ear of corn, it expands into a small niche with a pointed canopy, which joins with the fantastic parapet in at once relieving, and yet making more notable by its contrast, the weight of massy wall below.

The Ducal Palace is peculiar in these niches at the angles, which throughout the rest of the city appear on churches only; but some may perhaps have been removed by restorations, together with the parapets with which they were associated.

Of these roof parapets of Venice, the examples which remain differ from those of all other cities of Italy in their purely ornamental character. They are not battlements, properly so called; still less machicolated cornices, such as crown the fortress palaces of the great mainland nobles; but merely adaptations of the light and crown-like ornaments which crest the walls of the Arabian mosque. Nor are even these generally used on the main walls of the palaces themselves. They occur on the Ducal Palace, on the Casa d'Oro, and, some years back, were still standing on the Fondaco de' Turchi; but the majority of the Gothic palaces have the plain dog-tooth cornice under the tiled projecting roof; and the highly decorated parapet is employed only on the tops of walls which surround courts or gardens, and which, without such decoration, would have been utterly devoid of interest.

The parapets of the palaces themselves were lighter and more fantastic, consisting of narrow lance-like spires of marble, set between the broader pinnacles, which were in such cases generally carved into the form of a fleur-de-lis: the French words gives the reader the best idea of the form, though he must remember that this use of the lily for the parapets has nothing to do with France, but is the carrying out of the Byzantine system of floral ornamentation, which introduced the outline of the lily everywhere; so that I have found it convenient to call its most beautiful capitals, the *lily* capitals of St. Mark's. The decorations of the parapet were completed by attaching gilded

Palazzo Priuli. A nineteenth-century photograph showing (on the right)
the window that Ruskin used to illustrate
the fifth order window in its fully developed form (see p. 164).

balls of metal to the extremities of the leaves of the lilies, and of the intermediate spires, so as literally to form for the wall a diadem of silver touched upon the points with gold; the image being rendered still more distinct in the Casa d'Oro, by variation in the height of the pinnacles.

Very few of these light roof-parapets now remain: they are, of course, the part of the building which dilapidation first renders it necessary to remove. That of the Ducal Palace, however, though often, I doubt not, restored, retains much of the ancient form, and is exceedingly beautiful, though it has no appearance from below of being intended for protection, but serves only, by its extreme lightness, to relieve the eye when wearied by the breadth of wall beneath; it is nevertheless a most serviceable defence for any person walking along the edge of the roof. It has some appearance of insecurity, but I have never heard of its having been disturbed by anything short of an earthquake; and, as we have seen, even the great earthquake of 1511, though it much injured the battlements of the Casa d'Oro, and threw down several statues at St. Mark's, only shook one lily from the brow of the Ducal Palace.

Although, however, these light and fantastic forms appear to have been universal in the battlements meant primarily for decoration, there was another condition of parapet altogether constructed for the protection of persons walking on the roofs or in the galleries of the churches, and from these more substantial and simple defences, the BALCONIES, to which the Gothic palaces owe half of their picturesque effect, were immediately derived; the balcony being, in fact, nothing more than a portion of such roof parapets arranged round a projecting window-sill sustained on brackets, as in the central example of the annexed figure. We must, therefore, examine these defensive balustrades and the derivative balconies consecutively.

Obviously, a parapet with an unbroken edge, upon which the arm may rest, can be constructed only in one of three ways. It must either be (1) of solid stone, decorated, if at all, by mere surface sculpture as in the uppermost example in the annexed figure; or (2) pierced into some kind of tracery as in the second; or (3) composed of small pillars carrying a level bar of stone, as in the third; this last condition being, in a diseased and swollen form, familiar to us in the balustrades of our bridges.

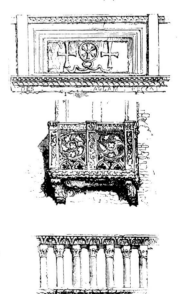

(1) Of these three kinds, the first, which is employed for the pulpit at Torcello and in the nave of St. Mark's, whence the uppermost example is taken, is beautiful when sculpture so rich can be employed upon it; but it is liable to objection, first, because it is heavy and unlike a parapet when seen from below; and, secondly, because it is inconvenient in use. The position of leaning over a balcony becomes cramped and painful if long continued, unless the foot can be sometimes advanced *beneath* the ledge on which the arm leans, *i.e.*, between the balusters or traceries, which of course

cannot be done in the solid parapet: it is also more agreeable to be able to see partially down through the penetrations, than to be obliged to lean far over the edge. The solid parapet was rarely used in Venice after the earlier ages.

(2) The Traceried Parapet is chiefly used in the Gothic of the North, from which the above example, in the Casa Contarini Fasan, is directly derived. It is, when well designed, the richest and most beautiful of all forms, and many of the best buildings of France and Germany are dependent for half their effect upon it; its only fault being a slight tendency to fantasticism. It was never frankly received in Venice, where the architects had unfortunately returned to the Renaissance forms before the flamboyant parapets were fully developed in the North; but, in the early stage of the Renaissance, a kind of pierced parapet was employed, founded on the old Byzantine interwoven traceries; that is to

say, the slab of stone was pierced here and there with holes, and then an interwoven pattern traced on the surface round them. The difference in system will be understood in a moment by comparing the uppermost example in the figure at the side, which is a Northern parapet from the Cathedral of Abbeville, with the lowest, from a secret chamber in the Casa Foscari. It will be seen that the Venetian one is far more simple and severe, yet singularly piquant, the black penetrations telling sharply on the plain broad surface. Far inferior in beauty, it has yet one point of superiority to that of Abbeville, that it proclaims itself more definitely to be stone. The other has rather the look of lace.

The intermediate figure is a panel of the main balcony of the Ducal Palace, and is introduced here as being an exactly transitional condition between the Northern and Venetian types. It was built when the German Gothic workmen were exercising considerable influence over those in Venice, and there was some chance of the Northern parapet introducing itself. It actually did so, as above shown, in the Casa Contarini Fasan, but was for the most part stoutly resisted and kept at bay by the Byzantine form, the lowest in the last figure, until that form itself was displaced by the common, vulgar, Renaissance baluster; a grievous loss, for the severe pierced type was capable of a variety as endless as the fantasticism of our own Anglo-Saxon manuscript ornamentation.

(3) The Baluster Parapet. Long before the idea of tracery had suggested itself to the minds either of Venetian or any other architects, it had, of course, been necessary to provide protection for galleries, edges of roofs, etc.: and the most natural form in which such protection could be obtained was that of a horizontal bar or hand-rail, sustained upon short shafts or balusters. This form was above all others likely to be adopted where variations of Greek or Roman pillared architecture were universal in the larger masses of the building; the parapet became itself a small series of columns, with capitals and architraves; and whether the crossbar laid upon them should be simply

Balconies.

horizontal, and in contact with their capitals, or sustained by mimic arches, round or pointed, depended entirely on the system adopted in the rest of the work. Where the large arches were round, the small balustrade arches would be so likewise; where those were pointed, these would become so in sympathy with them.

Unfortunately, wherever a balcony or parapet is used in an inhabited house, it is, of course, the part of the structure which first suffers from dilapidation, as well as that of which the security is most anxiously cared for. It is only, therefore, in the churches of Torcello, Murano, and St. Mark's, that the ancient forms of gallery defence may still be seen. In domestic architecture, the remains of the original balconies begin to occur first in the beginning of the fourteenth century, when the round arch had entirely disappeared; and the parapet consists, almost without exception, of a series of small trefoiled arches, cut boldly through a bar of stone which rests upon the shafts, at first very simple, and generally adorned with a cross at the point of each arch, as in fig. 7 on page 151, which gives the angle of such a balcony on a large scale; but soon enriched into the beautiful conditions, figs. 2 and 3, and sustained on brackets formed of lions' heads, as seen in the central example of their entire effect, fig. 1.

We have next to examine those features of the Gothic palaces in which the transitions of their architecture are most distinctly traceable: namely, the arches of the windows and doors.

It has already been repeatedly stated, that the Gothic style had formed itself completely on the mainland, while the Byzantines still retained their influence at Venice; and that the history of early Venetian Gothic is therefore not that of a school taking new forms independently of external influence, but the history of the struggle of the Byzantine manner with a contemporary style quite as perfectly organised as itself, and far more energetic. And this struggle is exhibited partly in the gradual change of the Byzantine architecture into other forms, and partly by isolated examples of genuine Gothic, taken prisoner, as it were, in the contest; or rather entangled among the enemy's forces, and maintaining their ground till their friends came up to sustain them. Let us follow the steps of the gradual change.

The uppermost shaded series of six forms of windows on page 153, represents, at a glance, the modifications of this feature in Venetian palaces, from the eleventh to the fifteenth century. Fig. 1 is Byzantine, of the eleventh and twelfth centuries; figs. 2 and 3 transitional, of the thirteenth and early fourteenth centuries; figs. 4 and 5 pure Gothic, of the thirteenth, fourteenth, and early fifteenth; and fig. 6 late Gothic, of the fifteenth century, distinguished by its added finial. Fig. 4 is the longest-lived of all these forms: it occurs first in the thirteenth century; and, sustaining modifications only in its mouldings, is found also in the middle of the fifteenth.

I shall call these the six orders of Venetian windows, and when I speak of a window of the fourth, second, or sixth order, the reader will only have to refer to the numerals at the top of page 153.

Then the series below shows the principal forms found in each period, belonging to each several order; except 1 b to 1 c, and the two lower series, numbered 7 to 16, which are types of Venetian doors.

The Orders of Venetian Arches.

Windows of the Fourth Order.

We shall now be able, without any difficulty, to follow the course of transition, beginning with the first order, 1 and 1 *a*, in the second row. The horse-shoe arch, 1 *b*, is the door-head commonly associated with it, and the other three in the same row occur in St. Mark's exclusively; 1 *c* being used in the nave, in order to give a greater appearance of lightness to its great lateral arcades, which at first the spectator supposes to be round-arched, but he is struck by a peculiar grace and elasticity in the curves for which he is unable to account, until he ascends into the galleries whence the true form of the arch is discernible. The other two, – 1 *d*, from the door of the southern transept, and 1 *c*, from that of the treasury, – sufficiently represent a group of fantastic forms derived from the Arabs, and of which the exquisite decoration is one of the most important features in St. Mark's. Their form is indeed permitted merely to obtain more fantasy in the curves of this decoration, or in their own curves. The reader can see in a moment, that, as pieces of masonry, or bearing arches, they are infirm or useless, and therefore never could be employed in any building in which dignity of structure was the primal object. It is just because structure is *not* the primal object in St. Mark's, because it has no severe weights to bear, and much loveliness of marble and sculpture to exhibit, that they are therein allowable. They are of course, like the rest of the building, built of brick and faced with marble, and their inner masonry, which must be very ingenious, is therefore not discernible. They have settled a little, as might have been expected, and the consequence is, that there is in every one of them, except the upright arch of the treasury, a small fissure across the marble of the flanks.

Though, however, the Venetian builders adopted these Arabian forms of arch where grace of ornamentation was their only purpose, they saw that such arrangements were unfit for ordinary work; and there is no instance, I believe, in Venice, of their having used any of them for a dwelling-house in the truly Byzantine period. But so soon as the Gothic influence began to be felt, and the pointed arch forced itself upon them, their first concession to its attack was the adoption, in preference to the round arch, of the form 3 *a*; the point of the Gothic arch forcing itself up, as it were, through the top of the semicircle which it was soon to supersede.

The woodcut above represents the door and two of the lateral windows of a house in the Corte del Remer, facing the Grand Canal, in the parish of the

Apostoli. It is remarkable as having its great entrance on the first floor, attained by a bold flight of steps, sustained on pure *pointed* arches wrought in brick. I cannot tell if these arches are contemporary with the building, though it must always have had an access of the kind. The rest of its aspect is Byzantine, except only that the rich sculptures of its archivolt show in combats of animals, beneath the soffit, a beginning of the Gothic fire and energy. The moulding of its plinth is of a Gothic profile, and the windows are pointed, not with a reversed curve, but in a pure straight gable, very curiously contrasted with the delicate bending of the pieces of marble armour cut for the shoulders of each arch. There is a two-lighted window, such as that seen in the vignette, on each side of the door, sustained in the centre by a basket-worked Byzantine capital: the mode of covering the brick archivolt with marble, both in the windows and doorway, is precisely like that of the true Byzantine palaces.

But as, even on a small scale, these arches are weak, if executed in brick-work, the appearance of this sharp point in the outline was rapidly accom-

panied by a parallel change in the method of building; and instead of constructing the arch of brick and coating it with marble, the builders formed it of three pieces of hewn stone inserted in the wall. Not, however, at first in this perfect form. The endeavour to reconcile the grace of the reversed arch with the strength of the round one, and still to build in brick, ended at first in conditions such as that represented at *a*, which is a window in the Calle del Pistor, close to the church of the Apostoli, a very interesting and perfect example. Here, observe, the poor

a   *b*

round arch is still kept to do all the hard work, and the fantastic ogee takes its pleasure above in the form of a moulding merely, a chain of bricks cast to the required curve. And this condition, translated into stonework, becomes a window of the second order (*b*): a form perfectly strong and serviceable, and of immense importance in the transitional architecture of Venice.

At *b* above, is given one of the earliest and simplest occurrences of the second order window (in a double group, exactly like the brick transitional form *a*), from a most important fragment of a defaced house in the Salizzada San Lio, close to the Merceria. It is associated with a fine *pointed* brick arch, indisputably of contemporary work, towards the close of the thirteenth century, and it is shown to be later than the previous example, *a*, by the greater development of its mouldings. The archivolt profile, indeed, is the simpler of the two, not having the sub-arch; as in the brick example; but the other mouldings are far more developed. *1* shows the arch profiles, *2* the capital profiles, *3* the basic-plinth profiles, of each window, *a* and *b*.

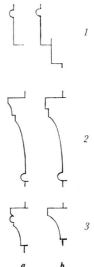

But the second order window soon attained nobler development. At once simple, graceful, and strong, it was received into all the architecture of the period, and there is hardly a street in Venice which does not exhibit some important remains of palaces built with this form of window in many stories, and in numerous groups. The most extensive and perfect is one upon the Grand Canal in the parish of the Apostoli, near the Rialto, covered with rich decoration, in the Byzantine manner, between the windows of its first story; but not completely characteristic of the transitional period, because still retaining the dentil in the arch mouldings, while the transitional houses all have the simple roll. Of the fully established type, one of the most extensive and perfect examples is in a court in the Calle di Rimedio, close to the Ponte dell' Angelo, near St. Mark's Place. Another looks out upon a small square garden, one of the few visible in the centre of Venice, close by the Corte Salviati. But, on the whole, the most interesting to the traveller is that of [the Casa Falier].

The advance of the Gothic spirit was, for a few years, checked by this compromise between the round and pointed arch. The truce, however, was at last broken, in consequence of the discovery that the keystone would do duty quite as well in the form *b* as in the form *a*; and the substitution of *b*, at the head of the arch, gives us the window of the third order, *3b*, *3d*, and *3e*, on page 153. The forms *3a* and *3c* are exceptional; the first occurring in the Corte del Remer, and in one other palace on the Grand Canal, close to the Church of St. Eustachio; the second only, as far as I know, in one house on the Canna-Reggio, belonging to the true Gothic period. The other three examples, *3b*, *3d*, *3e*, are generally characteristic of the third order; and it will be observed that they differ not merely in mouldings, but in slope of sides, and this latter difference is by far the most material. For in the example *3b* there is hardly any true Gothic expression; it is still the pure Byzantine arch, with a point thrust up through it; but the moment the flanks slope, as in *3d*, the Gothic expression is definite, and the entire school of the architecture is changed.

This slope of the flanks occurs, first, in so slight a degree as to be hardly perceptible, and gradually increases until, reaching the form *3e* at the close of the thirteenth century, the window is perfectly prepared for a transition into the fifth order.

The most perfect examples of the third order in Venice are the windows of the palace of Marco Querini, the father-in-law of Bajamonte Tiepolo, in consequence of whose conspiracy against the government this palace was ordered to be razed in 1310; but it was only partially ruined, and was afterwards used as the common shambles. Another example, less refined in workmanship, but, if possible, still more interesting, owing to the variety of its capitals, remains in the little piazza opening to the Rialto, on the St. Mark's side of the Grand Canal. The house faces the bridge, and its second story has been built in the thirteenth century, above a still earlier Byzantine cornice remaining, or perhaps introduced from some other ruined edifice, in the walls of the first floor. The windows of the second story are of pure third order; four of them are represented above, with their flanking pilaster, and capitals

varying in the form of the flower or leaf introduced between their volutes.

Another most important example exists in the lower story of the Casa Sagredo, on the Grand Canal, remarkable as having the early upright form (3 *b*, page 153) with a somewhat late moulding. Many others occur in the fragmentary ruins in the streets: but the two boldest conditions which I found in Venice are those of the Chapter-house of the Frari, in which the Doge Francesco Dandolo was buried circa 1339; and those of the flank of the Ducal Palace itself, absolutely corresponding with those of the Frari, and therefore of inestimable value in determining the date of the palace.

Contemporarily with these windows of the second and third orders, those of the fourth (4 *a*, and 4 *b*, on page 153) occur, at first in pairs, and with simple mouldings, precisely similar to those of the second order, but much more rare,

as in the example at the side, from the Salizzada San Liò; and then, enriching their mouldings as shown in the continuous series 4*c*, 4*d*, on page 153, associate themselves with the fifth-order windows of the perfect Gothic period. There is hardly a palace in Venice without some example, either early or late, of these fourth-order windows; but page 154 represents one of their purest groups at the close of the thirteenth century, from a house on the Grand Canal, nearly opposite the Church of the Scalzi. I have drawn it from the side, in order that the great depth of the arches may be seen, and the clear detaching of the shafts from the sheets of glass behind. The latter, as well as the balcony, are comparatively modern; but there is no doubt that if glass were used in the old window, it was set behind the shafts at the same depth. The entire modification of the interiors of all the Venetian houses by recent work has, however, prevented me from entering into any inquiry as to the manner in which the ancient glazing was attached to the interiors of the windows.

The fourth-order window is found in great richness and beauty at Verona, down to the latest Gothic times, as well as in the earliest, being then more frequent than any other form. It occurs, on a grand scale, in the old palace of the Scaligers, and profusely throughout the streets of the city. The series 4 *a* to 4 *e*, page 153, shows its most ordinary conditions and changes of arch-line: 4 *a* and 4 *b* are the early Venetian forms; 4 *c*, later, is general at Venice; 4 *d*, the best and most piquant condition, owing to its fantastic and bold projection of cusp, is common to Venice and Verona; 4 *e* is early Veronese.

The reader will see at once, in descending to the fifth row on page 153, representing the windows of the fifth order, that they are nothing more than a combination of the third and fourth. By this union they become the nearest approximation to a perfect Gothic form which occurs characteristically at Venice; and we shall therefore pause on the threshold of this final change, to glance back upon, and gather together, those fragments of purer pointed architecture which were above noticed as the forlorn hopes of the Gothic assault.

The little Campiello San Rocco is entered by a sotto-portico behind the Church of the Frari. Looking back, the upper traceries of the magnificent apse are seen towering above the irregular roofs and chimneys of the little square; and our lost Prout was enabled to bring the whole subject into an exquisitely picturesque composition, by the fortunate occurrence of four quaint trefoiled windows in one of the houses on the right. Those trefoils are among the most ancient efforts of Gothic art in Venice. They are built entirely of brick, except

the central shaft and capital, which are of Istrian stone. Their structure is the simplest possible; the trefoils being cut out of the radiating bricks which form the pointed arch, and the edge or upper limit of that pointed arch indicated by a roll moulding formed of cast bricks, in length of about a foot, and ground at the bottom so as to meet in one. The capital of the shaft is one of the earliest transitional forms; and observe the curious following out, even in this minor instance, of the great law of centralisation above explained with respect to the Byzantine palaces. There is a central shaft, a pilaster on each side, and then the wall. The pilaster has, by way of capital, a square flat brick projecting a little, and cast, at the edge, into the form of the first type of all cornices; and the shafts and pilasters all stand, without any added bases, on a projecting plinth of the same simple profile. These windows have been much defaced; but I have not the least doubt that their plinths are the original ones: and the whole group is one of the most

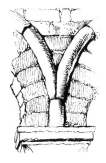

valuable in Venice, as showing the way in which the humblest houses, in the noble times, followed out the system of the larger palaces, as far as they could, in their rude materials. It is not often that the dwellings of the lower orders are preserved to us from the thirteenth century.

In the two upper lines of page 161 I have arranged some of the more delicate and finished examples of Gothic work of this period. Of these, fig. 4 is taken from the outer arcade of San Fermo of Verona, to show the condition of mainland architecture, from which all these Venetian types were borrowed. This arch, together with the rest of the arcade, is wrought in fine stone with a band of inlaid red brick, the whole chiselled and fitted with exquisite precision, all Venetian work being coarse in comparison. Throughout the streets of Verona, arches and windows of the thirteenth century are of continual occurrence, wrought, in this manner, with brick and stone; sometimes the brick alternating with the stones of the arch.

The arch from St. Fermo, however, fig. 4, page 161, corresponds more closely, in its entire simplicity, with the little windows from the Campiello San Rocco; and with the type 5 set beside it on page 161, from a very ancient house in the Corte del Forno at Santa Marina; while the upper examples, 1 and 2, show the use of the flat but highly enriched architrave. These windows (figs. 1 and 2, page 161) are from a narrow alley in a part of Venice now exclusively inhabited by the lower orders, close to the Arsenal; they are entirely wrought in brick, with exquisite mouldings, not cast, but *moulded in the clay by the hand*, so that there is not one piece of the arch like another; the pilasters and shafts being, as usual, of stone.

And now observe, as we pass from fig. 2 to fig. 3, and from fig. 5 to fig. 6, on page 161 a most interesting step of transition. As we saw above, the round arch yielding to the Gothic, by allowing a point to emerge at its summit, so here we have the Gothic conceding something to the form which had been assumed by the round; and itself slightly altering its outline so as to meet the condescension of the round arch half way. The small window here, fig. 6, is from the Campo Santa Maria Mater Domini, where the reversed curve at the head of the pointed arch is just perceptible and no more. The other examples, figs. 3 and 7, the first from a small but very noble house in the Merceria, the second from an isolated palace at Murano, show more advanced conditions of the reversed curve, which, though still employing the broad decorated architrave of the earlier examples, are in all other respects prepared for the transition to the simple window of the fifth order.

The next example, the uppermost of the three lower series on page 161, shows this order in its early purity; associated with intermediate decorations like those of the Byzantines, from a palace once belonging to the Erizzo family, near the Arsenal. The ornaments appear to be actually of Greek workmanship (except, perhaps, the two birds over the central arch, which are bolder, and more free in treatment), and built into the Gothic fronts; showing, however, the early date of the whole by the manner of their insertion, corresponding exactly with that employed in the Byzantine palaces, and by the covering of the intermediate spaces with sheets of marble, which, however, instead of being laid over the entire wall, are now confined to the immediate spaces between and above the windows, and are bounded by a dentil moulding.

In the example below this the Byzantine ornamentation has vanished, and the fifth order window is seen in its generic form, as commonly employed throughout the early Gothic period. Such arcades are of perpetual occurrence; the one in the Plate was taken from a small palace on the Grand Canal, nearly opposite the Casa Foscari. One point in it deserves especial notice, the increased size of the lateral window as compared with the rest: a circumstance

Windows of the Early Gothic Palaces.

which occurs in a great number of the groups of windows belonging to this period, and for which I have never been able to account.

Both these figures have been most carefully engraved; and the uppermost will give the reader a perfectly faithful idea of the general effect of the Byzantine sculptures, and of the varied alabaster among which they are inlaid, as well as of the manner in which these pieces are set together, every joint having been drawn on the spot: and the transition from the embroidered and silvery richness of this architecture, in which the Byzantine ornamentation was associated with the Gothic form of arch, to the simplicity of the pure Gothic arcade as seen in the lower figure, is one of the most remarkable phenomena in the history of Venetian art.

Such, then, is the simple fact at Venice, that from the beginning of the thirteenth century there is found a singular increase of simplicity in all architectural ornamentation; the rich Byzantine capitals giving place to a pure and severe type, and the rich sculptures vanishing from the walls, nothing but the marble facing remaining. One of the most interesting examples of this transitional state is a palace at San Severo, just behind the Casa Zorzi. This latter is a Renaissance building, utterly worthless in every respect, but known to the Venetian Ciceroni; and by inquiring for it, and passing a little beyond it down the Fondamenta San Severo, the traveller will see, on the other side of the canal, a palace which the Ciceroni never notice, but which is unique in Venice for the magnificence of the veined purple alabasters with which it has been decorated, and for the manly simplicity of the foliage of its capitals. Except in these, it has no sculpture whatever, and its effect is dependent entirely on colour. Disks of green serpentine are inlaid on the field of purple alabaster; and the pillars are alternately of red marble with white capitals, and of white marble with red capitals. Its windows appear of the third order; and the back of the palace, in a small and most picturesque court, shows a group of windows which are, perhaps, the most superb examples of that order in Venice. But the windows to the front have, I think, been of the fifth order, and their cusps have been cut away.

When the Gothic feeling began more decidedly to establish itself, it evidently became a question with the Venetian builders how the intervals between the arches, now left blank by the abandonment of the Byzantine sculptures, should be enriched in accordance with the principles of the new school. Two most important examples are left of the experiments made at this period: one at the Ponte del Forner, at San Cassano, a noble house in which the spandrils of the windows are filled by the emblems of the four Evangelists, sculptured in deep relief, and touching the edges of the arches with their expanded wings; the other now known as the Palazzo Cicogna, near the Church of San Sebastiano, in which a large space of wall above the windows is occupied by an intricate but rude tracery of involved quatrefoils. For the question as to the mode of decorating the interval between the arches was suddenly and irrevocably determined by the builder of the Ducal Palace, who, as we have seen, taking his first idea from the traceries of the Frari, and arranging those traceries as best fitted his own purpose, designed the great arcade (the lowest of the three on page 161), which thenceforward became the established model for every work of importance in Venice. The palaces built on this model, however, most of them not till the beginning of the fifteenth century, belong properly to the time of the Renaissance; and what little we have to note respecting them may be more clearly stated in connexion with other facts characteristic of that period.

I have given on page 164 examples of the fifth-order window, both in its earliest and in its fully developed form, completed from base to keystone. The upper example is a beautiful group from a small house, never of any size or pretension, and now inhabited only by the poor, in the Campiello della Strope, close to the Church of San Giacomo de Lorio. It is remarkable for its excessive purity of curve, and is of very early date, its mouldings being simpler than usual. The lower example is from the second story of a palace belonging to the Priuli family, near San Lorenzo, and shows one feature to which our attention has not hitherto been directed, namely, the penetration of the cusp, leaving only a silver thread of stone traced on the darkness of the window. I need not say that, in this condition, the cusp ceases to have any constructive use, and is merely decorative, but often exceedingly beautiful. Generally speaking, the condition in which the cusp is found is a useful test of age, when compared with other points; the more solid it is, the more ancient: but the massive form is often found associated with the perforated, as late as the beginning of the fourteenth century. In the Ducal Palace, the lower or bearing traceries have the solid cusp, and the upper traceries of the windows, which are merely decorative, have the perforated cusp, both with exquisite effect.

The smaller balconies between the great shafts in the lower example on page 164 are original and characteristic: not so the lateral one of the detached window, which has been restored; but by imagining it to be like that represented in fig. 1 page 151 above, which is a perfect window of the finest time of the fifth order, the reader will be enabled to form a complete idea of the external appearance of the principal apartments in the house of a noble of Venice, at the beginning of the fourteenth century.

There remains only one important feature to be examined, the entrance gate or door. We have already observed that the one seems to pass into the other, a sign of increased love of privacy rather than of increased humility, as the Gothic palaces assume their perfect form. In the Byzantine palaces the entrances appear always to have been rather great gates than doors, magnificent semicircular arches opening to the water, and surrounded by rich sculpture in the archivolts. Their sculpture is generally of grotesque animals scattered among leafage, without any definite meaning; but the great outer entrance of St. Mark's, which appears to have been completed some time after the rest of the fabric, differs from all others in presenting a series of subjects altogether Gothic in feeling, selection, and vitality of execution, and which show the occult entrance of the Gothic spirit before it had yet succeeded in effecting any modification of the Byzantine forms. These sculptures represent the months of the year employed in the avocations usually attributed to them throughout the whole compass of the Middle Ages. For the sake of the traveller in Venice, who should examine this archivolt carefully, I shall enumerate these sculptures in their order, noting such parallel representations as I remember in other work.

There are four successive archivolts, one within the other, forming the great

central entrance of St. Mark's. The first is a magnificent external arch, formed of obscure figures mingled among masses of leafage, as in ordinary Byzantine work; within this there is a hemispherical dome, covered with modern mosaic; and at the back of this recess the other three archivolts follow, two sculptured, one plain; the one with which we are concerned is the outermost.

It is carved both on its front and under surface or soffit; on the front are seventeen female figures bearing scrolls, from which the legends are unfortunately effaced. These figures were once gilded on a dark blue ground, as may still be seen in Gentile Bellini's picture of St. Mark's in the Accademia delle Belle Arti. The sculptures of the months are on the under-surface, beginning at the bottom on the left hand of the spectator as he enters, and following in succession round the archivolt; separated, however, into two groups, at its centre, by a beautiful figure of the youthful Christ, sitting in the midst of a slightly hollowed sphere covered with stars to represent the firmament, and with the attendant sun and moon, set one on each side, to rule over the day and over the night.

The months are personified as follows:–

1. JANUARY. *Carrying home a noble tree on his shoulders, the leafage of which nods forward, and falls nearly to his feet.* Superbly cut. This is a rare representation of him. More frequently he is represented as the two-headed Janus, sitting at a table, drinking at one mouth and eating at the other. Sometimes as an old man, warming his feet at a fire, and drinking from a bowl; though this type is generally reserved for February. His sign, Aquarius, is obscurely indicated in the archivolt by some wavy lines representing water, unless the figure has been broken away.

2. FEBRUARY. *Sitting in a carved chair, warming his bare feet at a blazing fire.* Generally, when he is thus represented, there is a pot hung over the fire, from the tops of the chimney. His sign, Pisces, is prominently carved above him.

3. MARCH. Here, as almost always in Italy, *a warrior*: the Mars of the Latins being, of course, in mediæval work, made representative of the military power of the place and period; and thus, at Venice, having the winged Lion painted upon his shield. His sign, the Ram, is very superbly carved above him in the archivolt.

4. APRIL. Here, *carrying a sheep upon his shoulder*. A rare representation of him. In Northern work he is almost universally gathering flowers, or holding them triumphantly in each hand.

5. MAY *is seated, while two young maidens crown him with flowers*. A very unusual representation, even in Italy; where, as in the North, he is almost always riding out hunting or hawking, sometimes playing on a musical instrument. In this archivolt there are only two heads to represent the zodiacal sign.

The summer and autumnal months are always represented in a series of agricultural occupations, which, of course, vary with the locality in which they occur; but generally in their order only. Thus, if June is mowing, July is reaping; if July is mowing, August is reaping; and so on. I shall give a parallel view of some of these varieties presently; but, meantime, we had better follow the St. Mark's series, as it is peculiar in some respects.

Windows of the Fifth Order.

6. JUNE. *Reaping*. The corn and sickle sculptured with singular care and precision, in bold relief, and the zodiacal sign, the Crab, above, also worked with great spirit.

7. JULY. *Mowing*. A very interesting piece of sculpture, owing to the care with which the flowers are wrought out among the long grass. I do not remember ever finding July but either reaping or mowing.

8. AUGUST. Peculiarly represented in this archivolt, *sitting in a chair, with his head upon his hand, as if asleep; the Virgin* (the zodiacal sign) *above him, lifting up her hand.* This appears to be a peculiarly Italian version of the proper employment of August.

9. SEPTEMBER. *Bearing home grapes in a basket.* Almost always sowing, in Northern work.

10. OCTOBER. *Wearing a conical hat, and digging busily with a long spade.* In Northern work he is sometimes a vintager, sometimes beating the acorns out of an oak to feed swine.

11. NOVEMBER. *Seems to be catching small birds in a net.* I do not remember him so employed elsewhere. He is nearly always killing pigs.

12. DECEMBER. *Killing swine.* It is hardly ever that this employment is not given to one or other of the terminal months of the year. If not so engaged, December is usually putting new loaves in the oven; sometimes killing oxen.

A series nearly similar to that of St. Mark's occurs on the door of the Cathedral of Lucca, and on that of the Baptistery of Pisa; in which, however, if I recollect rightly, February is fishing, and May has something resembling an umbrella in his hand, instead of a hawk. But, in all cases, the figures are treated with the peculiar spirit of the Gothic sculptors; and this archivolt is the first expression of that spirit which is to be found in Venice.

In the private palaces, the entrances soon admitted some concession to the Gothic form also. They pass through nearly the same conditions of change as the windows, with these three differences: first, that no arches of the fantastic fourth order occur in any doorways; secondly, that the pure pointed arch occurs earlier, and much oftener, in doorways than in window-heads; lastly, that the entrance itself, if small, is nearly always square-headed in the earliest examples, without any arch above, but afterwards the arch is thrown across above the lintel. The interval between the two, or tympanum, is filled with sculpture, or closed by iron bars, with sometimes a projecting gable, to form a porch, thrown over the whole.

Such are the principal circumstances to be noted in the external forms and details of the Gothic palaces; of their interior arrangements there is little left unaltered. The gateways which we have been examining almost universally lead, in the earlier palaces, into a long interior court, round which the mass of the palace is built; and in which its first story is reached by a superb external staircase, sustained on four or five pointed arches gradually increasing as they ascend, both in height and span, – this change in their size being, so far as I remember, peculiar to Venice, and visibly a consequence of the habitual admission of arches of different sizes in the Byzantine façades. These staircases are protected by exquisitely carved parapets, like those of the outer balconies,

Detail from the second archivolt of St. Mark's showing the sculpture of November.

Gentile Bellini A PROCESSION IN THE PIAZZA SAN MARCO,
showing the archivolts of the great central entrance to St. Mark's
as they were in the fifteenth century.

with lions or grotesque heads set on the angles and with true projecting balconies on their landing-places. In the centre of the court there is always a marble well; and these wells furnish some of the most superb examples of Venetian sculpture. I am aware only of one remaining from the Byzantine period; it is octagonal, and treated like the richest of our Norman fonts: but the

John Ruskin COURT OF THE DUCAL PALACE
'In the centre of the court there is always a marble well; and these furnish
some of the most superb examples of Venetian sculpture.'

Gothic wells of every date, from the thirteenth century downwards, are innumerable, and full of beauty, though their form is little varied; they being, in almost every case, treated like colossal capitals of pillars, with foliage at the angles, and the shield of the family upon their sides.

The interior apartments always consist of one noble hall on the first story, often on the second also, extending across the entire depth of the house, and lighted in front by the principal groups of its windows, while smaller apartments open from it on either side. The ceilings, where they remain untouched, are of bold horizontal beams, richly carved and gilded; but few of these are left from the true Gothic times, the Venetian interiors having, in almost every case, been remodelled by the Renaissance architects. This change, however, for once, we cannot regret, as the walls and ceilings, when so altered, were covered with the noblest works of Veronese, Titian, and Tintoret; nor the interior walls only, but, as before noticed, often the exteriors also. Of the colour decorations of the Gothic exteriors I have, therefore, at present taken no notice, as it will be more convenient to embrace this subject in one general view of the systems of colouring of the Venetian palaces, when we arrive at the period of its richest development. It remains for us, therefore, at present, only to review the history, fix the date, and note the most important particulars in the structure of the building which at once consummates and embodies the entire system of the Gothic architecture of Venice,–the DUCAL PALACE.

THE DUCAL PALACE

IT was stated in the commencement of the preceding chapter that the Gothic art of Venice was separated by the building of the Ducal Palace into two distinct periods; and that in all the domestic edifices which were raised for half a century after its completion, their characteristic and chiefly effective portions were more or less directly copied from it. The fact is, that the Ducal Palace was the great work of Venice at this period, itself the principal effort of her imagination, employing her best architects in its masonry, and her best painters in its decoration, for a long series of years; and we must receive it as a remarkable testimony to the influence which it possessed over the minds of those who saw it in its progress, that, while in the other cities of Italy every palace and church was rising in some original and daily more daring form, the majesty of this single building was able to give pause to the Gothic imagination in its full career; stayed the restlessness of innovation in an instant, and forbade the powers which had created it thenceforth to exert themselves in new directions, or endeavour to summon an image more attractive.

Before the reader can enter upon any inquiry into the history of this building, it is necessary that he should be thoroughly familiar with the arrangement and names of its principal parts, as it at present stands. I must do what I can, by the help of a rough plan and bird's-eye view [on page 173], to give him the necessary topographical knowledge.

The reader will observe that the Ducal Palace is arranged somewhat in the form of a hollow square, of which one side faces the Piazzetta, B, and another the quay called the Riva de' Schiavoni, R R; the third is on the dark canal called the 'Rio del Palazzo,' and the fourth joins the Church of St. Mark.

Of this fourth side, therefore, nothing can be seen. Of the other three sides we shall have to speak constantly; and they will be called, that towards the Piazzetta, the 'Piazzetta Façade;' that towards the Riva de' Schiavoni, the 'Sea Façade;' and that towards the Rio del Palazzo, the 'Rio Façade.'

We must now proceed to obtain some rough idea of the appearance and distribution of the palace itself; but its arrangement will be better understood by supposing ourselves raised some hundred and fifty feet above the point in

John Ruskin THE DUCAL PALACE, RENAISSANCE CAPITALS OF THE LOGGIA

the lagoon in front of it, so as to get a general view of the Sea Façade and Rio Façade (the latter in very steep perspective) and to look down into its interior court. In this drawing [omitting all details on the roofs, in order to avoid confusion] we have merely to notice that, of the two bridges seen on the right, the uppermost, above the black canal, is the Bridge of Sighs; the lower one is the Ponte della Paglia, the regular thoroughfare from quay to quay, and, I

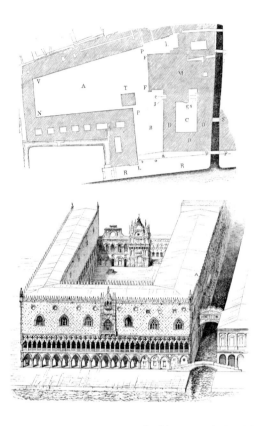

A. St. Mark's Place.
B. Piazzetta.
P. V. Procuratie Vecchie.
P. N. (opposite) Procuratie Nuove.
P. L. Libreria Vecchia.
I. Piazzetta de' Leoni.
T. Tower of St. Mark.
F. F. Great Façade of St. Mark's Church.
M. St. Mark's. (It is so united with the Ducal Palace, that the separation cannot be indicated in the plan, unless all the walls

had been marked, which would have confused the whole.)
D D D. Ducal Palace.
C. Court of Ducal Palace.
c. Porta della Carta.
p. p. Ponte della Paglia (Bridge of Straw).
S. Ponte de' Sospiri (Bridge of Sighs).
R. R. Riva de' Schiavoni.
g s. Giant's stair.
J. Judgment angle.
a. Fig-tree angle.

believe, called the Bridge of Straw, because the boats which brought straw from the mainland used to sell it at this place. The corner of the palace, rising above this bridge, and formed by the meeting of the Sea Façade and Rio Façade, will always be called the Vine angle, because it is decorated by a sculpture of the drunkenness of Noah. The angle opposite will be called the Fig-tree angle, because it is decorated by a sculpture of the Fall of Man. The long and narrow range of building, of which the roof is seen in perspective behind this angle, is the part of the palace fronting the Piazzetta; and the angle under the pinnacle most to the left of the two which terminate it will be called, for a reason presently to be stated, the Judgment angle. Within the square formed by the building is seen its interior court (with one of its wells), terminated by small and fantastic buildings of the Renaissance period, which face the Giant's Stair, of which the extremity is seen sloping down on the left.

The great façade which fronts the spectator looks southward. Hence the two traceried windows lower than the rest, and to the right of the spectator, may be conveniently distinguished as the 'Eastern Windows.' There are two others like them, filled with tracery, and at the same level, which look upon the narrow canal between the Ponte della Paglia and the Bridge of Sighs: these we may conveniently call the 'Canal Windows'. The reader will observe a vertical line in this dark side of the palace, separating its nearer and plainer wall from a long four-storied range of rich architecture. This more distant range is entirely Renaissance: its extremity is not indicated, because I have no accurate sketch of the small buildings and bridges beyond it, and we shall have nothing whatever to do with this part of the palace in our present inquiry. The nearer and undecorated wall is part of the older palace, though much defaced by modern opening of common windows, refittings of the brick-work, etc.

In the bird's-eye view it will be noticed that the two windows on the right are lower than the other four of the façade. In this arrangement there is one of the most remarkable instances I know of the daring sacrifice of symmetry to convenience, which was noticed in Chapter 7 as one of the chief noblenesses of the Gothic schools.

The part of the palace in which the two lower windows occur, was first built, and arranged in four stories in order to obtain the necessary number of apartments. Owing to circumstances it became necessary, in the beginning of the fourteenth century, to provide another large and magnificent chamber for the meeting of the Senate. That chamber was added at the side of the older building; but, as only one room was wanted, there was no need to divide the added portion into two stories. The entire height was given to the single chamber, being indeed not too great for just harmony with its enormous length and breadth. And then came the question how to place the windows, whether on a line with the two others, or above them.

The ceiling of the new room was to be adorned by the paintings of the best masters in Venice, and it became of great importance to raise the light near that gorgeous roof, as well as to keep the tone of illumination in the Council Chamber serene; and therefore to introduce light rather in simple masses than in many broken streams. A modern architect, terrified at the idea of violating external symmetry, would have sacrificed both the pictures and the peace of the Council. He would have placed the larger windows at the same level with the other two, and have introduced above them smaller windows, like those of the upper story in the older building, as if that upper story had been continued along the façade. But the old Venetian thought of the honour of the paintings, and the comfort of the Senate, before his own reputation. He unhesitatingly raised the large windows to their proper position with reference to the interior of the chamber, and suffered the external appearance to take care of itself. And

I believe the whole pile rather gains than loses in effect by the variation thus obtained in the spaces of wall above and below the windows.

On the party wall, between the second and third windows, which faces the eastern extremity of the Great Council Chamber, is painted the Paradise of Tintoret; and this wall will therefore be called the 'Wall of the Paradise.'

In nearly the centre of the Sea Façade, and between the first and second windows of the Great Council Chamber, is a large window to the ground, opening on a balcony, which is one of the chief ornaments of the palace, and will be called in future the 'Sea Balcony.'

The façade which looks on the Piazzetta is very nearly like this to the Sea, but the greater part of it was built in the fifteenth century, when people had become studious of their symmetries. Its side windows are all on the same level. Two light the west end of the Great Council Chamber, one lights a small room anciently called the Quarantia Civil Nuova; the other three, and the central one, with a balcony like that to the Sea, light another large chamber, called Sala del Scrutinio, or 'Hall of Inquiry,' which extends to the extremity of the palace above the Porta della Carta.

The reader is now well enough acquainted with the topography of the existing building, to be able to follow the accounts of its history.

We have seen above, that there were three principal styles of Venetian architecture; Byzantine, Gothic, and Renaissance.

The Ducal Palace was built successively in the three styles. There was a Byzantine Ducal Palace, a Gothic Ducal Palace, and a Renaissance Ducal Palace. The second superseded the first totally: a few stones of it (if indeed so much) are all that is left. But the third superseded the second in part only, and the existing building is formed by the union of the two.

In the year of the death of Charlemagne, 813, the Venetians determined to make the island of Rialto the seat of the government and capital of their state. Their Doge, Angelo or Agnello Participazio, instantly took vigorous means for the enlargement of the small group of buildings which were to be the nucleus of the future Venice. He appointed persons to superintend the raising of the banks of sand, so as to form more secure foundations, and to build wooden bridges over the canals. For the offices of religion, he built the Church of St. Mark; and on, or near, the spot where the Ducal Palace now stands, he built a palace for the administration of the government. The history of the Ducal Palace, therefore, begins with the birth of Venice.

Of the exact position and form of this palace of Participazio little is ascertained. Sansovino says that it was 'built near the Ponte della Paglia, and answeringly on the Grand Canal,' towards San Giorgio; that is to say, in the place now occupied by the Sea Façade; but this was merely the popular report of his day. We know, however, positively, that it was somewhere upon the site of the existing palace; and that it had an important front towards the Piazzetta, with which, as we shall see, the present palace at one period was incorporated.

There can be no doubt whatever that the palace at this period resembled and impressed the other Byzantine edifices of the city, such as the Fondaco de' Turchi, whose remains have been already described; and that, like them, it was covered with sculpture, and richly adorned with gold and colour.

In the year 1106, it was for the second time injured by fire, but repaired before 1116. Between 1173 and the close of the century, it seems to have been repaired and much enlarged by the Doge Sebastian Ziani and, after this, the palace seems to have remained untouched for a hundred years, until, in the commencement of the fourteenth century, the works of the Gothic Palace were begun. As, therefore, the old Byzantine building was, at the time when those works first interfered with it, in the form given to it by Ziani, I shall hereafter always speak of it as the *Ziani* Palace.

The reader, doubtless, recollects that the important change in the Venetian government which gave stability to the aristocratic power took place about the year 1297, under the Doge Pietro Gradenigo. The Serrar del Consiglio fixed the numbers of the Senate within certain limits, and it conferred upon them a dignity greater than they had ever before possessed. It was natural that the alteration in the character of the assembly should be attended by some change in the size, arrangement, or decoration of the chamber in which they sat.

We accordingly find it recorded by Sansovino, that 'in 1301 another saloon was begun on the Rio del Palazzo, *under the Doge Gradenigo*, and finished in 1309, *in which year the Grand Council first sat in it.*' In the first year, therefore, of the fourteenth century, the Gothic Ducal Palace of Venice was begun. Considered as the principal representation of the Venetian school of architecture, the Ducal Palace is the Parthenon of Venice, and Gradenigo its Pericles.

I wish the reader to remember the date 1301, as marking the commencement of a great architectural epoch, in which took place the first appliance of the energy of the aristocratic power, and of the Gothic style, to the works of the Ducal Palace. The operations then begun were continued, with hardly an interruption, during the whole period of the prosperity of Venice. We shall see the new buildings consume, and take the place of, the Ziani Palace, piece by piece: and when the Ziani Palace was destroyed, they fed upon themselves; being continued round the square, until, in the sixteenth century, they reached the point where they had been begun in the fourteenth, and pursued the track they had then followed some distance beyond the junction; destroying or hiding their own commencement, as the serpent, which is the type of eternity, conceals its tail in its jaws.

We cannot, therefore, *see* the extremity, wherein lay the sting and force of the whole creature, – the chamber, namely, built by the Doge Gradenigo; but the reader must keep that commencement and the date of it carefully in his mind. The body of the Palace Serpent will soon become visible to us.

The Gradenigo Chamber was somewhere on the Rio Façade, behind the present position of the Bridge of Sighs; *i.e.*, about the point marked on the roof by the dotted lines in the woodcut: it is not known whether low or high, but probably on a first story. The great façade of the Ziani Palace being, as above mentioned, on the Piazzetta, this chamber was as far back and out of the way as possible; secrecy and security being obviously the points first considered.

But the newly constituted Senate had need of other additions to the ancient palace besides the Council Chamber. A short, but most significant, sentence is added to Sansovino's account of the construction of that room. 'There were, *near it*,' he says, 'the Cancellaria, and the *Gheba* or *Gabbia*, afterwards called the Little Tower.'

Gabbia means a 'cage'; and there can be no question that certain apartments were at this time added at the top of the palace and on the Rio Façade, which were to be used as prisons. Whether any portion of the old Torresella still remains is a doubtful question; but the apartments at the top of the palace, in its fourth story, were still used for prisons as late as the beginning of the seventeenth century. The new chamber, then, and the prisons, being built, the Great Council first sat in their retired chamber on the Rio in the year 1309.

Now, observe the significant progress of events. They had no sooner thus established themselves in power than they were disturbed by the conspiracy of the Tiepolos, in the year 1310. In consequence of that conspiracy the Council of Ten was created, still under the Doge Gradenigo; who, having finished his work and left the artistocracy of Venice armed with this terrible power, died in the year 1312, some say by poison. He was succeeded by the Doge Marino Giorgio, who reigned only one year; and then followed the prosperous government of John Soranzo. There is no mention of any additions to the Ducal Palace during his reign, but he was succeeded by that Francesco Dandolo, the sculptures on whose tomb, still existing in the cloisters of the Salute, may be compared by any traveller with those of the Ducal Palace.

The Senate found their new Council Chamber inconveniently small, and, about thirty years after its completion, began to consider where a larger and more magnificent one might be built. The government was now thoroughly established, and it was probably felt that there was some meanness in the retired position, as well as insufficiency in the size, of the Council Chamber on the Rio.

It appears from the entry still preserved in the Archivio that it was on the 28th of December, 1340, that the commissioners appointed to decide on this important matter gave in their report to the Grand Council, and that the decree passed thereupon for the commencement of a new Council Chamber on the Grand Canal.

The room then begun is the one now in existence, and its building involved the building of all that is best and most beautiful in the present Ducal Palace, the rich arcades of the lower stories being all prepared for sustaining this Sala del Gran Consiglio.

In saying that it is the same now in existence, I do not mean that it has undergone no alterations; it has been refitted again and again, and some portions of its walls rebuilt; but in the place and form in which it first stood, it still stands. The Grand Council sat in the finished chamber for the first time in 1423. In that year the Gothic Ducal Palace of Venice was completed. It had taken, to build it, the energies of the entire period which I have above described as the central one of her life.

I must go back a step or two, in order to be certain that the reader understands clearly the state of the palace in 1423. The works of addition or renovation had now been proceeding, at intervals, during a space of a hundred and twenty-three years. Three generations at least had been accustomed to witness the gradual advancement of the form of the Ducal Palace into more stately symmetry, and to contrast the works of sculpture and painting with which it was decorated – full of the life, knowledge, and hope of the fourteenth century – with the rude Byzantine chiselling of the palace of the Doge Ziani.

The magnificent fabric just completed, of which the new Council Chamber was the nucleus, was now habitually known in Venice as the 'Palazzo Nuovo'; and the old Byzantine edifice, now ruinous, and more manifest in its decay by its contrast with the goodly stones of the building which had been raised at its side, was of course known as the 'Palazzo Vecchio.' That fabric, however, still occupied the principal position in Venice. The new Council Chamber had been erected by the side of it towards the sea; but there was not then the wide quay in front, the Riva dei Schiavoni, which now renders the Sea Façade as important as that to the Piazzetta. There was only a narrow walk between the pillars and the water; and the *old* palace of Ziani still faced the Piazzetta, and interrupted, by its decrepitude, the magnificence of the square where the nobles daily met. Every increase of the beauty of the new palace rendered the discrepancy between it and the companion building more painful; and then began to arise in the minds of all men a vague idea of the necessity of destroying the old palace, and completing the front of the Piazzetta with the same splendour as the Sea Façade. But no such sweeping measure of renovation had been contemplated by the Senate when they first formed the plan of their new Council Chamber. First a single additional room, then a gateway, then a larger room; but all considered merely as necessary additions to the palace, not as involving the entire reconstruction of the ancient edifice. The exhaustion of the treasury and the shadows upon the political horizon, rendered it more than imprudent to incur the vast additional expense which such a project involved; and the Senate, fearful of itself, and desirous to guard against the weakness of its own enthusiasm, passed a decree, like the effort of a man fearful of some strong temptation to keep his thoughts averted from the point of danger. It was a decree, not merely that the old palace should not be rebuilt, but that no one should *propose* rebuilding it. The feeling of the desirableness of doing so was too strong to permit fair discussion, and the Senate knew that to bring forward such a motion was to carry it.

The decree, thus passed in order to guard against their own weakness, forbade any one to speak of rebuilding the old palace, under the penalty of a thousand ducats. But they had rated their own enthusiasm too low: there was a man among them whom the loss of a thousand ducats could not deter from proposing what he believed to be for the good of the state.

Some excuse was given him for bringing forward the motion by a fire which occurred in 1419, and which injured both the Church of St. Mark's, and part of the old palace. What followed, I shall relate in the words of Sanuto.

'Therefore they set themselves with all diligence and care to repair and adorn sumptuously, first God's house: but in the Prince's house things went on more slowly, *for it did not please the Doge* [Tomaso Mocenigo] *to restore it in the form in which it was before*; and they could not rebuild it altogether in a better manner, so great was the parsimony of these old fathers; because it was forbidden by laws, which condemned in a penalty of a thousand ducats any one who should propose to throw down the *old* palace, and to rebuilt it more richly and with greater expense. But the Doge, who was magnanimous, and who desired above all things what was honourable to the city, had the thousand ducats carried into the Senate Chamber, and then proposed that the palace should be rebuilt.'

The new Council Chamber, at the time when Mocenigo brought forward his measure, had never yet been used. It was in the year 1422 that the decree passed to rebuild the palace: Mocenigo died in the following year, and Francesco Foscari was elected in his room. The Great Council Chamber was used for the first time on the day when Foscari entered the Senate as Doge, and the following year the first hammer was lifted up against the old palace of Ziani.

That hammer stroke was the first act of the period properly called the 'Renaissance.' It was the knell of the architecture of Venice,—and of Venice herself.

The central epoch of her life was past; the decay had already begun: I dated its commencement above from the death of Mocenigo. A year had not yet elapsed since that great Doge had been called to his account: his patriotism, always sincere, had been in this instance mistaken; in his zeal for the honour of future Venice, he had forgotten what was due to the Venice of long ago. A thousand palaces might be built upon her burdened islands, but none of them could take the place, or recall the memory, of that which was first built upon her unfrequented shore. It fell; and, as if it had been the talisman of her fortunes, the city never flourished again.

I have no intention of following out, in their intricate details, the operations which were begun under Foscari, and continued under succeeding Doges, till the palace assumed its present form, for I am not in this work concerned, except by occasional reference, with the architecture of the fifteenth century: but the main facts are the following. The palace of Ziani was destroyed; the existing façade to the Piazzetta built, so as both to continue and to resemble, in most particulars, the work of the Great Council Chamber. It was carried back from the Sea as far as the Judgment angle; beyond which is the Porta della Carta, begun in 1439, and finished in two years, under the Doge Foscari; the interior buildings connected with it were added by the Doge Christopher Moro (the Othello of Shakespeare) in 1462.

By reference to the figure the reader will see that we have now gone the round of the palace, and that the new work of 1462 was close upon the first piece of the Gothic palace, the *new* Council Chamber of 1301. Some remnants of the Ziani Palace were perhaps still left between the two extremities of the Gothic Palace; or, as is more probable, the last stones of it may have been swept away after the fire of 1419, and replaced by new apartments for the Doge. But whatever buildings, old or new, stood on this spot at the time of the completion of the Porta della Carta were destroyed by another great fire in 1479, together with so much of the palace on the Rio, that, though the saloon of Gradenigo, then known as the Sala de' Pregadi, was not destroyed, it became necessary to reconstruct the entire façades of the portion of the palace behind the Bridge of Sighs, both towards the court and canal. This work was entrusted to the best Renaissance architects of the close of the fifteenth and opening of the sixteenth centuries; Antonio Ricci executing the Giant's staircase, and, on his absconding with a large sum of the public money, Pietro Lombardo taking his place. The whole work must have been completed towards the middle of the sixteenth century. The architects of the palace, advancing round the square and led by fire, had more than reached the point from which they had set out; and the work of 1560 was joined to the work of

1301–1340, at the point marked by the conspicuous vertical line on the Rio Façade.

But the palace was not long permitted to remain in this finished form. Another terrific fire, commonly called the great fire, burst out in 1574, and destroyed the inner fittings and all the precious pictures of the Great Council Chamber, and of all the upper rooms on the Sea Façade, and most of those on the Rio Façade, leaving the building a mere shell, shaken and blasted by the flames. It was debated in the Great Council whether the ruin should not be thrown down, and an entirely new palace built in its stead. The opinions of all the leading architects of Venice were taken, respecting the safety of the walls, or the possibility of repairing them as they stood.

I cannot help feeling some childish pleasure in the accidental resemblance to my own name in that of the architect whose opinion was first given in favour of the ancient fabric, Giovanni Rusconi. Others, especially Palladio, wanted to pull down the old palace, and execute designs of their own; but the best architects in Venice, and, to his immortal honour, chiefly Francesco Sansovino, energetically pleaded for the Gothic pile, and prevailed. It was successfully repaired, and Tintoret painted his noblest picture on the wall from which the 'Paradise' of Guariento had withered before the flames.

The repairs necessarily undertaken at this time were however extensive, and interfere in many directions with the earlier work of the palace: still the only serious alteration in its form was the transposition of the prisons, formerly at the top of the palace, to the other side of the Rio del Palazzo; and the building of the Bridge of Sighs, to connect them with the palace, by Antonio da Ponte. The completion of this work brought the whole edifice into its present form; with the exception of alterations in doors, partitions, and staircases among the inner apartments.

Now, therefore, we are at liberty to examine some of the details of the Ducal Palace, without any doubt about their dates. First, then, the reader will observe that, as the building was very nearly square on the ground plan, a peculiar prominence and importance were given to its angles, which rendered it necessary that they should be enriched and softened by sculpture. It is to be noted that this principle of breaking the angle is peculiarly Gothic, arising partly out of the necessity of strengthening the flanks of enormous buildings, where composed of imperfect materials, by buttresses or pinnacles; partly out of the conditions of Gothic warfare, which generally required a tower at the angle; partly out of the natural dislike of the meagreness of effect in buildings which admitted large surfaces of wall, if the angle were entirely unrelieved. The Ducal Palace, in its acknowledgment of this principle, makes a more definite concession to the Gothic spirit than any of the previous architecture of Venice. No angle, up to the time of its erection, had been otherwise decorated than by a narrow fluted pilaster of red marble, and the sculpture was reserved always, as in Greek and Roman work, for the plane surfaces of the building, with, as far as I recollect, two exceptions only, both in St. Mark's; namely, the bold and grotesque gargoyle on its north-west angle, and the angles which project from the four inner angles under the main cupola; both of these arrangements being plainly made under Lombardic influence.

The Ducal Palace, however, accepts the principle in its completeness, and throws the main decoration upon its angles. The central window, which looks rich and important in the woodcut, was entirely restored in the Renaissance time under the Doge Steno; so that we have no traces of its early treatment; and the principal interest of the older palace is concentrated in the angle sculpture, which is arranged in the following manner. The pillars of the two bearing arcades are much enlarged in thickness at the angles, and their capitals increased in depth, breadth, and fulness of subject: above each capital, on the angle of the wall, a sculptural subject is introduced, consisting, in the great lower arcade, of two or more figures of the size of life; in the upper arcade, of a single angel holding a scroll: above these angels rise the twisted

Renaissance sculpture of the Judgment of Solomon at the
north-west corner of the Ducal Palace.

pillars with their crowning niches, already noticed in the account of parapets in the seventh chapter; thus forming an unbroken line of decoration from the ground to the top of the angle.

It was before noticed that one of the corners of the palace joins the irregular outer buildings connected with St. Mark's, and is not generally seen. There remain, therefore, to be decorated, only the three angles, above distinguished as the Vine angle, the Fig-tree angle, and the Judgment angle; and at these we have, according to the arrangement just explained,—

First, Three great bearing capitals (lower arcade).
Secondly, Three figure subjects of sculpture above them (lower arcade).
Thirdly, Three smaller bearing capitals (upper arcade).
Fourthly, Three angels above them (upper arcade).
Fifthly, Three spiral shafts with niches.

I shall describe the bearing capitals hereafter, in their order, with the others of the arcade; for the first point to which the reader's attention ought to be directed is the choice of subject in the great figure sculptures above them. These, observe, are the very corner stones of the edifice, and in them we may expect to find the most important evidences of the feeling, as well as of the skill, of the builder. If he has anything to say to us of the purpose with which he built the palace, it is sure to be said here; if there was any lesson which he wished principally to teach to those for whom he built, here it is sure to be inculcated; if there was any sentiment which they themselves desired to have expressed in the principal edifice of their city, this is the place in which we may be secure of finding it legibly inscribed.

Now the first two angles, of the Vine and Fig-tree, belong to the old, or true Gothic, Palace; the third angle belongs to the Renaissance imitation of it: therefore, at the first two angles, it is the Gothic spirit which is going to speak to us; and, at the third, the Renaissance spirit.

The reader remembers, I trust, that the most characteristic sentiment of all that we traced in the working of the Gothic heart, was the frank confession of its own weakness; and I must anticipate, for a moment, the results of our inquiry in subsequent chapters, so far as to state that the principal element in the Renaissance spirit, is its firm confidence in its own wisdom.

Here, then, the two spirits speak for themselves.

The first main sculpture of the Gothic Palace is on what I have called the angle of the Fig-tree:

Its subject is the FALL OF MAN.

The second sculpture is on the angle of the Vine:

Its subject is the DRUNKENNESS OF NOAH.

The Renaissance sculpture is on the Judgment angle:

Its subject is the JUDGMENT OF SOLOMON.

It is impossible to overstate, or to regard with too much admiration, the significance of this single fact. It is as if the palace had been built at various epochs, and preserved uninjured to this day, for the sole purpose of teaching us the difference in the temper of the two schools.

In the subjects of the Fall and the Drunkenness, the tree, which forms the chiefly decorative portion of the sculpture,—fig in the one case, vine in the other,—was a necessary adjunct. Its trunk, in both sculptures, forms the true outer angle of the palace; boldly cut separate from the stonework behind, and branching out above the figures so as to enwrap each side of the angle, for several feet, with its deep foliage. Nothing can be more masterly or superb than the sweep of this foliage on the Fig-tree angle; the broad leaves lapping round the budding fruit, and sheltering from sight, beneath their shadows, birds of the most graceful form and delicate plumage. The branches are, however, so strong, and the masses of stone hewn into leafage so large, that, notwithstanding the depth of the undercutting, the work remains nearly uninjured; not so at the Vine angle, where the natural delicacy of the vine-leaf and tendril having tempted the sculptor to greater effort, he has passed the proper limits of his art, and cut the upper stems so delicately that half of them have been broken away by the casualties to which the situation of the

Rafaelle Carloforti STUDY OF THE HEAD OF NOAH, THE VINE-TREE ANGLE, THE DUCAL PALACE
Carloforti, who was studying at the Accademia, drew
several studies of sculpture for Ruskin.

Suo Discepolo Ubbidiente
Raffaele Castaforti

sculpture necessarily exposes it. Although half of the beauty of the composition is destroyed by the breaking away of its central masses, there is still enough in the distribution of the variously bending leaves, and in the placing of the birds on the lighter branches, to prove to us the power of the designer. I have already referred to this as a remarkable instance of the Gothic Naturalism; and, indeed, it is almost impossible for the copying of nature to be carried further than in the fibres of the marble branches, and the careful finishing of the tendrils: note especially the peculiar expression of the knotty joints of the vine in the light branch which rises highest.

As must always be the case in early sculpture, the figures are much inferior to the leafage; yet so skilful in many respects, that it was a long time before I could persuade myself that they had indeed been wrought in the first half of the fourteenth century.

The figures of Adam and Eve, sculptured on each side of the Fig-tree angle, are more stiff than those of Noah and his sons, but are better fitted for their architectural service; and the trunk of the tree, with the angular body of the serpent writhed around it, is more nobly treated as a terminal group of lines than that of the vine.

The Renaissance sculptor of the figures of the Judgment of Solomon has very nearly copied the fig-tree from this angle, placing its trunk between the executioner and the mother, who leans forward to stay his hand. But, though the whole group is much more free in design than those of the earlier palace, and in many ways excellent in itself, so that it always strikes the eye of a careless observer more than the others, it is of immeasurably inferior spirit in the workmanship; the leaves of the tree, though far more studiously varied in flow than those of the fig-tree from which they are partially copied, have none of its truth to nature; they are ill set on the stems, bluntly defined on the edges, and their curves are not those of growing leaves, but of wrinkled drapery.

Above these three sculptures are set, in the upper arcade, the statues of the archangels Raphael, Michael, and Gabriel; the figure of Gabriel, which is by much the most beautiful feature of the Renaissance portion of the palace, has in its hand the Annunciation lily.

Such are the subjects of the main sculptures decorating the angles of the palace; notable, observe, for their simple expression of two feelings, the consciousness of human frailty, and the dependence upon Divine guidance and protection: this being, of course, the general purpose of the introduction of the figures of the angels. We have next to examine the course of divinity and of natural history embodied by the old sculptor in the great series of capitals which support the lower arcade of the palace; and which, being at a height of little more than eight feet above the eye, might be read, like the pages of a book, by those (the noblest men in Venice) who habitually walked beneath the shadow of this great arcade at the time of their first meeting each other for morning converse.

The principal sculptures of the capitals consist of personifications of the Virtues and Vices, the favourite subjects of decorative art, at this period, in all the cities of Italy; and I believe the reader may both happily and profitably rest for a little while beneath the first vault of the arcade, to review these symbols of the virtues.

We will take the pillars of the Ducal Palace in their order. It has already been mentioned (Chapter 1) that there are, in all, thirty-six great pillars supporting the lower story; and that these are to be counted from right to left, because then the more ancient of them come first: and that, thus arranged, the first, which is not a shaft, but a pilaster, will be the support of the Vine angle; the eighteenth will be the great shaft of the Fig-tree angle; and the thirty-sixth, that of the Judgment angle.

All their capitals, except that of the first, are octagonal, and are decorated by sixteen leaves, differently enriched in every capital, but arranged in the same way; eight of them rising to the angles, and there forming volutes; the eight others set between them, on the sides, rising half-way up the bell of the capital; there nodding forward, and showing above them, rising out of their luxuriance, the groups or single figures which we have to examine. In some instances, the intermediate or lower leaves are reduced to eight sprays of foliage; and the capital is left dependent for its effect on the bold position of the figures. In referring to the figures on the octagonal capitals, I shall call the outer side, fronting either the Sea or the Piazzetta, the first side; and so count round from left to right; the fourth side being thus, of course, the innermost. As, however, the first five arches were walled up after the great fire, only three sides of their capitals are left visible, which we may describe as the front and the eastern and western sides of each.

FIRST CAPITAL: *i.e.* of the pilaster at the Vine angle.

In front, towards the Sea. A child holding a bird before him, with its wings expanded, covering his breast.

On its eastern side. Children's heads among leaves.

On its western side. A child carrying in one hand a comb; in the other a pair of scissors.

It appears curious, that this, the principal pilaster of the façade, should have been decorated only by these graceful grotesques, for I can hardly suppose them anything more. There may be meaning in them, but I will not venture to conjecture any, except the very plain and practical meaning conveyed by the last figure to all Venetian children, which it would be well if they would act upon. For the rest, I have seen the comb introduced in grotesque work as early as the thirteenth century, but generally for the purpose of ridiculing too great care in dressing the hair, which assuredly is not its purpose here. The children's heads are very sweet and full of life, but the eyes sharp and small.

SECOND CAPITAL. Only three sides of the original work are left unburied by the mass of added wall. Each side has a bird, one web-footed, with a fish; one clawed, with a serpent, which opens its jaws, and darts its tongue at the bird's breast; the third pluming itself, with a feather between the mandibles of its bill. It is by far the most beautiful of the three capitals decorated with birds.

THIRD CAPITAL. Also has three sides only left. They have three heads, large, and very ill cut; one female, and crowned.

FOURTH CAPITAL. Has three children. The eastern one is defaced: the one in front holds a small bird, whose plumage is beautifully indicated, in its right hand; and with its left holds up half a walnut, showing the nut inside: the third holds a fresh fig, cut through, showing the seeds.

The hair of all the three children is differently worked: the first has luxuriant flowing hair, and a double chin; the second, light flowing hair falling in pointed locks on the forehead; the third, crisp curling hair, deep cut with drill holes.

This capital has been copied on the Renaissance side of the palace, only with such changes in the ideal of the children as the workman thought expedient and natural. It is highly interesting to compare the child of the fourteenth with the child of the fifteenth century. The early heads are full of youthful life, playful, humane, affectionate, beaming with sensation and vivacity, but with much manliness and firmness also, not a little cunning, and some cruelty perhaps, beneath all; the features small and hard, and the eyes keen. There is the making of rough and great men in them. But the children of the fifteenth century are dull smooth-faced dunces, without a single meaning line in the fatness of their stolid cheeks; and, although, in the vulgar sense, as handsome as the other children are ugly, capable of becoming nothing but perfumed coxcombs.

FIFTH CAPITAL. Still three sides only left, bearing three half-length statues of kings; this is the first capital which bears any inscription. In front, a king with a sword in his right hand points to a handkerchief embroidered and fringed, with a head on it, carved on the cavetto of the abacus. His name is written above, TITUS VESPASIAN IMPERATOR.

On eastern side, TRAJANUS IMPERATOR. Crowned, a sword in right hand, and sceptre in left.

On western, (OCT) AVIANUS AUGUSTUS IMPERATOR. The OCT is broken away. He bears a globe in his right hand, with MUNDUS PACIS upon it; a sceptre in his left, which I think has terminated in a human figure. He has a flowing beard and a singularly high crown; the face is much injured, but has once been very noble in expression.

SIXTH CAPITAL. Has large male and female heads, very coarsely cut, hard, and bad.

SEVENTH CAPITAL. This is the first of the series which is complete; the first open arch of the lower arcade being between it and the sixth. It begins the representation of the Virtues.

First side. Largitas, or Liberality: always distinguished from the higher Charity. A male figure, with his lap full of money, which he pours out of his hand. The coins are plain, circular, and smooth; there is no attempt to mark device upon them.

In the copy of this design on the twenty-fifth capital, instead of showering out the gold from his open hand, the figure holds it in a plate or salver, introduced for the sake of disguising the direct imitation. The changes thus made in the Renaissance pillars are always injuries.

The virtue is the proper opponent of Avarice; though it does not occur in the systems of Orcagna or Giotto, being included in Charity. It was a leading virtue with Aristotle and the other ancients.

Second side. Constancy; not very characteristic. An armed man with a sword in his hand.

This virtue is one of the forms of fortitude, and Giotto therefore sets as the vice opponent to Fortitude, 'Inconstantia', represented as a woman in loose drapery, falling from a rolling globe. The vision seen in the interpreter's house in the Pilgrim's Progress, of the man with a very bold countenance, who says to him who has the writer's ink-horn by his side, 'Set down my name', is the best personification of the Venetian 'Constantia' of which I am aware in literature.

Third side. Discord; holding up her finger, but needing the inscription above to assure us of her meaning.

Fourth side. Patience. A female figure, very expressive and lovely, in a hood, with her right hand on her breast, the left extended. She is one of the principal virtues in all the Christian systems.

Fifth side. Despair. A female figure thrusting a dagger into her throat, and tearing her long hair, which flows down among the leaves to the capital below her knees. One of the finest figures of the series. In the Renaissance copy she is totally devoid of expression, and appears, instead of tearing her hair, to be dividing it into long curls on each side.

This vice is the proper opposite of Hope. By Giotto she is represented as a woman hanging herself, a fiend coming for her soul.

Sixth side. Obedience: with her arms folded; meek, but rude and common-place, looking at a little dog standing on its hind legs and begging, with a collar round its neck.

This virtue is, of course, a principal one in the monkish systems; represented by Giotto at Assisi as 'an angel robed in black, placing the finger of his left hand on his mouth, and passing the yoke over the head of a Franciscan monk kneeling at his feet'.

Seventh side. Infidelity. A man in a turban, with a small image in his hand, or the image of a child.

By Giotto Infidelity is most nobly symbolised as a woman helmeted, the helmet having a broad rim which keeps the light from her eyes. She is covered with a heavy drapery, stands infirmly as if about to fall, is *bound by a cord round her neck to an image* which she carries in her hand, and has flames bursting forth at her feet.

Eighth side. Modesty; bearing a pitcher. (In the Renaissance copy, a vase like a coffee-pot.)

I do not find this virtue in any of the Italian series, except that of Venice.

EIGHTH CAPITAL. It has no inscriptions, and its subjects are not, by themselves, intelligible; but they appear to be typical of the degradation of human instincts.

First side. A caricature of Arion on his dolphin; he wears a cap ending in a long proboscis-like horn, and plays a violin with a curious twitch of the bow and wag of the head, very graphically expressed, but still without anything approaching to the power of Northern grotesque. His dolphin has a goodly row of teeth, and the waves beat over its back.

Second side. A human figure, with curly hair and the legs of a bear; the paws laid, with great sculptural skill, upon the foliage. It plays a violin, shaped like a guitar, with a bent double-stringed bow.

Third side. A figure with a serpent's tail and a monstrous head, founded on a Negro type, hollow-cheeked, large-lipped, and wearing a cap made of a serpent's skin, holding a fir-cone in its hand.

Fourth side. A monstrous figure, terminating below in a tortoise. It is devouring a gourd, which it grasps greedily with both hands; it wears a cap ending in a hoofed leg.

Fifth side. A centaur wearing a crested helmet, and holding a curved sword.

Sixth side. A knight, riding a headless horse, and wearing chain armour, with a triangular shield flung behind his back, and a two-edged sword.

Seventh side. A figure like that on the fifth, wearing a round helmet, and with the legs and tail of a horse. He bears a long mace with a top like a fir-cone.

Eighth side. A figure with curly hair, and an acorn in its hand, ending below in a fish.

NINTH CAPITAL. *First side.* Faith. She has her left hand on her breast, and the cross on her right. The Faith of Giotto holds the cross in her right hand; in her left, a scroll with the Apostles' Creed. She treads upon cabalistic books, and has a key suspended to her waist.

Second side. Fortitude. A long-bearded man [Samson?] tearing open a lion's jaw. The inscription is illegible, and the somewhat vulgar personification appears to belong rather to Courage than Fortitude. On the Renaissance copy it is inscribed FORTITUDO SUM VIRILIS. The Latin word has, perhaps, been received by the sculptor as merely signifying 'Strength', the rest of the perfect idea of this virtue having been given in 'Constantia' previously. But both these Venetian symbols together do not at all approach the idea of Fortitude as given generally by Giotto and the Pisan sculptors; clothed with a lion's skin, knotted about her neck, and falling to her feet in deep folds; drawing back her right hand, with the sword pointed towards her enemy; and slightly retired behind her immovable shield, which with Giotto is square, and rested on the ground like a tower, covering her up to above the shoulders; bearing on it a lion, and with broken heads of javelins deeply infixed.

Third side. Temperance; bearing a pitcher of water and a cup. In this somewhat vulgar and most frequent conception of this virtue, temperance is confused with mere abstinence, the opposite of Gula, or Gluttony; whereas the Greek Temperance, a truly cardinal virtue, is the moderator of *all* the passions, and so represented by Giotto, who has placed a bridle upon her lips, and a sword in her hand, the hilt of which she is binding to the scabbard. In his system, she is opposed among the vices, not by Gula, or Gluttony, but by Ira, Anger.

Fourth side. Humility with a veil upon her head, carrying a lamb in her lap.

This virtue is of course a peculiarly Christian one, hardly recognised in the Pagan systems, though carefully impressed upon the Greeks in early life.

Fifth side. Charity. A woman with her lap full of loaves (?), giving one to a child, who stretches his arm out for it across a broad gap in the leafage of the capital.

Again very far inferior to the Giottesque rendering of this virtue. In the Arena Chapel she is distinguished from all the other virtues by having a circular glory round her head, and a cross of fire; she is crowned with flowers, presents with her right hand a vase of corn and fruit, and with her left receives treasure from Christ, who appears above her, to provide her with the means of continual offices of beneficence, while she tramples under foot the treasures of the earth.

The peculiar beauty of most of the Italian conceptions of Charity is in the subjection of mere munificence to the glowing of her love, always represented by flames; here in the form of a cross, round her head.

Sixth side. Justice. Crowned, and with sword.

This idea was afterwards much amplified and adorned in the only good capital of the Renaissance series, under the Judgment angle. Giotto has also given his whole strength to the painting of this virtue, representing her as enthroned under a noble Gothic canopy, holding scales, not by the beam, but one in each hand; a beautiful idea, showing that the equality of the scales of Justice is not owing to natural laws, but to her own immediate weighing the opposed causes in her own hands. In one scale is an executioner beheading a criminal; in the other an angel crowning a man, who seems (in Selvatico's plate) to have been working at a desk or table.

Beneath her feet is a small predella, representing various persons riding securely in the woods, and others dancing to the sound of music.

Seventh side. Prudence. A man with a book and a pair of compasses, wearing the noble cap, hanging down towards the shoulder, and bound in a fillet round the brow, which occurs so frequently during the fourteenth century in Italy in the portraits of men occupied in any civil capacity.

This virtue is conceived under very different degrees of dignity, from mere worldly prudence up to heavenly wisdom, being opposed sometimes by Stultitia, sometimes by Ignorantia. Giotto expresses her vigilance and just measurement or estimate of all things by painting her as Janus-headed, and gazing into a convex mirror, with compasses in her right hand; the convex mirror showing her power of looking at many things in small compass.

Eighth side. Hope. A figure full of devotional expression, holding up its hands as in prayer, and looking to a hand which is extended towards it out of sunbeams. In the Renaissance copy this hand does not appear.

Of all the virtues, this is the most distinctively Christian (it could not, of course, enter definitely into any Pagan scheme); and above all others, it seems to me the *testing* virtue, – that by the possession of which we may most certainly determine whether we are Christians or not; for many men have charity, that is to say, general kindness of heart, or even a kind of faith, who have not any habitual *hope* of, or longing for, heaven. The Hope of Giotto is represented as winged, rising in the air, while an angel holds a crown before her.

TENTH CAPITAL. *First side.* Luxury (the opposite of Chastity). A woman with a jewelled chain across her forehead, smiling as she looks into a mirror, exposing her breast by drawing down her dress with one hand.

These subordinate forms of vice are not met with so frequently in art as those of the opposite virtues.

In fact, the proper and comprehensive expression of this vice is the Cupid of the ancients; and there is not any minor circumstance more indicative of the *intense* difference between the mediæval and the Renaissance spirit, than the mode in which this god is represented.

I have above said, that all great European art is rooted in the thirteenth century, and it seems to me that there is a kind of central year about which we may consider the energy of the middle ages to be gathered; a kind of focus of time, which, by what is to my mind a most touching and impressive Divine appointment, has been marked for us by the greatest writer of the middle ages, in the first words he utters; namely, the year 1300, the 'mezzo del cammin' of the life of Dante. Now, therefore, to Giotto, the contemporary of Dante, and who drew Dante's still existing portrait in this very year, 1300, we may always look for the central mediæval idea in any subject: and observe how he represents Cupid; as one of three, a terrible trinity, his companions being Satan and Death; and he himself 'a lean scarecrow, with bow, quiver, and fillet, and feet ending in claws,' thrust down into Hell by Penance, from the presence of Purity and Fortitude.

Second side. Gluttony. A woman in a turban, with a jewelled cup in her right hand. In her left, the clawed limb of a bird, which she is gnawing.

Third side. Pride. A knight, with a heavy and stupid face, holding a sword with three edges; his armour covered with ornaments in the form of roses, and with two ears attached to his helmet.

Fourth side. Anger. A woman tearing her dress open at her breast.

Fifth side. Avarice. An old woman with a veil over her forehead, and a bag of money in each hand. A figure very marvellous for power of expression. The throat is all made up of sinews with skinny channels deep between them, strained as by anxiety, and wasted by famine; the features hunger-bitten, the eyes hollow, the look glaring and intense, yet without the slightest caricature.

Sixth side. Idleness. Accidia. A figure much broken away, having had its arms round two branches of trees.

I do not know why Idleness should be represented as among trees, unless, in the Italy of the fourteenth century, forest country was considered as desert, and therefore the domain of Idleness.

Seventh side. Vanity. She is smiling complacently as she looks into a mirror in her lap. Her robe is embroidered with roses, and roses for her crown.

There is some confusion in the expression of this vice, between pride in the personal appearance and lightness of purpose. It is difficult to find this sin – which, after Pride, is the most universal, perhaps the most fatal, of all, fretting the whole depth of our humanity into storm – definitely expressed in art. The idea is, however, entirely worked out in the Vanity Fair of the 'Pilgrim's Progress'.

Eighth side. Envy. One of the noblest pieces of expression in the series. She is pointing malignantly with her finger; a serpent is wreathed about her head like a cap, another forms the girdle of her waist, and a dragon rests in her lap.

Giotto has, however, represented her, with still greater subtlety, as having her fingers terminating in claws, and raising her right hand with an expression partly of involuntary grasping; a serpent, issuing from her mouth, is about to bite her between the eyes; she has long membranous ears, horns on her head, and flames consuming her body.

ELEVENTH CAPITAL. Its decoration is composed of eight birds; these birds are all varied in form and action, but not so as to require special description.

TWELFTH CAPITAL. This has been very interesting, but is grievously defaced, four of its figures being entirely broken away, and the character of two others quite indecipherable. It has been copied in the thirty-third capital.

First side. Misery. A man with a wan face, seemingly pleading with a child who has its hands crossed on its breast. There is a buckle at his own breast in

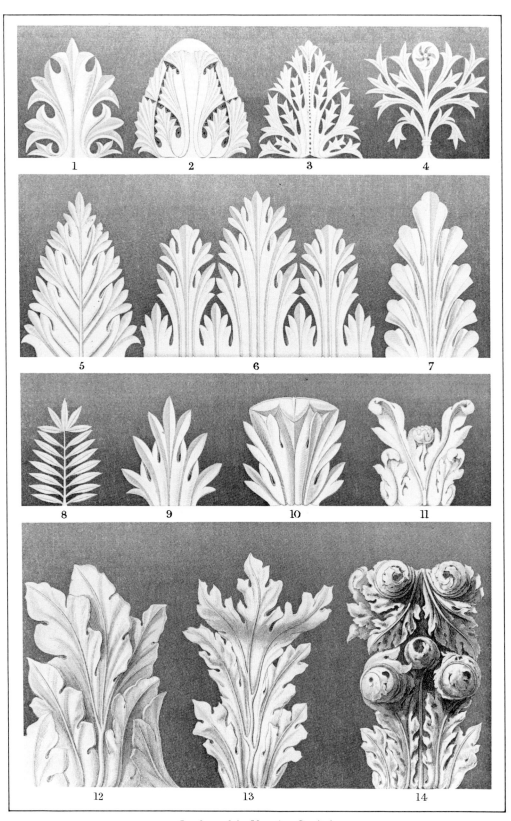

Leafage of the Venetian Capitals.

the shape of a cloven heart. The intention of this figure is not altogether apparent, as it is by no means treated as a vice; the distress seeming real, and like that of a parent in poverty mourning over his child. Yet it seems placed here as in direct opposition to the virtue of Cheerfulness, which follows next in order; rather, however, I believe, with the intention of illustrating human life, than the character of the vice which Dante placed in the circle of hell.

It is to be noticed, however, that in the Renaissance copy this figure is stated to be, not Miseria, but 'Misericordia' [compassion]. The contraction is a very moderate one, Misericordia being in old MS. written always as 'Mia'. If this reading be right, the figure is placed here rather as the companion, than the opposite, of Cheerfulness; unless, indeed, it is intended to unite the idea of Mercy and Compassion with that of Sacred Sorrow.

Second side. Cheerfulness. A woman with long flowing hair, crowned with roses, playing on a tambourine, and with open lips, as singing.

Third side. Destroyed; but, from the copy, we find it has been Stultitia, Folly; it is there represented simply as a man *riding*, a sculpture worth the consideration of the English residents who bring their horses to Venice. Giotto gives Stultitia a feather, cap and club. In early manuscripts he is always eating with one hand, and striking with the other; in later ones he has a cap and bells, or cap crested with a cock's head, whence the word 'coxcomb'.

Fourth side. Destroyed, all but a book, which identifies it with the 'Celestial Chastity' of the Renaissance copy; there represented as a woman pointing to a book (connecting the convent life with the pursuit of literature?).

Fifth side. Only a scroll is left; but, from the copy, we find it has been Honesty or Truth. It is very curious, that among all the Christian systems of the virtues, we should find this one in Venice only.

Sixth side. Falsehood. An old woman leaning on a crutch. Dante's fraud is the finest personification of all, but the description is too long to be quoted.

Seventh side. Injustice. An armed figure holding a halbert; so also in the copy. The figure used by Giotto with the particular intention of representing unjust government, is represented at the gate of an embattled castle in a forest, between rocks, while various deeds of violence are committed at his feet.

Eighth side. A man with a dagger looking scornfully at a child, who turns its back to him. I cannot understand this figure.

THIRTEENTH CAPITAL. It has lions' heads all round, coarsely cut.

FOURTEENTH CAPITAL. It has various animals, each sitting on its haunches. Three dogs, one a greyhound, one long-haired, one short-haired with bells about its neck; two monkeys, one with fan-shaped hair projecting on each side of its face; a noble boar, with its tusks, hoofs, and bristles sharply cut; and a lion and lioness.

FIFTEENTH CAPITAL. The pillar to which it belongs is thicker than the rest, as well as the one over it in the upper arcade.

The sculpture of this capital is also much coarser, and seems to me later than that of the rest; and it has no inscription, which is embarrassing, as its subjects have had much meaning; but I believe Selvatico is right in supposing it to have been intended for a general illustration of Idleness.

First side. A woman with a distaff; her girdle richly decorated, and fastened by a buckle.

Second side. A youth in a long mantle, with a rose in his hand.

Third side. A woman in a turban stroking a puppy, which she holds by the haunches.

Fourth side. A man with a parrot.

Fifth side. A woman in very rich costume, with braided hair, and dress thrown into minute folds, holding a rosary (?) in her left hand, her right on her breast.

Sixth side. A man with a very thoughtful face, laying his hand upon the leaves of the capital.

Seventh side. A crowned lady, with a rose in her hand.

Eighth side. A boy with a ball in his left hand, and his right laid on his breast.

SIXTEENTH CAPITAL. It is decorated with eight large heads, partly intended to be grotesque, and very coarse and bad, except only that in the sixth side, which is totally different from all the rest, and looks like a portrait. It is thin, thoughtful, and dignified; thoroughly fine in every way. It wears a cap surmounted by two winged lions; and, therefore, I think this head is certainly meant to express the superiority of the Venetian character over that of other nations. Nothing is more remarkable in all early sculpture than its appreciation of the signs of dignity of character in the features, and the way in which it can exalt the principal figure in any subject by a few touches.

SEVENTEENTH CAPITAL. This has been so destroyed by the sea wind, which sweeps at this point of the arcade round the angle of the palace, that its inscriptions are no longer legible, and great parts of its figures are gone. Selvatico states them as follows: Solomon, the wise; Priscian, the grammarian; Aristotle, the logician; Tully, the orator; Pythagoras, the philosopher; Archimedes, the mechanic; Orpheus, the musician; Ptolemy, the astronomer. The fragments actually remaining are the following:

First side. A figure with two books, in a robe richly decorated with circles of roses.

Second side. A man with one book, poring over it; he has had a long stick or reed in his hand.

Third side. ARISTOTLE: so inscribed. He has a peaked double beard and a flat cap, from under which his long hair falls down his back.

Fourth side. Destroyed.

Fifth side. Destroyed, all but a board with three (counters?) on it.

Sixth side. A figure with compasses.

Seventh side. Nothing is left but a guitar with its handle wrought into a lion's head.

Eighth side. Destroyed.

We have now arrived at the EIGHTEENTH CAPITAL, the most interesting and beautiful of the palace. It represents the planets, and the sun and moon, in those divisions of the zodiac known to astrologers as their 'houses'; and perhaps indicates, by the position in which they are placed, the period of the year at which this great corner-stone was laid. The inscriptions above have been in quaint Latin rhyme, but are now decipherable only in fragments, and that with the more difficulty because the rusty iron bar that binds the abacus has broken away, in its expansion, nearly all the upper portions of the stone, and with them the signs of contraction, which are of great importance.

It should be premised that, in modern astrology, the houses of the planets are thus arranged:

The house of the Sun	is	Leo.
,,	Moon	,,	Cancer.
,,	of Mars	,,	Aries and Scorpio.
,,	Venus	,,	Taurus and Libra.
,,	Mercury	,,	Gemini and Virgo.
,,	Jupiter	,,	Sagittarius and Pisces.
,,	Saturn	,,	Capricorn.
,,	Herschel	,,	Aquarius.

The Herschel planet being of course unknown to the old astrologers, we have only the other six planetary powers, together with the sun; and Aquarius is assigned to Saturn as his house. I could not find Capricorn at all; but this sign may have been broken away, as the whole capital is grievously defaced. The eighth side of the capital, which the Herschel planet would now have occupied, bears a sculpture of the Creation of Man: it is the most conspicuous side, the one set diagonally across the angle; or the eighth in our usual mode of reading the capitals, from which I shall not depart.

The *first side*, then, or that towards the Sea, has Aquarius, as the house of Saturn, represented as a seated figure beautifully draped, pouring a stream of water out of an amphora over the leaves of the capital.

Second side. Jupiter, in his houses Sagittarius and Pisces, represented throned, with an upper dress disposed in radiating folds about his neck, and hanging down upon his breast, ornamented by small pendent trefoiled studs or bosses. He wears the drooping bonnet and long gloves; but the folds about the neck, shot forth to express the rays of the star, are the most remarkable characteristic of the figure. He raises his sceptre in his left hand over Sagit-

Detail from the eighteenth capital, showing the Moon.

tarius, represented as the centaur Chiron; and holds two thunnies in his right. Something rough, like a third fish, has been broken away below them; the more easily because this part of the group is entirely undercut, and the two fish glitter in the light, relieved on the deep gloom below the leaves.

Third side. Mars, in his houses Aries and Scorpio. Represented as a very ugly knight in chain mail, seated sideways on the ram, whose horns are broken away, and having a large scorpion in his left hand, whose tail is broken also, to the infinite injury of the group, for it seems to have curled across to the angle leaf, and formed a bright line of light, like the fish in the hand of Jupiter. The knight carries a shield, on which fire and water are sculptured, and bears a banner upon his lance, with the word DEFEROSUM, which puzzled me for some time. It should be read, I believe, 'De ferro sum'; which would be good *Venetian* Latin for 'I am of iron'.

Fourth side. The sun, in his house Leo. Represented under the figure of Apollo, sitting on the Lion, with rays shooting from his head, and the world in his hand.

Fifth side. Venus in her houses Taurus and Libra. The most beautiful figure of the series. She sits upon the bull, who is deep in the dewlap, and better cut than most of the animals, holding a mirror in her right hand, and the scales in her left. Her breast is very nobly and tenderly indicated under the folds of her drapery, which is exquisitely studied in its fall.

Sixth side. Mercury, represented as wearing a pendent cap, and holding a book: he is supported by three children in reclining attitudes, representing his houses Gemini and Virgo.

Seventh side. The Moon, in her house Cancer. This sculpture, which is turned towards the Piazzetta, is the most picturesque of the series. The moon is represented as a woman in a boat upon the sea, who raises the crescent in her right hand, and with her left draws a crab out of the waves, up the boat's side. The moon was, I believe, represented in Egyptian sculptures as in a boat; but I rather think the Venetian was not aware of this, and that he meant to express the peculiar sweetness of the moonlight at Venice, as seen across the lagoons. Whether this was intended by putting the planet in the boat, may be questionable, but assuredly the idea was meant to be conveyed by the dress of the figure. For all the draperies of the other figures on this capital, as well as on the rest of the façade, are disposed in severe but full folds, showing little of the forms beneath them; but the moon's drapery *ripples* down to her feet, so as exactly to suggest the trembling of the moonlight on the waves. This beautiful idea is highly characteristic of the thoughtfulness of the early sculptors: five hundred men may be now found who could have cut the drapery, as such, far better, for one who would have disposed its folds with this intention.

Eighth side. God creating man. Represented as a throned figure, with a glory round the head, laying his left hand on the head of a naked youth, and sustaining him with his right hand. I imagine the whole of this capital, therefore – the principal one of the old palace, – to have been intended to signify, first, the formation of the planets for the service of man upon the earth; secondly, the entire subjection of the fates and fortune of man to the will of God, as determined from the time when the earth and stars were made, and, in fact, written in the volume of the stars themselves.

Thus interpreted, the doctrines of judicial astrology were not only consistent with, but an aid to, the most spiritual and humble Christianity.

In the workmanship and grouping of its foliage, this capital is, on the whole, the finest I know in Europe. The sculptor has put his whole strength into it.

NINETEENTH CAPITAL. This is, of course, the second counting from the Sea, on the Piazzetta side of the palace, calling that of the Fig-tree angle the first.

It is the most important capital, as a piece of evidence in point of dates, in the whole palace. Great pains have been taken with it, and in some portion of the accompanying furniture or ornaments of each of its figures a small piece of coloured marble has been inlaid, with peculiar significance: for the capital represents the *arts of sculpture and architecture;* and the inlaying of the coloured stones (which are far too small to be effective at a distance, and are found in this one capital only of the whole series) is merely an expression of the architect's feeling of the essential importance of this art of inlaying, and of the value of colour generally in his own art.

First side. ST. SIMPLICIUS: so inscribed. A figure working with a pointed chisel on a small oblong block of green serpentine, about four inches long by one wide, inlaid in the capital. The chisel is, of course, in the left hand, but the right is held up open, with the palm outwards.

Second side. A crowned figure, carving the image of a child on a small statue, with a ground of red marble. The sculptured figure is highly finished, and is in type of head much like the Ham or Japheth at the Vine angle. Inscription effaced.

Third side. An old man, uncrowned, but with curling hair, at work on a small column, with its capital complete, and a little shaft of dark red marble, spotted with paler red. The capital is precisely of the form of that found in the palace of the Tiepolos and the other thirteenth century work of Venice. This one figure would be quite enough, without any other evidence whatever, to determine the date of this flank of the Ducal Palace as not later, at all events, than the first half of the fourteenth century. Its inscription is broken away, all but DISIPULO.

Fourth side. A crowned figure; but the object on which it has been working is broken away, and all the inscription except ST. E(N?)AS.

Fifth side. A man with a turban and a sharp chisel, at work on a kind of panel or niche, the back of which is of red marble.

Sixth side. A crowned figure, with hammer and chisel, employed *on a little range of windows of the fifth order,* having roses set, instead of orbicular ornaments, between the spandrils, with a rich cornice, and a band of purple marble inserted above. This sculpture assures us of the date of the fifth-order window, which it shows to have been universal in the early fourteenth century.

There are also five arches in the block on which the sculptor is working, marking the frequency of the number five in the window groups of the time.

Seventh side. A figure at work on a pilaster, with Lombardic thirteenth century capital, the shaft of dark red spotted marble.

Eighth side. A figure with a rich open crown, working on a delicate recumbent statue, the head of which is laid on a pillow covered with a rich chequer pattern; the whole supported on a block of dark red marble. There appear altogether to have been five saints, two of them popes, if Simplicius is the pope of that name (three in front, two on the fourth and sixth sides), alternating with the three uncrowned workmen in the manual labour of sculpture.

TWENTIETH CAPITAL. It is adorned with heads of animals, and is the finest of the whole series in the broad massiveness of its effect. In spite of the sternness of its plan, however, it is wrought with great care in surface detail; and the ornamental value of the minute chasing obtained by the delicate plumage of the birds, and the clustered bees on the honeycomb in the bear's mouth, opposed to the strong simplicity of its general form, cannot be too much admired. There are also more grace, life, and variety in the sprays of foliage on each side of it, and under the heads, than in any other capital of the series, though the earliness of the workmanship is marked by considerable hardness and coldness in the larger heads. A Northern Gothic workman, better acquainted with bears and wolves than it was possible to become in St. Mark's Place, would have put far more life into these heads, but he could not have composed them more skilfully.

First side. A lion with a stag's haunch in his mouth. Those readers who have the folio plate, should observe the peculiar way in which the ear is cut into the shape of a ring, jagged or furrowed on the edge; an archaic mode of treatment peculiar, in the Ducal Palace, to the lions' heads of the fourteenth century. The moment we reach the Renaissance work, the lions' ears are smooth. Inscribed simply, LEO.

Second side. A wolf with a dead bird in his mouth, its body wonderfully true in expression of the passiveness of death. The feathers are each wrought with a central quill and radiating filaments.

Third side. A fox, not at all like one, with a dead cock in his mouth, its comb and pendent neck admirably designed so as to fall across the great angle leaf of the capital, its tail hanging down on the other side, its long straight feathers exquisitely cut.

Fourth side. Entirely broken away.

Fifth side. APER. Well tusked, with a head of maize in his mouth; at least I suppose it to be maize, though shaped like a pine-cone.

Sixth side. CHANIS. With a bone, very ill cut; and a bald-headed species of dog, with ugly flap ears.

Seventh side. MUSCIPULUS. With a rat (?) in his mouth.

Eighth side. URSUS. With a honeycomb, covered with large bees.

TWENTY-FIRST CAPITAL. Represents the principal inferior professions.

First side. An old man, with his brow deeply wrinkled, and very expressive features, beating in a kind of mortar with a hammer.

Second side. I believe, a goldsmith; he is striking a small flat bowl or patera, on a pointed anvil, with a light hammer. The inscription is gone.

Third side. A shoemaker, with a shoe in his hand, and an instrument for cutting leather suspended beside him. Inscription undecipherable.

Fourth side. Much broken. A carpenter planing a beam resting on two horizontal logs.

Fifth side. A figure shovelling fruit into a tub; the latter very carefully carved from what appears to have been an excellent piece of cooperage. Two thin laths cross each other over the top of it.

Sixth side. A man, with a large hoe, breaking the ground, which lies in irregular furrows and clods before him.

Seventh side. A man, in a pendent cap, writing on a large scroll which falls over his knee. Inscribed NOTARIUS SUM.

Eighth side. A smith forging a sword or scythe-blade: he wears a large skull-cap; beats with a large hammer on a solid anvil.

TWENTY-SECOND CAPITAL. The Ages of Man; and the influence of the planets on human life.

First side. The moon, governing infancy for four years, according to Selvatico. I have no note of this side, having, I suppose, been prevented from raising the ladder against it by some fruit-stall or other impediment in the regular course of my examination; and then forgotten to return to it.

Second side. A child with a tablet, and an alphabet inscribed on it.

Third side. An older youth, with another tablet, but broken.

Selvatico misses this side altogether, as I did the first, so that the lost planet is irrecoverable, as the inscription is now defaced.

Fourth side. A youth with a hawk on his fist.

Fifth side. A man sitting, helmed, with a sword over his shoulder.

Sixth side. A very graceful and serene figure, in the pendent cap.

Seventh side. An old man in a skull-cap, praying.

Eighth side. The dead body lying on a mattress.

Shakespeare's Seven Ages are of course merely the expression of this early and well-known system. He has deprived the dotage of its devotion; but I think wisely, as the Italian system would imply that devotion was, or should be, always delayed until dotage.

TWENTY-THIRD CAPITAL. I agree with Selvatico in thinking this has been restored. It is decorated with large and vulgar heads.

TWENTY-FOURTH CAPITAL. This belongs to the large shaft which sustains the great party wall of the Sala del Gran Consiglio. The shaft is thicker than the rest; but the capital, though ancient, is coarse and somewhat inferior in design to the others of the series. It represents the history of marriage: the lover first seeing his mistress at a window, then addressing her, bringing her presents; then the bridal, the birth and the death of a child.

TWENTY-FIFTH CAPITAL. We have here the employments of the months, with which we are already tolerably acquainted. There are, however, one or two varieties worth noticing in this series.

First side. March. Sitting triumphantly in a rich dress, as the beginning of the year.

Second side. April and May. April with a lamb: May with a feather fan in her hand.

Third side. June. Carrying cherries in a basket.

I did not give this series with the others in the previous chapter, because this representation of June is peculiarly Venetian. It is called 'the month of cherries,' mese delle ceriese, in the popular rhyme on the conspiracy of Tiepolo.

Fourth side. July and August. The first reaping; the *leaves* of the straw being given, shooting out from the tubular stalk. August, opposite, beats (the grain?) in a basket.

Fifth side. September. A woman standing in a wine-tub, and holding a branch of vine. Very beautiful.

Sixth side. October and November. I could not make out their occupation; they seem to be roasting or boiling some root over a fire.

Seventh side. December. Killing pigs, as usual.

Eighth side. January warming his feet, and February frying fish. This last employment is again as characteristic of the Venetian winter as the cherries are of the Venetian summer.

This is the last of the capitals of the early palace; the next, or twenty-sixth capital, is the first of those executed in the fifteenth century under Foscari; and hence to the Judgment angle the traveller has nothing to do but to compare the base copies of the earlier work with their originals, or to observe the total want of invention in the Renaissance sculptor, wherever he has depended on his own resources. This, however, always with the exception of the twenty-seventh and of the last capital, which are both fine.

I shall merely enumerate the subjects and point out the plagiarisms of these capitals, as they are not worth description.

TWENTY-SIXTH CAPITAL. Copied from the fifteenth, merely changing the succession of the figures.

TWENTY-SEVENTH CAPITAL. I think it possible that this may be part of the old work displaced in joining the new palace with the old: at all events, it is well designed, though a little coarse. It represents eight different kinds of fruit, each in a basket; the characters well given, and groups well arranged, but without much care or finish.

TWENTY-EIGHTH CAPITAL. Copied from the seventh.

TWENTY-NINTH CAPITAL. Copied from the ninth.

THIRTIETH CAPITAL. Copied from the tenth. The 'Accidia' is noticeable as having the inscription complete; and the 'Luxuria' for its utter want of expression, having a severe and calm face, a robe up to the neck, and her hand upon her breast.

THIRTY-FIRST CAPITAL. Copied from the eighth.

THIRTY-SECOND CAPITAL. Has no inscription, only fully robed figures laying their hands, without any meaning, on their own shoulders, heads, or chins, or on the leaves around them.

THIRTY-THIRD CAPITAL. Copied from the twelfth.

THIRTY-FOURTH CAPITAL. Copied from the eleventh.

THIRTY-FIFTH CAPITAL. Has children, with birds or fruit, pretty in features, and utterly inexpressive, like the cherubs of the eighteenth century.

THIRTY-SIXTH CAPITAL. This is the last of the Piazzetta façade, the elaborate one under the Judgment angle. Its foliage is copied from the eighteenth at the opposite side, with an endeavour on the part of the Renaissance sculptor to refine upon it, by which he has merely lost some of its truth and force. This capital will, however, be always thought, at first, the most beautiful of the whole series: and indeed it is very noble; its groups of figures most carefully studied, very graceful, and much more pleasing than those of the earlier work, though with less real power in them; and its foliage is only inferior to that of the magnificent Fig-tree angle. It represents, on its front or first side, Justice enthroned, seated on two lions; and on the seven other sides examples of acts of justice or good government, or figures of lawgivers, in the following order:

Second side. Aristotle, with two pupils, giving laws.

Third side. I have mislaid my note of this side: Selvatico and Lazari call it 'Isidor'(?). Can they have mistaken the ISIPIONE of the fifth side for the word Isidore?

Fourth side. Solon with his pupils. One of the seated pupils in this sculpture is remarkably beautiful in the sweep of his flowing drapery.

Fifth side. The chastity of Scipio. A soldier in a plumed bonnet presents a kneeling maiden to the seated Scipio, who turns thoughtfully away.

Sixth side. Numa Pompilius building churches. Numa, in a kind of hat with a

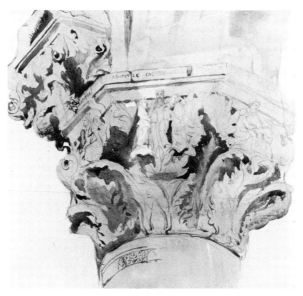

John Ruskin CAPITAL 36 OF THE DUCAL PALACE:
'very noble; its groups of figures most carefully studied, very graceful . . .'

crown above it, directing a soldier in Roman armour (note this, as contrasted with the mail of the earlier capitals). They point to a tower of three stories filled with tracery.

Seventh side. Moses receiving the law. Moses kneels on a rock, whence springs a beautifully fancied tree, with clusters of three berries in the centre of three leaves, sharp and quaint, like fine Northern Gothic. The half figure of the Deity comes out of the abacus, the arm meeting that of Moses, both at full stretch, with the stone tablets between.

Eighth side. Trajan doing justice to the Widow. He is riding spiritedly, his mantle blown out behind; the widow kneeling before his horse.

The reader will observe that this capital is of peculiar interest in its relation to the much disputed question of the character of the later government of Venice. It is the assertion by that government of its belief that Justice only could be the foundation of its stability, as these stones of Justice and Judgment are the foundation of its halls of council. And this profession of their faith may be interpreted in two ways. Most modern historians would call it, in common with the continual reference to the principles of justice in the political and judicial language of the period, nothing more than a cloak for consummate violence and guilt; and it may easily be proved to have been so in myriads of

200

instances. But in the main, I believe the expression of feeling to be genuine. I do not believe, of the majority of the leading Venetians of this period whose portraits have come down to us, that they were deliberately and everlastingly hypocrites. I see no hypocrisy in their countenances. Much capacity of it, much subtlety, much natural and acquired reserve; but no meanness. On the contrary, infinite grandeur, repose, courage, and the peculiar unity and tranquillity of expression which come of sincerity or *wholeness* of heart, and which it would take much demonstration to make me believe could by any possibility be seen on the countenance of an insincere man. I trust, therefore, that these Venetian nobles of the fifteenth century did, in the main, desire to do judgment and justice to all men; but, as the whole system of morality had been by this time undermined by the teaching of the Romish Church, the idea of justice had become separated from that of truth, so that dissimulation in the interest of the state assumed the aspect of duty. We had, perhaps, better consider, with some carefulness, the mode in which our own government is carried on, and the occasional difference between parliamentary and private morality, before we judge mercilessly of the Venetians in this respect. The secrecy with which their political and criminal trials were conducted, appears to modern eyes like a confession of sinister intentions; but may it not also be considered, and with more probability, as the result of an endeavour to do justice in an age of violence?—the only means by which Law could establish its footing in the midst of feudalism. Might not Irish juries at this day justifiably desire to conduct their proceedings with some greater approximation to the judicial principles of the Council of Ten? Finally, if we examine, with critical accuracy, the evidence on which our present impressions of Venetian government are founded, we shall discover, in the first place, that two-thirds of the traditions of its cruelties are romantic fables: in the second, that the crimes of which it can be proved to have been guilty differ only from those committed by the other Italian powers in being done less wantonly, and under profounder conviction of their political expediency: and lastly, that the final degradation of the Venetian power appears owing not so much to the principles of its government, as to their being forgotten in the pursuit of pleasure.

We have now examined the portions of the palace which contain the principal evidence of the feeling of its builders. The capitals of the upper arcade are exceedingly various in their character; their design is formed, as in the lower series, of eight leaves, thrown into volutes at the angles, and sustaining figures at the flanks; but these figures have no inscriptions, and though evidently not without meaning, cannot be interpreted without more knowledge than I possess of ancient symbolism. Many of the capitals towards the Sea appear to have been restored, and to be rude copies of the ancient ones; others, though apparently original, have been somewhat carelessly wrought; but those of them which are both genuine and carefully treated are even finer in composition than any, except the eighteenth, in the lower arcade. The traveller in Venice ought to ascend into the corridor, and examine with great care the series of capitals which extend on the Piazzetta side from the Fig-tree angle to the pilaster which carries the party wall of the Sala del Gran Consiglio. As examples of graceful composition in massy capitals meant for hard service and distant effect, these are among the finest things I know in

Gothic art; and that above the fig-tree is remarkable for its sculptures of the four winds; each on the side turned towards the wind represented. Levante, the east wind; a figure with rays round its head, to show that it is always clear weather when that wind blows, raising the sun out of the sea: Hotro, the south wind; crowned, holding the sun in its right hand: Ponente, the west wind; plunging the sun into the sea: and Tramontana, the north wind; looking up at the north star. I may also especially point out the bird feeding its three young ones on the seventh pillar on the Piazzetta side; but there is no end to the fantasy of these sculptures; and the traveller ought to observe them all carefully, until he comes to the great pilaster or complicated pier which sustains the party wall of the Sala del Consiglio; that is to say, the forty-seventh capital of the whole series, counting from the pilaster of the Vine angle inclusive, as in the series of the lower arcade. The forty-eighth, forty-ninth, and fiftieth are bad work, but they are old; the fifty-first is the first Renaissance capital of the upper arcade; the first new lion's head with smooth ears, cut in the time of Foscari, is over the fiftieth capital; and that capital, with its shaft, stands on the apex of the eighth arch from the Sea, on the Piazzetta side, of which one spandril is masonry of the fourteenth and the other of the fifteenth century.

The reader who is not able to examine the building on the spot may be surprised at the definiteness with which the point of junction is ascertainable; but a glance at the lowest range of leaves on page 191 will enable him to judge of the grounds on which the above statement is made. Fig. 12 is a cluster of leaves from the capital of the Four Winds; early work of the finest time. Fig. 13 is a leaf from the great Renaissance capital at the Judgment angle, worked in imitation of the older leafage. Fig. 14 is a leaf from one of the Renaissance capitals of the upper arcade, which are all worked in the natural manner of the period. It will be seen that it requires no great ingenuity to distinguish between such design as that of fig. 12 and that of fig. 14.

It is very possible that the reader may at first like fig. 14 the best. I shall endeavour, in the next chapter, to show why he should not; but it must also be noted, that fig. 12 has lost, and fig. 14 gained, both largely, under the hands of the engraver. All the bluntness and coarseness of feeling in the workmanship of fig. 14 have disappeared on this small scale, and all the subtle refinements in the broad masses of fig. 12 have vanished.

This early sculpture of the Ducal Palace, then, represents the state of Gothic work in Venice at its central and proudest period, *i.e.* circa 1350.

And as, under the shadow of these nodding leaves, we bid farewell to the great Gothic spirit, here also we may cease our examination of the details of the Ducal Palace; for above its upper arcade there are only the four traceried windows, and one or two of the third order on the Rio Façade, which can be depended upon as exhibiting the original workmanship of the older palace. I examined the capitals of the four other windows of the façade, and of those on the Piazzetta, one by one, with great care, and I found them all to be of far inferior workmanship to those which retain their traceries: I believe the stone framework of these windows must have been so cracked and injured by the flames of the great fire, as to render it necessary to replace it by new traceries: and that the present mouldings and capitals are base imitations of the original ones. The traceries were at first, however, restored in their complete form, as the holes for the bolts which fastened the bases of their shafts are still to be seen in the window-sills, as well as the marks of the inner mouldings on the soffits. How much the stone facing of the façade, the parapets, and the shafts and niches of the angles retain of their original masonry, it is also impossible to determine; but there is nothing in the workmanship of any of them demanding

John Ruskin EXTERIOR OF THE DUCAL PALACE

especial notice; still less in the large central windows on each façade which are entirely of Renaissance execution. All that is admirable in these portions of the building is the disposition of their various parts and masses, which is without doubt the same as in the original fabric, and calculated, when seen from a distance, to produce the same impression.

Not so in the interior. All vestige of the earlier modes of decoration was here, of course, destroyed by the fires; and the severe and religious work of Guariento and Bellini has been replaced by the wildness of Tintoret and the luxury of Veronese. But in this case, though widely different in temper, the art of the renewal was at least intellectually as great as that which had perished; and though the halls of the Ducal Palace are no more representative of the character of the men by whom it was built, each of them is still a colossal casket of priceless treasure. So precious, indeed, and so full of majesty, that sometimes when walking at evening on the Lido, whence the great chain of the Alps, crested with silver clouds, might be seen rising above the front of the Ducal Palace, I used to feel as much awe in gazing on the building as on the hills, and could believe that God had done a greater work in breathing into the narrowness of dust the mighty spirits by whom its haughty walls had been raised, and its burning legends written, than in lifting the rocks of granite higher than the clouds of heaven, and veiling them with their various mantle of purple flower and shadowy pine.

EARLY RENAISSANCE

I TRUST that the reader has been enabled, by the preceding chapters, to form some conception of the magnificence of the streets of Venice during the course of the thirteenth and fourteenth centuries. Yet by all this magnificence she was not supremely distinguished above the other cities of the middle ages. Her early edifices have been preserved to our times by the circuit of her waves; while continual recurrences of ruin have defaced the glory of her sister cities. I am not aware of any town of wealth and importance in the middle ages, in which some proof does not exist that, at its period of greatest energy and prosperity, its streets were inwrought with rich sculpture, and even (though in this, as before noticed, Venice always stood supreme) glowing with colour and with gold. Now, therefore, let the reader,—forming for himself as vivid and real a conception as he is able, either of a group of Venetian palaces in the fourteenth century, or, if he likes better, of one of the more fantastic but even richer street scenes of Rouen, Antwerp, Cologne, or Nuremberg, and keeping this gorgeous image before him,—go out into any thoroughfare representative, in a general and characteristic way, of the feeling for domestic architecture in modern times: let him, for instance, if in London, walk once up and down Harley Street or Gower Street; and then, looking upon this picture and on this, set himself to consider what have been the causes which have induced so vast a change in the European mind.

Renaissance architecture is the school which has conducted men's inventive and constructive faculties from the Grand Canal to Gower Street; from the marble shaft, and the lancet arch, and the wreathed leafage, and the glowing and melting harmony of gold and azure, to the square cavity in the brick wall. We have now to consider the causes and the steps of this change; and, as we endeavoured above to investigate the nature of Gothic, here to investigate also the nature of Renaissance.

Although Renaissance architecture assumes very different forms among different nations, it may be conveniently referred to three heads:—Early Renaissance, consisting of the first corruptions introduced into the Gothic schools: Central or Roman Renaissance, which is the perfectly formed style; and Grotesque Renaissance, which is the corruption of the Renaissance itself.

The manner of the debasement of all schools of art is in all ages the same; luxuriance of ornament, refinement of execution, and idle subtleties of fancy, taking the place of true thought and firm handling: and I do not intend to delay the reader long by the Gothic sick-bed. Nevertheless, it is necessary to the completeness of our view of the architecture of Venice, as well as to our understanding of the manner in which the Central Renaissance obtained its universal dominion, that we glance briefly at the principal forms into which Venetian Gothic first declined. They are two: one the corruption of the Gothic itself; the other a partial return to Byzantine forms: for the Venetian mind having carried the Gothic to a point at which it was dissatisfied, tried to retrace its steps, fell back first upon Byzantine types, and through them passed to the first Roman. But in thus retracing its steps, it does not recover its own lost energy.

The two principal causes of natural decline in any school are over-luxuriance and over-refinement. The corrupt Gothic of Venice furnishes us with a curious instance of the one, and the corrupt Byzantine of the other. We shall examine them in succession.

Now, observe, first, I do not mean by *luxuriance* of ornament *quantity* of ornament. In the best Gothic in the world there is hardly an inch of stone left unsculptured. But I mean that character of extravagance in the ornament itself which shows that it was addressed to jaded faculties; a violence and coarseness in curvature, a depth of shadow, a lusciousness in arrangement of line, evidently arising out of an incapability of feeling the true beauty of chaste form and restrained power. I do not know any character of design which may be more easily recognised at a glance than this over-lusciousness; and yet it seems to me that at the present day there is nothing so little understood as the essential difference between chasteness and extravagance, whether in colour, shade, or lines.

In a word, then, the safeguard of highest beauty, in all visible work, is exactly that which is also the safeguard of conduct in the soul, – Temperance, in the broadest sense; the Temperance which we have seen sitting on an equal throne with Justice amidst the Four Cardinal virtues, and, wanting which, there is not any other virtue which may not lead us into desperate error.

In curvature, which is the cause of loveliness in all form, the bad designer does not enjoy it more than the great designer, but he indulges in it till his eye is satiated, and he cannot obtain enough of it to touch his jaded feeling for grace. But the great and temperate designer does not allow himself any violent curves; he works much with lines in which the curvature, though always existing, is long before it is perceived. He dwells on all these subdued curvatures to the uttermost, and opposes them with still severer lines to bring them out in fuller sweetness; and, at last, he allows himself a momentary curve of energy, and all the work is, in an instant, full of life and grace.

Fig. 1, on page 207, is a piece of ornamentation from a Norman-French manuscript of the thirteenth century, and fig. 2 from an Italian one of the fifteenth. Observe in the first its stern moderation in curvature; the gradually united lines *nearly straight*, though none quite straight, used for its main limb, and contrasted with the bold but simple offshoots of its leaves, and the noble spiral from which it shoots, these in their turn opposed by the sharp trefoils and thorny cusps. And see what a reserve of resource there is in the whole; how easy it would have been to make the curves more palpable and the foliage more rich, and how the noble hand has stayed itself, and refused to grant one wave of motion more.

Then observe the other example, in which, while the same idea is continually repeated, excitement and interest are sought for by means of violent and continual curvatures wholly unrestrained, and rolling hither and thither in confused wantonness. Compare the character of the separate lines in these two examples carefully, and be assured that wherever this redundant and luxurious curvature shows itself in ornamentation, it is a sign of jaded energy and failing invention. Do not confuse it with fulness or richness. Wealth is not necessarily wantonness: a Gothic moulding may be buried half a foot deep in thorns and leaves, and yet will be chaste in every line; and a late Renaissance moulding may be utterly barren and poverty-stricken, and yet will show the disposition to luxury in every line.

Page 191, though prepared for the special illustration of the notices of capitals, becomes peculiarly interesting when considered in relation to the points at present under consideration. The four leaves in the upper row are Byzantine; the two middle rows are transitional, all but fig. 11 which is of the formed Gothic; fig. 12 is perfect Gothic of the finest time (Ducal Palace, oldest part); fig. 13 is Gothic beginning to decline; fig. 14 is Renaissance Gothic in complete corruption.

Now observe, first, the Gothic naturalism advancing gradually from the Byzantine severity; how from the sharp, hard, formalised conventionality of the upper series the leaves gradually expand into more free and flexible animation, until in fig. 12 we have the perfect living leaf as if just fresh gathered out of the dew. And then, in the last two examples, and partly in fig. 11, observe how the forms which can advance no longer in animation, advance, or rather decline, into luxury and effeminacy as the strength of the school expires.

Finally, observe—and this is very important—how one and the same character in the work may be a sign of totally different states of mind, and therefore in one case bad, and in the other good. The examples, fig. 3 and fig. 12, are both equally pure in line; but one is subdivided in the extreme, the other broad in the extreme, and both are beautiful. The Byzantine mind delighted in the delicacy of subdivision which nature shows in the fern-leaf or parsley-leaf; and so, also, often the Gothic mind, much enjoying the oak, thorn, and thistle. But the builder of the Ducal Palace used great breadth in his foliage, in order to harmonise with the broad surface of his mighty wall, and delighted in this breadth as nature delights in the sweeping freshness of the dock-leaf or water-lily. Both breadth and subdivision are thus noble, when they are contemplated or conceived by a mind in health; and both become ignoble, when conceived by a mind jaded and satiated. The subdivision in fig. 13, as compared with the type, fig. 12, which it was intended to improve, is the sign, not of a mind which loved intricacy, but of one which could not relish simplicity, which had not strength enough to enjoy the broad masses of the earlier leaves, and cut them to pieces idly, like a child tearing the book which, in its weariness, it cannot read. And on the other hand, we shall continually

Temperance and Intemperance in Curvature.

find, in other examples of work of the same period, an unwholesome breadth or heaviness, which results from the mind having no longer any care for refinement or precision, nor taking any delight in delicate forms, but making all things blunted, cumbrous, and dead, losing at the same time the sense of the elasticity and spring of natural curves. It is as if the soul of man, itself severed from the root of its health, and about to fall into corruption, lost the perception of life in all things around it; and could no more distinguish the wave of the strong branches, full of muscular strength and sanguine circulation, from the lax bending of a broken cord, nor the sinuousness of the edge of the leaf, crushed into deep folds by the expansion of its living growth, from the wrinkled contraction of its decay. Thus, in morals, there is a care for trifles which proceeds from love and conscience, and is most holy; and a care for trifles which comes of idleness and frivolity, and is most base.

The date at which this corrupt form of Gothic first prevailed over the early simplicity of the Venetian types can be determined in an instant on the steps of the choir of the Church of St. John and Paul. On our left hand, as we enter, is the tomb of the Doge Marco Cornaro, who died in 1367. It is rich and fully developed Gothic, with crockets and finials, but not yet attaining any extravagant development. Opposite to it is that of the Doge Andrea Morosini, who died in 1382. Its Gothic is voluptuous, and overwrought: the crockets are bold and florid, and the enormous finial represents a statue of St. Michael. There is no excuse for the antiquaries who, having this tomb before them, could have attributed the severe architecture of the Ducal Palace to a later date; for every one of the Renaissance errors is here in complete development, though not so grossly as entirely to destroy the loveliness of the Gothic forms. In the Porta della Carta, 1423, the vice reaches its climax.

Against this degraded Gothic, then, came up the Renaissance armies; and their first assault was in the requirement of universal perfection. For the first time since the destruction of Rome, the world had seen, in the work of the greatest artists of the fifteenth century,—in the painting of Ghirlandajo, Masaccio, Francia, Perugino, Pinturicchio, and Bellini; in the sculpture of Mino da Fiesole, of Ghiberti, and Verrocchio,—a perfection of execution and fulness of knowledge which cast all previous art into the shade, and which, being in the work of those men united with all that was great in that of former days, did indeed justify the utmost enthusiasm with which their efforts were, or could be, regarded. But when this perfection had once been exhibited in anything, it was required in everything; the world could no longer be satisfied with less exquisite execution, or less disciplined knowledge. The first thing that it demanded in all work was, that it should be done in a consummate and learned way; and men altogether forgot that it was possible to consummate what was contemptible, and to know what was useless. Imperatively requiring dexterity of touch, they gradually forgot to look for tenderness of feeling; imperatively requiring accuracy of knowledge, they gradually forgot to ask for originality of thought. The thought and the feeling which they despised departed from them, and they were left to felicitate themselves on their small science and their neat fingering. This is the history of the first attack of the Renaissance upon the Gothic schools, and of its rapid results; more fatal and immediate in architecture than in any other art, because there the demand for perfection was less reasonable, and less consistent with the capabilities of the workman; being utterly opposed to that rudeness or savageness on which, as we saw above, the nobility of the elder schools in great part depends. But, inasmuch as the innovations were founded on some of the most beautiful examples of art, and headed by some of the greatest men that the world ever saw, and as the Gothic with which they interfered was corrupt and valueless, the first appearance of the Renaissance feeling had the appearance of a healthy movement. A new energy replaced whatever weariness or dulness had affected the Gothic mind; an exquisite taste and refinement, aided by extended knowledge, furnished the first models of the new school; and over the whole of Italy a style arose, generally now known as cinque-cento, which in sculpture and painting, as I just stated, produced the noblest masters whom the world ever saw, headed by Michael Angelo, Raphael, and Leonardo; but which failed of doing the same in architecture, because, as we have seen above, perfection is therein not possible, and failed more totally than it would otherwise have done, because the classical enthusiasm had destroyed the best types of architectural form.

I hope enough has been advanced, in the chapter on the Nature of Gothic, to show the reader that perfection is *not* to be had from the general workman, but at the cost of everything, – of his whole life, thought, and energy. And Renaissance Europe thought this a small price to pay for manipulative perfection. Men like Verrocchio and Ghiberti were not to be had every day, nor in every place; and to require from the common workman execution or knowledge like theirs, was to require him to become their copyist. Their strength was great enough to enable them to join science with invention, method with emotion, finish with fire; but in them the invention and the fire were first, while Europe saw in them only the method and the finish. This was new to the minds of men, and they pursued it to the neglect of everything else. 'This,' they cried, 'we must have in all our work henceforward': and they were obeyed. The lower workman secured method and finish, and lost, in exchange for them, his soul.

Now, therefore, do not let me be misunderstood when I speak generally of the evil spirit of the Renaissance. The reader may look through all I have written, from first to last, and he will not find one word but of the most profound reverence for those mighty men who could wear the Renaissance armour of proof, and yet not feel it encumber their living limbs, – Leonardo and Michael Angelo, Ghirlandajo and Masaccio, Titian and Tintoret. But I speak of the Renaissance as an evil time, because, when it saw those men go burning forth into the battle, it mistook their armour for their strength; and forthwith encumbered with the painful panoply every stripling who ought to have gone forth only with his own choice of three smooth stones out of the brook.

So soon as the classical enthusiasm required the banishment of Gothic forms, it was natural that the Venetian mind should turn back with affection to the Byzantine models in which the round arches and simple shafts, necessitated by recent law, were presented under a form consecrated by the usage of their ancestors. And, accordingly, the first distinct school of architecture which arose under the new dynasty was one in which the method of inlaying marble, and the general forms of shaft and arch, were adopted from the buildings of the twelfth century, and applied with the utmost possible refinements of modern skill. Both at Verona and Venice the resulting architecture is exceedingly beautiful. At Venice it is severe, but yet adorned with sculpture which, for sharpness of touch and delicacy of minute form, cannot be rivalled, and rendered especially brilliant and beautiful by the introduction of those inlaid circles of coloured marble, serpentine, and porphyry, by which Phillippe de Commynes was so much struck on his first entrance into the city. The two most refined buildings in this style in Venice are, the small Church of the Miracoli, and the Scuola di San Marco beside the Church of St. John and St. Paul. The noblest is the Rio Façade of the Ducal Palace. The Casa Dario, and Casa Manzoni, on the Grand Canal, are exquisite examples of the school, as applied to domestic architecture; and, in the reach of the Canal between the Casa Foscari and the Rialto, there are several palaces, of which the Casa Contarini (called 'delle Figure') is the principal, belonging to the same group, though somewhat later, and remarkable for the association of the Byzantine principles of colour with the severest lines of the Roman pediment, gradually superseding the round arch. The precision of chiselling and delicacy of proportion in the ornament and general lines of these palaces cannot be too highly praised; and I believe that the traveller in Venice, in general, gives them rather too little attention than too much. But while I would ask him to stay his gondola beside each of them long enough to examine their every line, I must also warn him to observe most carefully the peculiar feebleness and want of soul in the conception of their ornament, which mark them as belonging to a period of decline; as well as the absurd mode of introduction of their pieces of coloured marble; these, instead of being simply and naturally inserted in the masonry, are placed in small circular or oblong frames of sculpture, like mirrors or pictures, and are represented as suspended by ribands against the wall; a pair of wings being generally fastened on to the circular tablets, as if to relieve the ribands and knots from their weight, and the whole series tied under the chin of a little cherub at the top, who is nailed against the façade like a hawk on a barn door.

But chiefly let him notice, in the Casa Contarini delle Figure, one most strange incident, seeming to have been permitted, like the choice of the subjects at the three angles of the Ducal Palace, in order to teach us, by a single lesson, the true nature of the style in which it occurs. In the intervals of the windows of the first story, certain shields and torches are attached, in the form of trophies, to the stems of two trees whose boughs have been cut off, and only one or two of their faded leaves left, scarcely observable, but delicately sculptured here and there, beneath the insertions of the severed boughs. It is as if the workman had intended to leave us an image of the expiring naturalism of the Gothic school.

It was above stated, that the principal difference in general form and treatment between the Byzantine and Gothic palaces was the contraction of the marble facing into the narrow spaces between the windows, leaving large fields of brick wall perfectly bare. The reason for this appears to have been, that the Gothic builders were no longer satisfied with the faint and delicate hues of the veined marble; they wished for some more forcible and piquant mode of decoration, corresponding more completely with the gradually advancing splendour of chivalric costume and heraldic device. What I have said of the simple habits of life of the thirteenth century, in nowise refers either to costumes of state or of military service; and any illumination of the thirteenth and early fourteenth centuries (the great period being, it seems to me, from 1250 to 1350), while it shows a peculiar majesty and simplicity in the fall of the robes (often worn over the chain armour), indicates, at the same time, an exquisite brilliancy of colour and power of design in the hems and borders, as well as in the armorial bearings with which they are charged; and while, as we have seen, a peculiar simplicity is found also in the *forms* of the architecture, corresponding to that of the folds of the robes, its *colours* were constantly increasing in brilliancy and decision, corresponding to those of the quartering of the shield, and of the embroidery of the mantle.

Whether, indeed, derived from the quarterings of the knights' shields, or from what other source, I know not; but there is one magnificent attribute of the colouring of the late twelfth, the whole thirteenth, and the early fourteenth century, which I do not find definitely in any previous work, nor afterwards in general art, though constantly, and necessarily, in that of great colourists, namely, the union of one colour with another by reciprocal interference: that is to say, if a mass of red is to be set beside a mass of blue, a piece of the red will be carried into the blue, and a piece of the blue carried into the red; sometimes in nearly equal portions, as in a shield divided into four quarters, of which the uppermost on one side will be of the same colour as the lowermost on the other; sometimes in smaller fragments, but, in the periods above named, always definitely and grandly, though in a thousand various ways. And I call it a magnificent principle, for it is an eternal and universal one, not in art only, but in human life. It is the great principle of Brotherhood, not by equality, nor by likeness, but by giving and receiving; the souls that are unlike, and the nations that are unlike, and the natures that are unlike, being bound into one noble whole by each receiving something from and of the others' gifts and the others' glory. I have not space to follow out this thought,—it is of infinite extent and application,—but I note it for the reader's pursuit, because I have long believed that in whatever has been made by the Deity externally delightful to the human sense of beauty, there is some type of God's nature or of God's laws; nor are any of His laws, in one sense, greater than the appointment that the most lovely and perfect unity shall be obtained by the taking of one nature into another. I trespass upon too high ground; and yet I cannot fully show the reader the extent of this law, but by leading him thus far.

It is perfectly inconceivable, until it has been made a subject of special inquiry, how perpetually Nature employs this principle in the distribution of her light and shade; how by the most extraordinary adaptations, apparently accidental, but always in exactly the right place, she contrives to bring darkness into light, and light into darkness; and that so sharply and decisively, that at the very instant when one object changes from light to dark, the thing

Overleaf: Gentile Bellini THE MIRACLE OF THE CROSS
'Happily, in the pictures of Gentile Bellini, the fresco colouring of the
Gothic Palaces is recorded ... a field of subdued russet quartered with broad
sculptured masses of white and gold.'

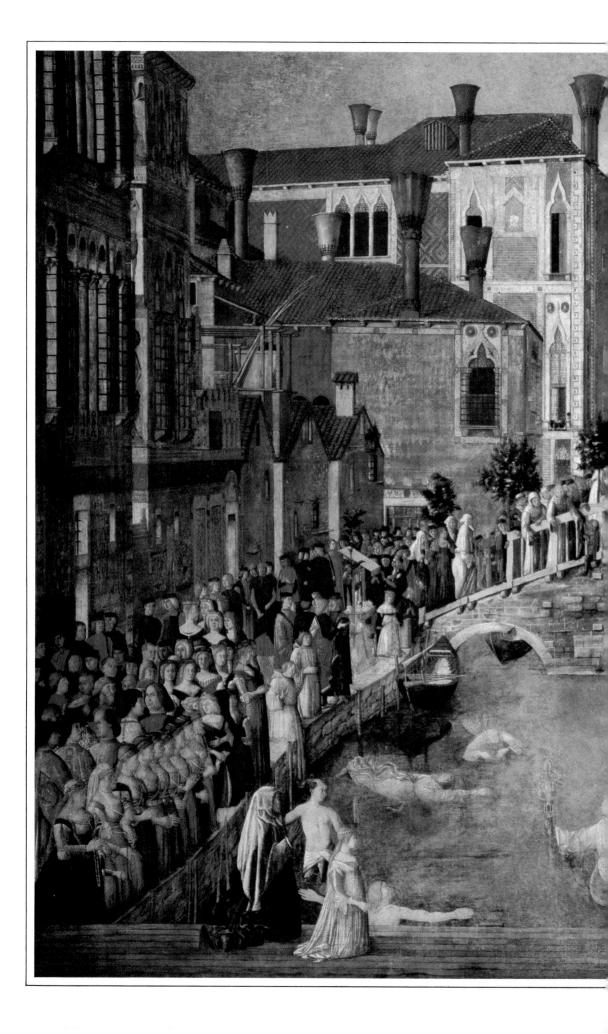

relieved upon it will change from dark to light, and yet so subtly that the eye will not detect the transition till it looks for it. The secret of a great part of the grandeur in all the noblest compositions is the doing of this delicately in *degree*, and broadly in *mass*; in colour it may be done much more decisively than in light and shade, and, according to the simplicity of the work, with greater frankness of confession, until, in purely decorative art, as in the illumination and heraldry of the great periods, we find it reduced to segmental accuracy. Its greatest masters, in high art, are Tintoret, Veronese, and Turner.

Together with this great principle of quartering is introduced another, also of very high value as far as regards the delight of the eye, though not of so profound meaning. As soon as colour began to be used in broad and opposed fields, it was perceived that the mass of it destroyed its brilliancy, and it was *tempered* by chequering it with some other colour or colours in smaller quantities, mingled with minute portions of pure white. The two moral principles of which this is the type are those of Temperance and Purity; the one requiring the fulness of the colour to be subdued, and the other that it shall be subdued without losing either its own purity or that of the colours with which it is associated.

Hence arose the universal and admirable system of the diapered or chequered backgrounds of early ornamental art. They are completely developed in the thirteenth century, and extend through the whole of the fourteenth, gradually yielding to landscape and other pictorial backgrounds, as the designers lost perception of the purpose of their art, and of the value of colour. The chromatic decoration of the Gothic palaces of Venice was of course founded on these two great principles, which prevailed constantly wherever the true chivalric and Gothic spirit possessed any influence. The windows, with their intermediate spaces of marble, were considered as the objects to be relieved, and variously quartered with vigorous colour. The whole space of the brick wall was considered as a background; it was covered with stucco, and painted in fresco, with diaper patterns.

I am not sure if I am right in applying the term 'stucco' to the ground of fresco; but this is of no consequence: the reader will understand that it was white, and that the whole wall of the palace was considered as the page of a book to be illuminated: but he will understand also that the sea winds are bad librarians; that, when once the painted stucco began to fade or to fall, the unsightliness of the defaced colour would necessitate its immediate restoration; and that therefore, of all the chromatic decoration of the Gothic palaces, there is hardly a fragment left.

Happily, in the pictures of Gentile Bellini, the fresco colouring of the Gothic palaces is recorded, as it still remained in his time; not with rigid accuracy, but quite distinctly enough to enable us, by comparing it with the existing coloured designs in the manuscripts and glass of the period, to ascertain precisely what it must have been.

The walls were generally covered with chequers of very warm colour, a russet inclining to scarlet more or less relieved with white, black, and grey; as still seen in the only example which, having been executed in marble, has been perfectly preserved, the front of the Ducal Palace. This, however, owing to the nature of its materials, was a peculiarly simple example; the ground is white, crossed with double bars of pale red, and in the centre of each chequer there is a cross, alternately black with a red centre and red with a black centre where the arms cross. In painted work the grounds would be, of course, as varied and complicated as those of manuscripts.

On these russet or crimson backgrounds the entire space of the series of windows was relieved, for the most part as a subdued white field of alabaster; and on this delicate and veined white were set the circular disks of purple and green. The arms of the family were of course blazoned in their own proper colours, but I think generally on a pure azure ground; the blue colour is still left behind the shields in the Casa Priuli and one or two more of the palaces which are unrestored, and the blue ground was used also to relieve the sculptures of religious subjects. Finally, all the mouldings, capitals, cornices, cusps, and traceries, were either entirely gilded or profusely touched with gold.

The whole front of a Gothic palace in Venice may, therefore, be simply described as a field of subdued russet, quartered with broad sculptured masses of white and gold; these latter being relieved by smaller inlaid fragments of blue, purple, and deep green.

Before leaving these last palaces over which the Byzantine influence extended itself, there is one more lesson to be learned from them of much importance to us. Though in many respects debased in style, they are consummate in workmanship, and unstained in honour; there is no imperfection in them, and no dishonesty. That there is absolutely *no* imperfection, is indeed, as we have seen above, a proof of their being wanting in the highest qualities of architecture; but, as lessons in masonry, they have their value, and may well be studied for the excellence they display in methods of levelling stones, for the precision of their inlaying, and other such qualities, which in them are indeed too principal, yet very instructive in their particular way.

The Rio Façade of the Ducal Palace, though very sparing in colour, is yet, as an example of finished masonry in a vast building, one of the finest things, not only in Venice, but in the world. It differs from other work of the Byzantine Renaissance, in being on a very large scale; and it still retains one pure Gothic character, which adds not a little to its nobleness, that of perpetual variety. There is hardly one window of it, or one panel, that is like another; and this continual change so increases its apparent size by confusing the eye, that, though presenting no bold features, or striking masses of any kind, there are few things in Italy more impressive than the vision of it overhead, as the gondola glides from beneath the Bridge of Sighs. And lastly (unless we are to blame these buildings for some pieces of very childish perspective) they are magnificently honest, as well as perfect.

ROMAN RENAISSANCE

O F all the buildings in Venice, later in date than the final additions to the Ducal Palace, the noblest is, beyond all question, the Casa Grimani. It is composed of three stories of the Corinthian order, at once simple, delicate, and sublime; but on so colossal a scale, that the three-storied palaces on its right and left only reach to the cornice which marks the level of its first floor. There is not an erring line, nor a mistaken proportion, throughout its noble front; and the exceeding fineness of the chiselling gives an appearance of lightness to the vast blocks of stone out of whose perfect union that front is composed. The decoration is sparing, but delicate: the first story only simpler than the rest, in that it has pilasters instead of shafts, but all with Corinthian capitals, rich in leafage, and fluted delicately; the rest of the walls flat and smooth, and their mouldings sharp and shallow, so that the shafts look like crystals of beryl running through a rock of quartz.

This palace is the principal type at Venice, and one of the best in Europe, of the central architecture of the Renaissance schools; that carefully studied and perfectly executed architecture to which those schools owe their principal claims to our respect, and which became the model of most of the important works subsequently produced by civilised nations. I have called it the Roman Renaissance, because it is founded, both in its principles of superimposition, and in the style of its ornament, upon the architecture of classic Rome at its best period.

It is this style, in its purity and fullest form, – represented by such buildings as the Town Hall at Vicenza (by Palladio), St. Peter's at Rome (by Michael Angelo), St. Paul's and Whitehall in London (by Wren and Inigo Jones) — which is the true antagonist of the Gothic school. The intermediate, or corrupt conditions of it, though multiplied over Europe, are no longer admired by architects, or made the subjects of their study; but the finished work of this central school is still, in most cases, the model set before the student of the nineteenth century, as opposed to those Gothic, Romanesque, or Byzantine

Casa Grimani: '*Of all the buildings in Venice, later in date than the final additions to the Ducal Palace, the noblest is beyond all question, the Casa Grimani.*'

forms which have long been considered barbarous, and are so still by most of the leading men of the day. That they are, on the contrary, most noble and beautiful, and that the antagonistic Renaissance is, in the main, unworthy and unadmirable, whatever perfection of a certain kind it may possess, it was my principal purpose to show, when first I undertook the labour of this work. It has been attempted already to put before the reader the various elements which unite in the Nature of Gothic, and to enable him thus to judge, not merely of the beauty of the forms which that system has produced already, but of its future applicability to the wants of mankind, and endless power over their hearts. I would now endeavour, in like manner, to set before the reader the Nature of Renaissance, and thus to enable him to compare the two styles under the same light, and with the same enlarged view of their relations to the intellect, and capacities for the service, of man.

It will not be necessary for me to enter at length into any examination of its external form. It uses, whether for its roofs of aperture or roofs proper, the low gable or circular arch: but it differs from Romanesque work in attaching great importance to the horizontal lintel or architrave *above* the arch; transferring the energy of the principal shafts to the supporting of this horizontal beam, and thus rendering the arch a subordinate, if not altogether a superfluous, feature. But it is not the form of this architecture against which I would plead. Its defects are shared by many of the noblest forms of earlier building, and might have been entirely atoned for by excellence of spirit. But it is the moral nature of it which is corrupt, and which it must, therefore, be our principal business to examine and expose.

The moral, or immoral, elements which unite to form the spirit of Central Renaissance architecture are, I believe, in the main, two—Pride and Infidelity; but the pride resolves itself into three main branches—Pride of Science, Pride of State, and Pride of System: and thus we have four separate mental conditions which must be examined successively.

PRIDE OF SCIENCE. It would have been more charitable, but more confusing, to have added another element to our list, namely the *Love* of Science. But, whether pursued in pride or in affection, the first notable characteristic of the Renaissance central school is its introduction of accurate knowledge into all its work, so far as it possesses such knowledge; and its evident conviction that such science is necessary to the excellence of the work, and is the first thing to be expressed therein.

The whole function of the artist in the world is to be a seeing and feeling creature; to be an instrument of such tenderness and sensitiveness, that no shadow, no hue, no line, no instantaneous and evanescent expression of the visible things around him, nor any of the emotions which they are capable of conveying to the spirit which has been given him, shall either be left unrecorded, or fade from the book of record. It is not his business either to think, to judge, to argue, or to know. His place is neither in the closet, nor on the bench, nor at the bar, nor in the library. They are for other men, and other work. He may think, in a by-way; reason, now and then, when he has nothing better to do; know, such fragments of knowledge as he can gather without stooping, or reach without pains; but none of these things are to be his care. The work of his life is to be two-fold only; to see, to feel.

No science of perspective, or of anything else, will enable us to draw the simplest natural line accurately, unless we see it and feel it. Science is soon at her wits' end. All the professors of perspective in Europe could not, by perspective, draw the line of curve of a sea-beach; nay, could not outline one pool of the quiet water left among the sand. The eye and hand can do it, nothing else.

The other day I showed a fine impression of Albert Durer's 'St. Hubert' to a modern engraver, who had never seen it nor any other of Albert Durer's works. He looked at it for a minute contemptuously, then turned away: 'Ah, I see that man did not know much about aerial perspective!' All the glorious work and thought of the mighty master, all the redundant landscape, the living vegetation, the magnificent truth of line, were dead letters to him, because he happened to have been taught one particular piece of knowledge which Durer despised.

If there is any one lesson in the book which stands forth more definitely than another, it is of the holy and humbling influence of natural science on the human heart. And yet, even here, it is not the science, but the perception, to which the good is owing; and the natural sciences may become as harmful as any others, when they lose themselves in classification and catalogue-making. Still, the principal danger is with the sciences of words and methods; and it was exactly into those sciences that the whole energy of men during the Renaissance period was thrown. The sciences ceased at once to be anything more than different kinds of grammars,–grammar of language, grammar of logic, grammar of ethics, grammar of art; and the tongue, wit, and invention of the human race were supposed to have found their utmost and most divine mission in syntax and syllogism, perspective and five orders.

Of such knowledge as this, nothing but pride could come; and, therefore, I have called the first mental characteristic of the Renaissance schools the 'pride' of science. It was enough, of itself, to have cast it into swift decline: but it was aided by another form of pride, which was above called the Pride of State; and which we have next to examine.

PRIDE OF STATE. It is easy to understand how an architecture which appealed not less to the lowest instincts of dulness than to the subtlest pride of learning, rapidly found acceptance with a large body of mankind; and how the spacious pomp of the new manner of design came to be eagerly adopted by the luxurious aristocracies, not only of Venice, but of the other countries of Christendom, now gradually gathering themselves into that insolent and festering isolation, against which the cry of the poor sounded hourly in more ominous unison, bursting at last into thunder (mark where–first among the planted walks and plashing fountains of the palace wherein the Renaissance luxury attained its utmost height in Europe, Versailles); that cry, mingling so much piteousness with its wrath and indignation, 'Our soul is filled with the scornful reproof of the wealthy, and with the despitefulness of the proud.'

But of all the evidence bearing upon this subject presented by the various art of the fifteenth century, none is so interesting or so conclusive as that deduced from its tombs. For, exactly in proportion as the pride of life became more insolent, the fear of death became more servile; and the difference in the manner in which the men of early and later days adorned the sepulchre, confesses a still greater difference in their manner of regarding death. To those he came as the comforter and the friend, rest in his right hand, hope in his left; to these as the humiliator, the spoiler, and the avenger. And, therefore, we find the early tombs at once simple and lovely in adornment, severe and solemn in their expression; confessing the power, and accepting the peace, of death, openly and joyfully; and in all their symbols marking that the hope of resurrection lay only in Christ's righteousness; signed always with this simple utterance of the dead, 'I will lay me down in peace, and take my rest; for it is thou, Lord, only that makest me dwell in safety.' But the tombs of the later ages are a ghastly struggle of mean pride and miserable terror: the one mustering the statues of the Virtues about the tomb, disguising the sar-

The tomb of Jacopo and Lorenzo Tiepolo
'which is peculiarly illustrative of the simplicity of these earlier ages'.

cophagus with delicate sculpture, polishing the false periods of the elaborate epitaph, and filling with strained animation the features of the portrait statue; and the other summoning underneath, out of the niche or from behind the curtain, the frowning skull, or scythed skeleton, or some other more terrible image of the enemy in whose defiance the whiteness of the sepulchre had been set to shine above the whiteness of the ashes.

This change in the feeling with which sepulchral monuments were designed, from the eleventh to the eighteenth centuries, has been common to the whole of Europe. But, as Venice is in other respects the centre of the Renaissance system, so also she exhibits this change in the manner of the sepulchral monument under circumstances peculiarly calculated to teach us its true character. For the severe guard which, in earlier times, she put upon every tendency to personal pomp and ambition, renders the tombs of her ancient monarchs as remarkable for modesty and simplicity as for their religious feeling; so that, in this respect, they are separated by a considerable interval from the more costly monuments erected at the same periods to the kings or nobles of other European states.

Of the simple sarcophagus tomb there are many exquisite examples both at Venice and Verona; the most interesting in Venice are those which are set in the recesses of the rude brick front of the Church of St. John and Paul, ornamented only, for the most part, with two crosses set in circles, and the legend with the name of the dead and an 'Orate pro anima' in another circle in the centre.

Among the tombs in front of the Church of St. John and Paul there is one which is peculiarly illustrative of the simplicity of these earlier ages. It is on the left of the entrance, a massy sarcophagus with low horns as of an altar, placed in a rude recess of the outside wall, shattered and worn, and here and there entangled among wild grass and weeds. Yet it is the tomb of two Doges, Jacopo and Lorenzo Tiepolo, by one of whom nearly the whole ground was given for the erection of the noble church.

Towards the beginning of the fourteenth century, in Venice, the recumbent figure begins to appear on the sarcophagus, the first dated example being also

John Ruskin THE TOMB OF ARNOLDO TENTONINO IN SANTA MARIA GLORIOSA DEI FRARI.
'I do not know of any other tomb in Venice of which the conception is so beautiful.'

one of the most beautiful; the statue of the prophet Simeon, sculptured upon the tomb which was to receive his relics in the church dedicated to him under the name of San Simeone Grande. So soon as the figure appears, the sarcophagus becomes much more richly sculptured, but always with definite religious purpose.

At Verona, where the great Pisan school had strong influence, the monumental sculpture is immeasurably finer; and so early as about the year 1335, the consummate form of the Gothic tomb occurs in the monument of Can Grande della Scala at Verona.

Let us now return to Venice, where, in the second chapel counting from right to left, at the west end of the Church of the Frari, there is a very early fourteenth, or perhaps late thirteenth, century tomb, another exquisite example of the perfect Gothic form. It is a knight's; but there is no inscription upon it, and his name is unknown. It consists of a sarcophagus, supported on bold brackets against the chapel wall, bearing the recumbent figure, protected by a simple canopy in the form of a pointed arch, pinnacled by the knight's crest; beneath which the shadowy space is painted dark blue, and strewn with stars. The statue itself is rudely carved; but its lines, as seen from the intended distance, are both tender and masterly. The knight is laid in his mail, only the hands and face being bare. The hauberk and helmet are of chain-mail, the armour for the limbs of jointed steel; a tunic, fitting close to the breast, and marking the noble swell of it by two narrow embroidered lines, is worn over the mail; his dagger is at his right side; his long cross-belted sword, not seen by the spectator from below, at his left. His feet rest on a hound (the hound being his crest), which looks up towards its master. In general, in tombs of this kind, the face of the statue is slightly turned towards the spectator; in this monument, on the contrary, it is turned away from him, towards the depth of the arch: for there, just above the warrior's breast, is carved a small image of St. Joseph bearing the infant Christ, who looks down upon the resting figure; and to this image its countenance is turned. The appearance of the entire tomb is as if the warrior had seen the vision of Christ in his dying moments, and had fallen back peacefully upon his pillow, with his eyes still turned to it, and his hands clasped in prayer.

On the opposite side of this chapel is another very lovely tomb, to Duccio degli Alberti, a Florentine ambassador at Venice; noticeable chiefly as being the first in Venice on which any images of the Virtues appear. We shall return to it presently, but some account must first be given of the more important among the other tombs in Venice belonging to the perfect period. Of these, by far the most interesting, though not the most elaborate, is that of the great Doge Francesco Dandolo, whose ashes, it might have been thought, were honourable enough to have been permitted to rest undisturbed in the chapter-house of the Frari, where they were first laid.

Of the tomb of the Doge Andrea Dandolo, in St. Mark's, I have spoken before. It is one of the first in Venice which presents, in the canopy, the Pisan idea of angels withdrawing curtains, as of a couch, to look down upon the dead. The sarcophagus is richly decorated with flower-work: the usual figures of the Annunciation are at the sides; an enthroned Madonna in the centre; and two bas-reliefs, one of the martyrdom of the Doge's patron saint, St. Andrew, occupy the intermediate spaces. The hair of the angels has here been gilded, their wings bedropped with silver, and their garments covered with the most exquisite arabesques. This tomb, and that of St. Isidore in another chapel of St. Mark's, which was begun by this very Doge, Andrea Dandolo, and completed after his death in 1354, are both nearly alike in their treatment, and are, on the whole, the best examples of Venetian monumental sculpture.

Of much ruder workmanship, though still most precious, and singularly interesting, from its quaintness, is a sarcophagus in the northernmost chapel, beside the choir of St. John and Paul, charged with two bas-reliefs and many figures, but which bears no inscription. It has, however, a shield with three dolphins on its brackets; and, as at the feet of the Madonna in its centre there is a small kneeling figure of a Doge, we know it to be the tomb of the Doge Giovanni Dolfino [who died in 1359].

Seven years later, a very noble monument was placed on the north side of the choir of St. John and Paul, to the Doge Marco Cornaro, chiefly, with respect to our present subject, noticeable for the absence of religious imagery from the sarcophagus, which is decorated with roses only; three very beautiful statues of the Madonna and two saints are, however, set in the canopy above.

Opposite this tomb, though about fifteen years later in date, is the richest monument of the Gothic period in Venice; that of the Doge Michele Morosini, who died in 1382. It consists of a highly florid canopy,—an arch crowned by a gable, with pinnacles at the flanks, boldly crocketed, and with a huge finial at the top representing St. Michael,—a medallion of Christ set in the gable; under the arch, a mosaic, representing the Madonna presenting the Doge to Christ upon the cross; beneath, as usual, the sarcophagus, with a most noble recumbent figure of the Doge, his face meagre and severe, and sharp in its lines, but exquisite in the form of its small and princely features. The sarcophagus is adorned with elaborate wrinkled leafage, projecting in front of it into seven brackets, from which the statues are broken away; but by which—for there can be no doubt that these last statues represented the theological and cardinal Virtues—we must for a moment pause.

It was noticed above, that the tomb of the Florentine ambassador, Duccio, was the first in Venice which presented images of the Virtues. Its small lateral statues of Justice and Temperance are exquisitely beautiful, and were, I have no doubt, executed by a Florentine sculptor; the whole range of artistical power and religious feeling being in Florence full half a century in advance of that of Venice. But this is the first truly Venetian tomb which has the Virtues. The face of the statue is resolute, thoughtful, serene, and full of beauty; and we must, therefore, for once allow the somewhat boastful introduction of the Virtues to have been perfectly just: though the whole tomb is most notable, as furnishing not only the exactly intermediate condition in style between the pure Gothic and its final Renaissance corruption, but, at the same time, the exactly intermediate condition of *feeling* between the pure calmness of early Christianity, and the boastful pomp of the Renaissance faithlessness; for here we have still the religious humility remaining in the mosaic of the canopy, which shows the Doge kneeling before the cross, while yet this tendency to self-trust is shown in the surrounding of the coffin by the Virtues.

The next tomb by the side of which they appear is that of Jacopo Cavalli, in the same chapel of St. John and Paul which contains the tomb of the Doge Delfin. It is peculiarly rich in religious imagery, adorned by boldly cut types of the four Evangelists, and of two saints, while, on projecting brackets in front of it, stood three statues of Faith, Hope and Charity, now lost, but drawn in Zanotto's work. It is all rich in detail, and its sculptor has been proud of it, thus recording his name below the epitaph:

QST OPERA DINTALGIO E FATTO IN PIERA,
UNVENICIAN LAFE CHANOME POLO,
NATO DI JACHOMEL CHATAIAPIERA.

This work of sculpture is done in stone;
A Venetian did it, named Paul,
Son of Jachomel the stone-cutter.

Of the tomb of [Tomaso Mocenigo] mention has before been made. Here, as in Morosini's, the images of the Virtues have no ironical power, although their great conspicuousness marks the increase of the boastful feeling in the treatment of monuments. For the rest, this tomb is the last in Venice which can be considered as belonging to the Gothic period. Its mouldings are already rudely classical, and it has meaningless figures in Roman armour at the angles; but its tabernacle above is still Gothic, and the recumbent figure is very beautiful. It was carved by two Florentine sculptors in 1423.

Tomaso Mocenigo was succeeded by the renowned Doge, Francesco Foscari, under whom, it will be remembered, the last additions were made to the Gothic Ducal Palace; additions which in form only, not in spirit, corresponded to the older portions; since, during his reign, the transition took place which permits us no longer to consider the Venetian architecture as Gothic at all. He died in 1457, and his tomb is the first important example of Renaissance art.

Not, however, a good characteristic example. It is remarkable chiefly as introducing all the faults of the Renaissance at an early period, when its merits, such as they are, were yet undeveloped. Its claim to be rated as a classical composition is altogether destroyed by the remnants of Gothic feeling which cling to it here and there in their last forms of degradation; and of which, now that we find them thus corrupted, the sooner we are rid the better. Thus the sarcophagus is supported by a species of trefoiled arches; the bases of the shafts have still their spurs; and the whole tomb is covered by a pediment, with crockets and a pinnacle. We shall find that the perfect Renaissance is at least pure in its insipidity, and subtle in its vice; but this monument is remarkable as showing the refuse of one style encumbering the embryo of another, and all principles of life entangled either in the swaddling clothes or the shroud.

With respect to our present purpose, however, it is a monument of enormous importance. We have to trace, be it remembered, the pride of state in its gradual intrusion upon the sepulchre; and the consequent and correlative vanishing of the expressions of religious feeling and heavenly hope, together with the more and more arrogant setting forth of the virtues of the dead. Now this tomb is the largest and most costly we have yet seen; but its means of religious expression are limited to a single statue of Christ, small, and used merely as a pinnacle at the top. The rest of the composition is as curious as it is vulgar. The conceit of angels withdrawing the curtains of the couch to look down upon the dead, was brought forward with increasing prominence by every succeeding sculptor; but, as we draw nearer to the Renaissance period, we find that the *angels* become of less importance, and the *curtains* of more. With the Pisans, the curtains are introduced as a motive for the angels; with the Renaissance sculptors, the angels are introduced merely as a motive for the curtains, which become every day more huge and elaborate. In the monument of Mocenigo, they have already expanded into a tent, with a pole in the centre of it: and in that of Foscari, for the first time, the *angels are absent altogether*; while the curtains are arranged in the form of an enormous French tent-bed, and are sustained at the flanks by two diminutive figures in Roman armour; substituted for the angels, merely that the sculptor might *show his knowledge* of classical costume.

Under the canopy is placed the sarcophagus with its recumbent figure. The statues of the Virgin and the saints have disappeared from it. In their stead, its panels are filled with half-length figures of Faith, Hope, and Charity; while Temperance and Fortitude are at the Doge's feet, Justice and Prudence at his head, figures now the size of life, yet nevertheless recognizable only by their attributes: for, except that Hope raises her eyes, there is no difference in the character or expression of any of their faces,—they are nothing more than

Above: The seventeenth-century tomb of Doge Giovanni Pesaro:
'*We have here, at last, the horrible images of death in violent contrast with the
defiant monument, which pretends to bring the resurrection down to the earth.*'
Below: The tomb of Jacopo Cavalli.

handsome Venetian women, in rather full and courtly dresses, and tolerably well thrown into postures for effect from below. Fortitude could not of course be placed in a graceful one without some sacrifice of her character, but that was of no consequence in the eyes of the sculptors of this period, so she leans back languidly, and nearly overthrows her own column; while Temperance, and Justice opposite to her, as neither the left hand of the one nor the right hand of the other could be seen from below, have been *left with one hand each.*

Still, these figures, coarse and feelingless as they are, have been worked with care, because the principal effect of the tomb depends on them. But the effigy of the Doge, of which nothing but the sign is visible, has been utterly neglected; and the ingenuity of the sculptor is not so great, at the best, as that he can afford to be slovenly. There is, indeed, nothing in the history of Foscari which would lead us to expect anything particularly noble in his face; but I trust, nevertheless, it has been misrepresented by this despicable carver; for no words are strong enough to express the baseness of the portraiture.

We now approach that period of the early Renaissance which was noticed in the preceding chapter as being at first a very visible improvement on the corrupted Gothic. The tombs executed during the period of the Byzantine Renaissance exhibit, in the first place, a consummate skill in handling the chisel, perfect science of drawing and anatomy, high appreciation of good classical models, and a grace of composition and delicacy of ornament derived, I believe, principally from the great Florentine sculptors. But, together with this science, they exhibit also, for a short time, some return to the early religious feeling, forming a school of sculpture which corresponds to that of the school of the Bellini in painting; and the only wonder is that there should not have been more workmen in the fifteenth century doing in marble what Perugino, Francia, and Bellini did on canvas. There are, indeed, some few, as I have just said, in whom the good and pure temper shows itself: but the sculptor was necessarily led sooner than the painter to an exclusive study of classical models, utterly adverse to the Christian imagination; and he was also deprived of the great purifying and sacred element of colour, besides having much more of merely mechanical and therefore degrading labour to go through in the realization of his thought. Hence I do not know any example of sculpture at this period, at least in Venice, which has not conspicuous faults (not faults of imperfection, as in early sculpture, but of purpose and senti-ment), staining such beauties as it may possess; and the whole school soon falls away, and merges into vain pomp and meagre metaphor.

The most celebrated monument of this period is that to the Doge Andrea Vendramin, in the Church of St. John and Paul, sculptured about 1480, and before alluded to in the first chapter.

Of far other workmanship are the tombs of Pietro and Giovanni Mocenigo, in St. John and Paul, and of Pietro Bernardo in the Frari; in all which the details are as full of exquisite fancy as they are perfect in execution: and in the two former, and several others of similar feeling, the old religious symbols return; the Madonna is again seen enthroned under the canopy, and the sarcophagus is decorated with legends of the saints. But the fatal errors of sentiment are, nevertheless, always traceable. But the most significant change in the treatment of these tombs, with respect to our immediate object, is in the form of the sarcophagus. In the earliest times, as we have seen, it was a gloomy mass of stone; gradually it became charged with religious sculpture; but never with the slightest desire to disguise its form, until towards the middle of the fifteenth century. It then becomes enriched with flower-work and hidden by the Virtues; and, finally, losing its four-square form, it is modelled on graceful types of ancient vases, made as little like a coffin as possible, and refined away in various elegances, till it becomes, at last, a mere pedestal or stage for the portrait statue. This statue, in the meantime, has been gradually coming back to life, through a curious series of transitions. The Vendramin monument is one of the last which shows, or pretends to show, the recumbent figure laid in death. A few years later, this idea became disagreeable to polite minds; and, lo! the figures, which before had been laid at rest upon the tomb pillow, raised themselves on their elbows, and began to look round them. The soul of the sixteenth century dared not contemplate its body in death.

The statue did not long remain in this partially recumbent attitude. Even the expression of peace became painful to the frivolous and thoughtless Italians, and they required the portraiture to be rendered in a manner that should induce no memory of death. The statue rose up, and presented itself in front of the tomb, like an actor upon a stage, surrounded now not merely, or not at all, by the Virtues, but by allegorical figures of Fame and Victory, by genii and muses, by personifications of humbled kingdoms and adoring nations, and by every circumstance of pomp, and symbol of adulation, that flattery could suggest or insolence could claim.

As of the intermediate monumental type, so also of this, the last and most gross, there are unfortunately many examples in our own country; but the most wonderful, by far, are still at Venice. I shall, however, particularise only two; the first, that of the Doge John Pesaro, in the Frari. We have passed over a considerable interval of time; we are now in the latter half of the seventeenth century; the progress of corruption has in the meantime been incessant, and sculpture has here lost its taste and learning as well as its feeling. We have here, at last, the horrible images of death in violent contrast with the defiant monument, which pretends to bring the resurrection down to earth; and it seems impossible for false taste and base feeling to sink lower. Yet even this monument is surpassed by one in St. John and Paul.

But before we pass to this, the last with which I shall burden the reader's attention, let us for a moment, and that we may feel the contrast more forcibly, return to a tomb of the early times.

In a dark niche in the outer wall of the outer corridor of St. Mark's,—not even in the church, observe, but in the atrium or porch of it, and on the north side of the church,—is a solid sarcophagus of white marble, raised only about two feet from the ground on four stunted square pillars. Its lid is a mere slab of stone; on its extremities are sculptured two crosses; in front of it are two rows of rude figures, the uppermost representing Christ with the Apostles: the lower row is of six figures only, alternately male and female, holding up their hands in the usual attitude of benediction; the sixth is smaller than the rest, and the midmost of the other five has a glory round its head. I cannot tell the meaning of these figures, but between them are suspended censers attached to crosses: a most beautiful symbolic expression of Christ's mediatorial function. The whole is surrounded by a rude wreath of vine leaves, proceeding out of the foot of a cross. It is the tomb of the Doge Marino Morosini, who reigned from 1249 to 1252.

From before this rude and solemn sepulchre let us pass to the southern aisle of the church of St. John and Paul; and there, towering from the pavement to the vaulting of the church, behold a mass of marble, sixty or seventy feet in height, of mingled yellow and white, the yellow carved into the form of an enormous curtain, with ropes, fringes, and tassels, sustained by cherubs; in front of which, in the now usual stage attitudes, advance the statues of the Doge Bertuccio Valier, his son the Doge Silvester Valier, and his son's wife Elisabeth. The statues of the Doges, though mean and Polonius-like, are partly redeemed by the Ducal robes; but that of the Dogaressa is a consummation of grossness, vanity, and ugliness;—the figure of a large and wrinkled woman, with elaborate curls in stiff projection round her face, covered from her shoulders to her feet with ruffs, furs, lace, jewels, and embroidery. Beneath and around are scattered Virtues, Victories, Fames, genii,—the entire company of the monumental stage assembled, as before a drop scene,—executed by various sculptors, and deserving attentive study as exhibiting every condition of false taste and feeble conception. The Victory in the centre is peculiarly interesting; the lion by which she is accompanied, springing on a dragon, has been intended to look terrible, but the incapable sculptor could not conceive any form of dreadfulness, could not even make the lion look angry. It looks only lachrymose; and its lifted forepaws, there being no spring nor motion in its body, give it the appearance of a dog begging. The inscriptions under the two principal statues are as follows:

> Bertucius Valier, Duke,
> Great in wisdom and eloquence,
> Greater in his Hellespontic victory,
> Greatest in the Prince his son,
> Died in the year 1658.

> Elisabeth Quirina,
> The wife of Silvester,
> Distinguished by Roman virtue,
> By Venetian piety,
> And by the Ducal crown,
> Died 1708.

The writers of this age were generally anxious to make the world aware that they understood the degrees of comparison, and a large number of epitaphs are principally constructed with this object: but the latter of these epitaphs is also interesting, from its mention, in an age now altogether given up to the pursuit of worldly honour, of that 'Venetian piety' which once truly distinguished the city from all others; and of which some form and shadow, remaining still, served to point an epitaph, and to feed more cunningly the pride which could not be satiated with the sumptuousness of the sepulchre.

Thus far, then, of the second element of the Renaissance spirit, the Pride of State; nor need we go farther to learn the reason of the fall of Venice. She was already likened in her thoughts, and was therefore to be likened in her ruin, to the Virgin of Babylon. The Pride of State and the Pride of Knowledge were no new passions: the sentence against them had gone forth from time everlasting.

PRIDE OF SYSTEM. I might have illustrated these evil principles from a thousand other sources, but I have not time to pursue the subject farther, and must pass to the third element above named, the Pride of System. It need not detain us so long as either of the others, for it is at once more palpable and less dangerous. The manner in which the pride of the fifteenth century corrupted the sources of knowledge, and diminished the majesty, while it multiplied the trappings, of state, is in general little observed; but the reader is probably already well and sufficiently aware of the curious tendency to formulization and system which, under the name of philosophy, encumbered the minds of the Renaissance schoolmen.

In the beginning of teaching, it is possible to say that this or that must or must not be done; and laws of colour and shade may be taught, as laws of harmony are to the young scholar in music. But the moment a man begins to be anything deserving the name of an artist, all this teachable law has become a matter of course with him, and if, thenceforth, he boast himself anywise in the law, or pretend that he lives and works by it, it is a sure sign that he is merely tithing cummin, and that there is no true art nor religion in him. For the true artist has that inspiration in him which is above all law, or rather, which is continually working out such magnificent and perfect obedience to supreme law, as can in nowise be rendered by line and rule. There are more laws perceived and fulfilled in the single stroke of a great workman, than could be written in a volume. His science is inexpressibly subtle, directly taught him by his Maker, not in anywise communicable or imitable. Neither can any written or definitely observable laws enable us to do any great thing. It is possible, by measuring and administering quantities of colour, to paint a room wall so that it shall not hurt the eye; but there are no laws by observing which we can become Titians. Out of the picture, once produced, men may elicit laws by the volume, and study them with advantage, to the better understanding of the existing picture; but no more paint another, than by discovering laws of vegetation they can make a tree to grow. And therefore, wheresoever we find the system and formality of rules much dwelt upon, and spoken of as anything else than a help for children, there we may be sure that noble art is not even understood, far less reached. And thus it was with all the common and public mind in the fifteenth and sixteenth centuries. The greater men, indeed, broke through the thorn hedges; and though much time was lost by the learned among them in writing Latin verses and anagrams, and arranging the framework of quaint sonnets and dexterous syllogisms, still they tore their way through the sapless thicket by force of intellect or of piety; for it was not possible that, either in literature or in painting, rules could be received by any strong mind, so as materially to interfere with its originality: and the crabbed discipline and exact scholarship became an advantage to the men who could pass through and despise them; so that in spite of the rules of the drama we had Shakespeare, and in spite of the rules of art we had Tintoret,—both of them, to this day, doing perpetual violence to the vulgar scholarship and dim-eyed proprieties of the multitude.

But in architecture it was not so; for that was the art of the multitude, and was affected by all their errors; and the great men who entered its field, like

Michael Angelo, found expression for all the best part of their minds in sculpture, and made the architecture merely its shell. So the simpletons and sophists had their way with it; and the reader can have no conception of the inanities and puerilities of the writers who, with the help of Vitruvius, re-established its 'five orders', determined the proportions of each, and gave the various recipes for sublimity and beauty, which have been thenceforward followed to this day, but which may, I believe, in this age of perfect machinery, be followed out still farther.

These, then, were the three principal directions in which the Renaissance pride manifested itself, and its impulses were rendered still more fatal by the entrance of another element, inevitably associated with pride. For, as it is written, 'He that trusteth in his own heart is a fool,' so also it is written, 'The fool hath said in his heart, There is no God;' and the self-adulation which influenced not less the learning of the age than its luxury, led gradually to the forgetfulness of all things but self, and to an infidelity only the more fatal because it still retained the form and language of faith.

INFIDELITY. In noticing the more prominent forms in which this faithless-ness manifested itself, it is necessary to distinguish justly between that which was the consequence of respect for Paganism, and that which followed from the corruption of Catholicism. For as the Roman architecture is not to be made answerable for the primal corruption of the Gothic, so neither is the Roman philosophy to be made answerable for the primal corruption of Christianity. Year after year, as the history of the life of Christ sank back into the depth of time, and became obscured by the misty atmosphere of the history of the world,—as intermediate actions and incidents multiplied in number, and countless changes in men's modes of life, and tones of thought rendered it more difficult for them to imagine the facts of distant time,—it became daily, almost hourly, a greater effort for the faithful heart to apprehend the entire veracity and vitality of the story of its Redeemer; and more easy for the thoughtless and remiss to deceive themselves as to the true character of the belief they had been taught to profess.

The renewal of the study of Pagan writers found the faith of Christendom already weakened and divided; and therefore it was itself productive of an effect tenfold greater than could have been apprehended from it at another time. It acted first in leading the attention of all men to words instead of things; for it was discovered that the language of the middle ages had been corrupt, and the primal object of every scholar became now to purify his style. To this study of words, that of forms being added, both as of matters of the first importance, half the intellect of the age was at once absorbed in the base sciences of grammar, logic, and rhetoric; studies utterly unworthy of the serious labour of men, and necessarily rendering those employed upon them incapable of high thoughts or noble emotion. Of the debasing tendency of philology, no proof is needed beyond once reading a grammarian's notes on a great poet: logic is unnecessary for men who can reason; and about as useful to those who cannot as a machine for forcing one foot in due succession before the other would be to a man who could not walk: while the study of rhetoric is one for men who desire to deceive or be deceived; he who has the truth at his heart need never fear the want of persuasion on his tongue, or, if he fear it, it is because the base rhetoric of dishonesty keeps the truth from being heard.

The study of these sciences, therefore, naturally made men shallow and dishonest in general. The faith which had been undermined by the genius of Pagans, was overthrown by the crimes of Christians; and the ruin which was begun by scholarship, was completed by sensuality. The civilised world is at this moment, collectively, just as Pagan as it was in the second century.

I believe that in a few years more we shall wake from all these errors in astonishment, as from evil dreams; having been preserved, in the midst of their madness, by those hidden roots of active and earnest Christianity which God's grace has bound in the English nation with iron and brass. But in the Venetian those roots themselves had withered; and, from the palace of their ancient religion, their pride cast them forth hopelessly to the pasture of the brute. From pride to infidelity, from infidelity to the unscrupulous and insatiable pursuit of pleasure, and from this to irremediable degradation, the transitions were swift, like the falling of a star. The great palaces of the haughtiest nobles of Venice were stayed, before they had risen far above their foundations, by the blast of a penal poverty; and the wild grass, on the unfinished fragments of their mighty shafts, waves at the tide-mark where the power of the godless people first heard the 'Hitherto shalt thou come.' And the regeneration in which they had so vainly trusted,—the new birth and clear dawning, as they thought it, of all art, all knowledge, and all hope,—became to them as that dawn which Ezekiel saw on the hills of Israel: 'Behold the Day; behold, it is come. The rod hath blossomed, pride hath budded, violence is risen up into a rod of wickedness. None of them shall remain, nor of their multitude; let not the buyer rejoice, nor the seller mourn, for wrath is upon all the multitude thereof.'

Once more, and for the last time, let me refer the reader to the important epoch of the death of the Doge Tomaso Mocenigo in 1423, long ago indicated as the commencement of the decline of the Venetian power. That commencement is marked not merely by the words of the dying Prince, but by a great and clearly legible sign. It is recorded, that on the accession of his successor, Foscari, to the throne, SI FESTEGGIO DALLA CITTA UNO ANNO INTERO: The city kept festival for a whole year. Venice had in her childhood sown, in tears, the harvest she was to reap in rejoicing. She now sowed in laughter the seeds of death.

Thenceforward, year after year, the nation drank with deeper thirst from the fountains of forbidden pleasure, and dug for springs, hitherto unknown, in the dark places of the earth. In the ingenuity of indulgence, in the varieties of vanity, Venice surpassed the cities of Christendom, as of old she had surpassed them in fortitude and devotion; and as once the powers of Europe stood before her judgment-seat, to receive the decisions of her justice, so now the youth of Europe assembled in the halls of her luxury, to learn from her the arts of delight.

It is as needless as it is painful to trace the steps of her final ruin. The ancient curse was upon her, the curse of the Cities of the Plain, 'Pride, fulness of bread, and abundance of idleness.' By the inner burning of her own passions, as fatal as the fiery rain of Gomorrah, she was consumed from her place among the nations; and her ashes are choking the channels of the dead, salt sea.

CONCLUSION

I n examining the nature of Gothic, we concluded that one of the chief
elements of power in that, and in *all good* architecture, was the acceptance
of uncultivated and rude energy in the workman. In examining the nature
of Renaissance, we concluded that its chief element of weakness was that
pride of knowledge which not only prevented all rudeness in expression,
but gradually quenched all energy which could only be rudely expressed; nor
only so, but, for the motive and matter of the work itself, preferred science to
emotion, and experience to perception.

Here let me finally and firmly enunciate the great principle to which all that
has hitherto been stated is subservient:– that art is valuable or otherwise, only
as it expresses the personality, activity, and living perception of a good and
great human soul; that it may express and contain this with little help from
execution, and less from science; and that if it have not this, if it show not the
vigour, perception, and invention of a mighty human spirit, it is worthless.
Worthless, I mean, as *art*; it may be precious in some other way, but, as art, it is
nugatory. For as a photograph is not a work of art, though it requires certain
delicate manipulations of paper and acid, and subtle calculations of time, in
order to bring out a good result; so, neither would a drawing *like* a photograph,
made directly from nature, be a work of art, although it would imply many
delicate manipulations of the pencil and subtle calculations of effects of colour
and shade.

We usually fall into much error by considering the intellectual powers as
having dignity in themselves, and separable from the heart; whereas the truth
is, that the intellect becomes noble or ignoble according to the food we give it,
and the kind of subjects with which it is conversant. It is not the reasoning
power which, of itself, is noble, but the reasoning power occupied with its
proper objects. Half of the mistakes of metaphysicians have arisen from their
not observing this; namely, that the intellect, going through the same proces-
ses, is yet mean or noble according to the matter it deals with, and wastes itself
away in mere rotatory motion, if it be set to grind straws and dust.

And therefore let us take no pride in our knowledge. We may, in a certain
sense, be proud of being immortal; we may be proud of loving, thinking,

seeing, and of all that we are by no human teaching: but not of what we have been taught by rote; not of the ballast and freight of the ship of the spirit, but only of its pilotage, without which all the freight will only sink it faster, and strew the sea more richly with its ruin.

There is not at this moment a junior student in our schools of painting, who does not know fifty times as much about the art as Giotto did; but he is not for that reason greater than Giotto; no, nor his work better, nor fitter for our beholding. Let him go on to know all that the human intellect can discover and contain in the term of a long life, and he will not be one inch, one line, nearer to Giotto's feet. But let him leave his academy benches, and, innocently, as one knowing nothing, go out into the highways and hedges, and there rejoice with them that rejoice, and weep with them that weep; and in the next world, among the companies of the great and good, Giotto will give his hand to him, and lead him into their white circle, and say, 'This is our brother.'

We have seen that all great art is the work of the whole living creature, body and soul, and chiefly of the soul. But it is not only *the work* of the whole creature, it likewise *addresses* the whole creature. That in which the perfect being speaks must also have the perfect being to listen. I am not to spend my utmost spirit, and give all my strength and life to my work, while you, spectator or hearer, will give me only the attention of half your soul. You must be all mine, as I am all yours; it is the only condition on which we can meet each other. All your faculties, all that is in you of greatest and best, must be awake in you, or I have no reward. The painter is not to cast the entire treasure of his human nature into his labour merely to please a part of the beholder: not merely to delight his senses, not merely to amuse his fancy, not merely to beguile him into emotion, not merely to lead him into thought; but to do *all* this. Senses, fancy, feeling, reason, the whole of the beholding spirit, must be stilled in attention or stirred with delight; else the labouring spirit has not done its work well. For observe, it is not merely its *right* to be thus met, face to face, heart to heart; but it is its *duty* to evoke this answering of the other soul: its trumpet call must be so clear, that though the challenge may by dulness or indolence be unanswered, there shall be no error as to the meaning of the appeal; there must be a summons in the work, which it shall be our own fault if we do not obey. We require this of it, we beseech this of it. Most men do not know what is in them till they receive this summons from their fellows: their hearts die within them, sleep settles upon them, the lethargy of the world's miasmata; there is nothing for which they are so thankful as that cry, 'Awake, thou that sleepest.' And this cry must be most loudly uttered to their noblest faculties; first of all, to the imagination, for that is the most tender, and the soonest struck into numbness by the poisoned air: so that one of the main functions of art, in its service to man, is to rouse the imagination from its palsy, like the angel troubling the Bethesda pool; and the art which does not do this is false to its duty, and degraded in its nature. It is not enough that it be well imagined, it must task the beholder also to imagine well; and this so imperatively, that if he does not choose to rouse himself to meet the work, he shall not taste it, nor enjoy it in any wise. Once that he is well awake, the guidance which the artist gives him should be full and authoritative: the beholder's imagination should not be suffered to take its own way, or wander hither and thither; but neither must it be left at rest; and the right point of realization, for any given work of art, is that which will enable the spectator to complete it for himself, in the exact way the artist would have him, but not that which will save him the trouble of effecting the completion. So soon as the idea is entirely conveyed, the artist's labour should cease; and every touch which he adds beyond the point when, with the help of the beholder's imagination, the story ought to have been told, is a degradation to his work. So that the art is wrong which either realizes its subject completely, or fails in giving such definite aid as shall enable it to be realized by the beholding imagination.

If, then, considering these things, any of my readers should determine, according to their means, to set themselves to the revival of a healthy school of architecture in England, and wish to know in few words how this may be done, the answer is clear and simple. First, let us cast out utterly whatever is connected with the Greek, Roman, or Renaissance architecture, in principle or in form. We have seen above, that the whole mass of the architecture, founded on Greek and Roman models, which we have been in the habit of building for the last three centuries, is utterly devoid of all life, virtue, honourableness, or power of doing good. It is base, unnatural, unfruitful, unenjoyable, and impious. Pagan in its origin, proud and unholy in its revival, paralyzed in its old age, yet making prey in its dotage of all the good and living things that were springing around it in their youth; an architecture invented, as it seems, to make plagiarists of its architects, slaves of its workmen, and sybarites of its inhabitants; an architecture in which intellect is idle, invention impossible, but in which all luxury is gratified, and all insolence fortified;—the first thing we have to do is to cast it out, and shake the dust of it from our feet for ever. Whatever has any connection with the five orders, or with any one of the orders,—whatever is Doric, or Ionic, or Tuscan, or Corinthian, or Composite, or in anywise Grecized or Romanized; whatever betrays the smallest respect for Vitruvian laws, or conformity with Palladian work,—that we are to endure no more. To cleanse ourselves of these 'cast clouts and rotten rags' is the first thing to be done in the court of our prison.

There need be no limits to our hope or our confidence; and I believe it to be possible for us, not only to equal, but far to surpass, in some respects, any Gothic yet seen in Northern countries. In the introduction of figure-sculpture, we must, indeed, for the present, remain utterly inferior, for we have no figures to study from. No architectural sculpture was ever good for anything which did not represent the dress and persons of the people living at the time; and our modern dress will *not* form decorations for spandrils and niches. But in floral sculpture we may go far beyond what has yet been done, as well as in refinement of inlaid work and general execution. For, although the glory of Gothic architecture is to receive the rudest work, it refuses not the best; and, when once we have been content to admit the handling of the simplest workman, we shall soon be rewarded by finding many of our simple workmen become cunning ones: and, with the help of modern wealth and science, we may do things like Giotto's campanile, instead of like our own rude cathedrals; but better than Giotto's campanile, insomuch as we may adopt the pure and perfect forms of the Northern Gothic, and work them out with the Italian refinement. It is hardly possible at present to imagine what may be the splendour of buildings designed in the forms of English and French thirteenth century *surface* Gothic, and wrought out with the refinement of Italian art in the details, and with a deliberate resolution, since we cannot have figure-sculpture, to display in them the beauty of every flower and herb of the English fields, each by each; doing as much for every tree that roots itself in our rocks, and every blossom that drinks our summer rains, as our ancestors did for the oak, the ivy, and the rose. Let this be the object of our ambition, and let us begin to approach it, not ambitiously, but in all humility, accepting help from the feeblest hands; and the London of the nineteenth century may yet become as Venice without her despotism, and as Florence without her dispeace.

INDEX

The author and publishers wish to thank the following for permission to reproduce photographs:

Ashmolean Museum, Oxford, title page and pages 115, 141, 170 and 203; Mr Peter Bellew, pages 70 and 87; Osvaldo Bohm, pages 13, 48, 194 and 225 *above*; The Brantwood Trust, Coniston, pages 32, 82/83, 93, 98 and 113; The Courtauld Institute of Art, pages 51 *left*, 51 *right*, 167, 181, 220, and 225 *below*; Fitzwilliam Museum, Cambridge, cover; Susan Griggs Agency, pages 57 and 79 *below* (photos Adam Woolfitt); John Hillelson Agency, page 75 (photo Inge Morath); Mansell Collection, pages 148 and 217; Metropolitan Museum of Art, New York, Rogers Fund, 1908, page 172; National Portrait Gallery, London, page 9; The Ruskin Galleries, Bembridge School, pages 14, 15, 16, 60, 73, 76, 103, 110, 144/145, 183, 200 and 221; Scala, Florence, pages 39, 43, 49, 64 *above*, 64 *below*, 79 *above*, 91, 94/95, 129, 168/169 and 212/213; Mr Sean Sexton, pages 24/25 and 29; The Tate Gallery, London, page 10/11; Yale Center for British Art, Paul Mellon Collection, page 59.

All other pictures are from the 1886 edition of *The Stones of Venice*, volumes I, II and III.